THE
ULTIMATE
GARDEN
DESIGNER

THE
ULTIMATE
GARDEN
DESIGNER

TIM NEWBURY

B.A. (Hons) (Architecture), B. Phil. (Landscape Design)

CASSELL
ILLUSTRATED

First published in the United Kingdom in 1995 by
Ward Lock

This paperback edition first published in 2000 by
Seven Dials, Cassell & Co

Reprinted 2002 by
Cassell Illustrated
A Member of Octopus Publishing Group Ltd
2-4 Heron Quays
London E14 4JP

Distributed in the United States of America by
Sterling Publishing Co., Inc.
387 Park Avenue South,
New York, NY 10016-8810

A CIP catalogue record for this book is available
from the British Library

ISBN 1 84188 113 9

Commissioning Editor: Stuart Cooper
Project Editor: Jane Birch
Designer: Anne Fisher
Typesetting and page make-up:
Associated Print Production Ltd (London)
Printed and bound by Craft Print in Singapore

CONTENTS

PREFACE

Good garden design relies on a well-balanced combination of flair, knowledge and experience on the part of the designer, attributes drawn from many disciplines, including horticulture, landscape architecture and even engineering. If you want to design your own garden, having to become proficient in some or perhaps all of these skills can be a daunting prospect, requiring a major investment of your time, energy and even money.

If you are one of the many who do not relish this prospect, then this is the book for you. It does not set out to turn you into a garden designer – what it will do, though, is present you with a wide range of beautiful 'off-the-peg' designs for both complete gardens and individual garden features to suit a whole range of tastes, plots and pockets. Whether you are looking for a low-maintenance family garden, a jungly wilderness full of foliage or a garden in the Japanese style; whether your plot of land is rectangular or triangular, hot and sunny or cool and shady – this book provides a host of design solutions.

The text is illustrated throughout with superb watercolour paintings of the gardens and features, plus clear, simple line drawings and sketches showing the layouts, construction details and planting schemes. A detailed plant directory describes a selection of popular plants, together with illustrations and notes on cultivation and maintenance.

In fact, all these features combine to make this book the next best thing to hiring a garden designer!

GARDEN DESIGN

Your needs as a person or family will determine the form your garden takes. These may be practical, such as providing a large lawn and patio area for the children to play on, or they may be purely visual, as in a traditional Japanese garden – more often than not, you will probably want to strike a happy medium. However, the way in which the various elements are put together will have a radical effect on the final outcome.

DESIGN CONSTRAINTS
Having established your needs, you must look at these in the light of certain constraints. One of these is financial, both in terms of the cost of initial construction and also long-term maintenance. How much or how little you wish to spend will clearly affect the scale and complexity of your design. Another constraint relates to the physical nature of the site and includes a whole range of factors that must be considered, such as soil type, aspect, topography, drainage, climate, location and existing features, whether natural or man-made.

These physical considerations will, first, influence the plan of the garden, so that, for example, you may wish to locate your patio in the sunniest corner of the garden and place the ornamental pond where it can be seen from the living room. You might then discover that you have a conflict, because the ideal spots for these two features happen to coincide. Second, these constraints will have a direct effect on the planting in your garden. For example, while your choice of species for a light, sunny border with good, well-drained soil may be extensive, that for a dark shady spot at the base of a large yew tree will be extremely limited. So any visions you may have had of a glorious

Plant colour and texture are two of the factors that should be considered when designing a garden.

Left: Successful garden design brings together hard and soft elements to create a harmonious effect.

Opposite: The beautiful and informal appearance of this cottage garden is not simply a happy accident. It is the result of a carefully thought-out design which combines the planting with a graceful stone urn and old paving.

display beneath the yew tree will be curtailed because there just aren't enough suitable plants that will thrive there.

These two simple examples demonstrate how the concept of garden design is one of constantly balancing the ideal against the reality.

A UNIFIED DESIGN

It is helpful if your garden can be designed as a complete package, even if you are not able to build it all in one go, so that over a period of time you can gradually add a pond, a rockery or a pergola, confident in the knowledge that the final effect is going to be as you envisaged it. Without an overall design in mind, you may well end up with a piece-meal effect, made up of a number of random and unrelated elements.

The overall visual effect will also be influenced by the colours and textures of the materials and plants used in the design, as will the mood or atmosphere that they create. Bright reds, oranges and yellows will generate feelings of warmth and vitality in a plant design. Blues, soft pinks and white tend to have a subdued, cooling effect and can give a greater impression of depth in a garden.

One way to unify a number of different elements or features in your garden is to develop a theme that is common to them all. This could take the form of a material such as red brick used, for example, as an edge to the lawn, the path from the lawn to the patio and as a coping to the raised pool. Alternatively, a less tangible but just as effective unifying theme could be the use of a shape or pattern on the ground – for example, making the beds, lawn and paved areas into a series of different sized squares, which could also be echoed in the square pattern of a trellis screen.

Taking note of the materials of adjacent walls, fences and buildings and repeating or complementing these in your garden layout is another effective way to make your design fit comfortably into its surroundings. You might, for instance, stain or paint your pergola in a colour to match the window and door frames of the house.

Above all, everything in a garden, must have a purpose, whether it is practical, such as a nicely detailed trellis screen to hide the bin store; artistic, such as a beautifully laid out herbaceous border; or even humorous, like the stone frog sitting by the pond.

Ultimately, the success of your garden will be measured by how satisfied you are with the final result and it is hoped that this book will make it possible for you to achieve this goal.

HOW TO USE THIS BOOK

Part 1 of the book, **Complete Gardens,** is divided into chapters that each cover a basic style or function of a garden, so that the reader can choose one broadly suited to his or her own tastes or needs. A selection of designs is then provided, depicting variations on that particular style or function. For example, under Cottage Gardens the designs depict a small, traditional garden; a contemporary garden for family use; and a garden in town. The overall visual effect of each design is shown by a colour illustration, alongside which is a

A colour photograph shows a further example of the garden style.

PART I

Introductory text describes the design of the garden, its main features and plants.

A colour illustration shows a view of the garden, typically the view that is seen from the house.

A three-dimensional colour illustration shows the complete garden, including the features and the planting schemes. Use this to select the garden style that most appeals to you.

A plan identifies the individual features of the garden and the planting scheme. A planting key lists the major plants used.

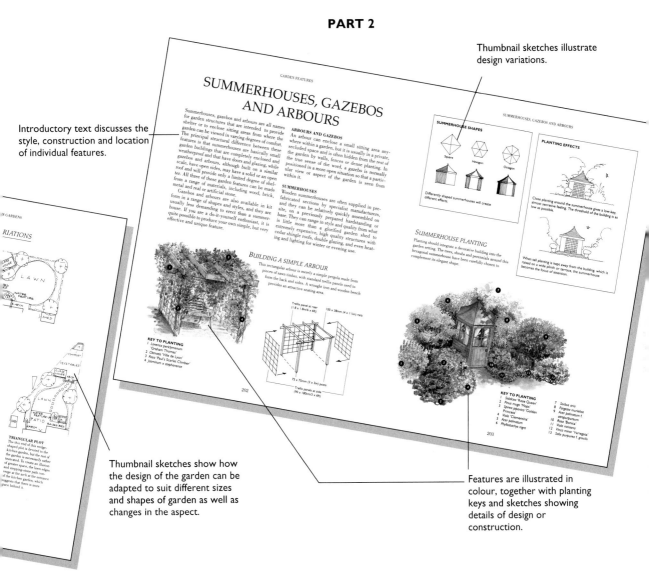

Introductory text discusses the style, construction and location of individual features.

Thumbnail sketches illustrate design variations.

Thumbnail sketches show how the design of the garden can be adapted to suit different sizes and shapes of garden as well as changes in the aspect.

Features are illustrated in colour, together with planting keys and sketches showing details of design or construction.

straightforward plan of the garden, identifying the various structural elements. The plans are key numbered to a planting list. Further annotation identifies the various elements of the garden, for which the reader can refer to the relevant section of Part 2 of the book, where details of the design and construction of various garden features can be found. Following the main colour illustration and plan is a series of sketches, which show how the basic elements of the garden can be rearranged or modified to suit, for example, different shapes or sizes of garden or changes in aspect.

Part 2, **Garden Features**, covers the various elements of a garden under headings such as Pools, Streams and Water Features, Pergolas and

Arches, or Patios and Paving. Each chapter gives examples of the planning and layout of the particular garden feature, providing a number of alternatives based on cost, style or ease of construction. The features are illustrated with watercolour paintings and colour photographs. Simple sketches show details of the construction, as well as variations that are possible in the design.

The **Plant Directory** lists and describes a selection of popular 'value-for-money' plants used in the garden designs in Part 1.

Taken together, the different sections of the book will enable you to mix and match designs and features, plants and plantings to create a unique garden suited to your own tastes and requirements.

Part One

COMPLETE

GARDENS

COTTAGE GARDENS

For many gardeners one of the attractions of a cottage garden is its seemingly uncontrolled nature, which allows plants, especially perennials, biennials and annuals, to spread gradually and thrive where conditions suit them best. This evolution of a garden can take time, however, and so the first example in this chapter illustrates how to achieve a traditional cottage-garden effect without having to wait many years.

Cottage gardens of this kind are, by their nature, not ideally suited to everyone's needs, especially children, and the second design therefore takes the 'feel' of a cottage garden and puts it into a situation that is far more practical in terms of a modern lifestyle.

The final scheme does away with the myth that cottage gardens are purely for country gardeners and illustrates an example of a small town garden laid out in a cottage style.

A random selection of geraniums, campanulas, astrantias and gladioli captures perfectly the essence of a traditional cottage garden.

A SMALL TRADITIONAL GARDEN

THE DESIGN

Cottage gardens owe their origins to the days of self-sufficiency when gardeners maintained their own supplies of fruit, vegetables and flowers as well as keeping livestock. The wonderfully satisfying array of plants that we now associate with such a garden, therefore, came about as a result of the cottage garden developing over many years. The design for this small back garden enables you to re-create this old-fashioned theme over a much shorter period of time.

The paved area around the house is deliberately irregular in outline, yet it is just large enough to sit out on, and it has access to the back door and to the side gate leading to the front garden.

An informal path leads down the centre of the garden and through a rustic rose arch, which is flanked on either side by tall flowering shrubs. This arch makes an attractive centrepiece, framing the view beyond and at the same time helping to create a sense of division between the ornamental area near the house and the more practical area further down the garden, where there is space for growing some fruit and vegetables. Here there is an additional area set aside for growing annual flowers for cutting, while tucked away in one corner behind the kitchen garden and screened from the house by tall shrubs is a paved area that contains a compact tool shed, a compost heap and, possibly, a cold frame for growing on young plants and seedlings.

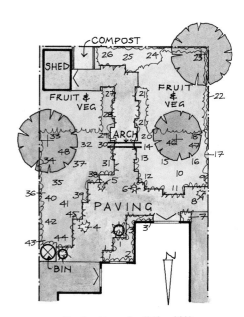

Garden 11m x 9m (36ft x 29ft)

THE PLANTING

The beds against the house and pockets in the paving, made by leaving out odd flagstones, are ideal for sun-loving herbs, perennials and shrubs such as rosemary (**Rosmarinus**), lavender (**Lavandula**) and catmint (**Nepeta**). Creeping plants such as prostrate thyme (**Thymus serpyllum**) can be grown in the paving joints if they are

KEY TO PLANTING

1 *Iris* 'Frost and Flame'
2 *Rosmarinus officinalis* 'Miss Jessopp's Upright'
3 *Lavandula angustifolia* 'Munstead'
4 *Thymus serpyllum*
5 *Arabis ferdinandi-coburgi* 'Variegata'
6 *Saxifraga* 'Flowers of Sulphur'
7 *Lonicera periclymenum* 'Belgica'
8 *Nepeta mussinii*
9 *Acanthus spinosus*
10 *Rudbeckia fulgida* var. *sullivantii* 'Goldsturm'
11 *Festuca scoparia*
12 *Alchemilla mollis*
13 *Aster novi-belgii* 'Jenny'
14 *Rosa* 'Golden Showers'
15 *Lupinus* 'My Castle'
16 *Rosa glauca*
17 *Jasminum officinale* f. *affine*
18 *Viburnum opulus* 'Compactum'
19 *Berberis darwinii*
20 *Chaenomeles* x *superba* 'Pink Lady'
21 Annuals
22 *Clematis montana alba*
23 *Prunus* x *subhirtella* 'Autumnalis'
24 *Taxus baccata* 'Semperaurea'
25 *Ilex aquifolium* 'Handsworth New Silver'
26 *Buxus sempervirens*
27 *Skimmia laureola*
28 *Potentilla fruticosa* 'Primrose Beauty'
29 *Philadelphus* 'Avalanche'
30 *Rosa* 'Golden Showers'
31 *Ligularia* 'The Rocket'
32 *Viburnum* x *bodnantense* 'Dawn'
33 *Sorbus* 'Joseph Rock'
34 *Ilex* x *altaclerensis* 'Golden King'
35 *Spiraea arguta*
36 *Hedera helix* 'Silver Queen'
37 *Paeonia lactiflora* 'Bowl of Beauty'
38 *Geranium* x *oxonianum* 'Wargrave Pink'
39 *Pulmonaria officinalis* 'Sissinghurst White'
40 *Thuja plicata* 'Stoneham Gold'
41 *Campanula persicifolia*
42 *Hydrangea arborescens* 'Annabelle'
43 *Clematis* 'Rouge Cardinal'
44 *Rosa* 'Nevada'
45 *Liriope muscari*
46 *Malus* x *robusta* 'Red Sentinel'
47 *Alcea rosea*
48 *Digitalis purpurea*

filled with a gritty mixture of good topsoil, and these will also provide a home for self-seeding annuals such as calendulas and alyssum.

Immediately beyond the main paved area on either side of the path, a mixture of small to medium-sized flowering shrubs and perennials provides a continuing display from early spring right through to late autumn, with taller shrubs such as **Viburnum** x **bodnantense** 'Dawn' on either side of the arch providing not only height and screening, but also late winter and early spring interest.

The boundary walls and fences are used to support a collection of traditional climbers including clematis and honeysuckle (**Lonicera**) as well as variegated ivies (**Hedera**) for year-round colour, while the arch provides an ideal frame for two pillar roses (**Rosa** 'Golden Showers').

The choice of trees is very important if they are to remain manageable and not outgrow their allocated space, and so a mountain ash (**Sorbus** 'Joseph Rock'), crab apple (**Malus** x **robusta** 'Red Sentinel') and a winter-flowering cherry (**Prunus** x

Opposite: View from the house.
Above: Three-dimensional view of the garden.

*This well-balanced mix of climbers, perennials and annuals is
the ideal complement to the old stone and brick paving.*

subhirtella 'Autumnalis') have been chosen.
These three trees are well suited to any small garden in both size and habit, and between them give
long and valuable displays of flowers, berries and
autumn colour.

THE FEATURES
Built from old, worn sandstone flags in a mixture of
sizes and laid with an irregular, staggered edge, the
sitting area creates an informal effect where it
meets the planting. Occasional small flags are
omitted to allow plants to be mixed in with the
paving itself, softening the lines of the joints and
providing further contrast. Notice, though, how
these 'spot' plants are carefully positioned to avoid
disrupting the main body of the paving where
chairs and table would be placed.

The narrow central path giving access to the
bottom of the garden is laid using the same flags as
the sitting area and careful selection of these stones
allows slight variations in the width of the path,
enhancing the general air of informality. The

paving from the side gate to the back door is dis-
tinguished from the rest by being built from old red
bricks, which are laid in a herringbone pattern and
are brushed over roughly with dry sand to fill the
joints. This will allow the occasional self-seeded
foxglove (**Digitalis**) or hollyhock (**Alcea**) to become
established where the brick paving meets the house
wall.

In keeping with the general style of the rest of
the garden, the central rose arch is made from
round, peeled larch poles, which have been pressure treated for maximum life. The simple sawn
and nailed joints may seem crude initially, but will
quickly blend into the background as the roses
mature and the tone of the wood mellows with age.
Climbers such as clematis and honeysuckle
(**Lonicera**), which are not truly self-clinging, are
supported by horizontal galvanized wires at vertical
intervals of 300–400mm (12–16in) held by vine
eyes screwed directly into the wooden fence post
or, alternatively, into the brick wall, which must
first be drilled and plugged.

DESIGN VARIATIONS

DIFFERENT ASPECT
The main sitting area is moved to the far end of the garden to catch the sun, with the utility area brought nearer to the house, although it is still screened from it. This creates extra space in the far corner of the garden for fruit and vegetables.

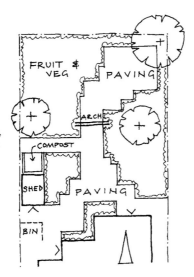

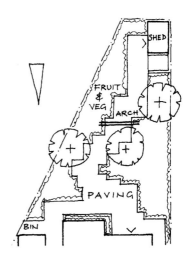

TRIANGULAR PLOT
The basic layout is relatively unchanged, but the central path is staggered to disguise the long, narrow appearance of the garden. The thin, wedge shape at the far end of the garden is ideal for the utility area.

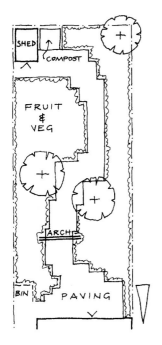

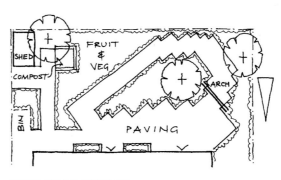

WIDE, SHALLOW PLOT
Setting the paving at an angle to the house diverts the eye away from the lack of depth. The arch and tree act as focal points and hide an area behind, while the path forms a circular route for additional interest.

LONG, NARROW PLOT
Staggering the path helps to break up the long view down the garden, and the view is further disrupted by bringing the arch into the foreground and by positioning two trees across the path to create what is, in effect, another 'arch'.

A CONTEMPORARY
COTTAGE GARDEN

THE DESIGN

Old-fashioned cottage gardens can be delightful places in which to work or relax, but they are not all suited to the demands of the modern-day family. In this larger plot, although the principal aim is to create a cottage-garden effect, consideration is also given to more practical requirements.

The comfortably sized patio adjoins a simple, central lawn, which provides adequate space for children to play on as well as for general entertainment or relaxation. The strongly curving style of the lawn is reflected in a brick path, which leads from the patio to a small kitchen-garden area, which has space for a small shed and compost heap. The kitchen garden is screened from the house, partly by shrub planting and partly by a number of climber-covered arches over the path.

At the back of the garage a simple lean-to construction with a light roof, which provides outside storage for bicycles, lawnmowers and logs, is carefully screened from the rest of the garden and house by a rustic trellis screen. This screen also acts as a backdrop to a raised bed on the corner of the patio, separating it from the storage area. This raised bed is ideal for use as a herb garden, being in a sunny position and conveniently placed near the back door.

THE PLANTING

The planting design is carefully thought out to give the overall impression of a cottage garden but

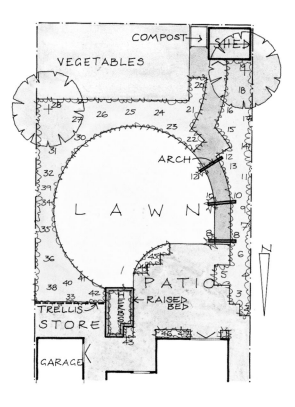

Garden 17m x 12m (56ft x 39ft)

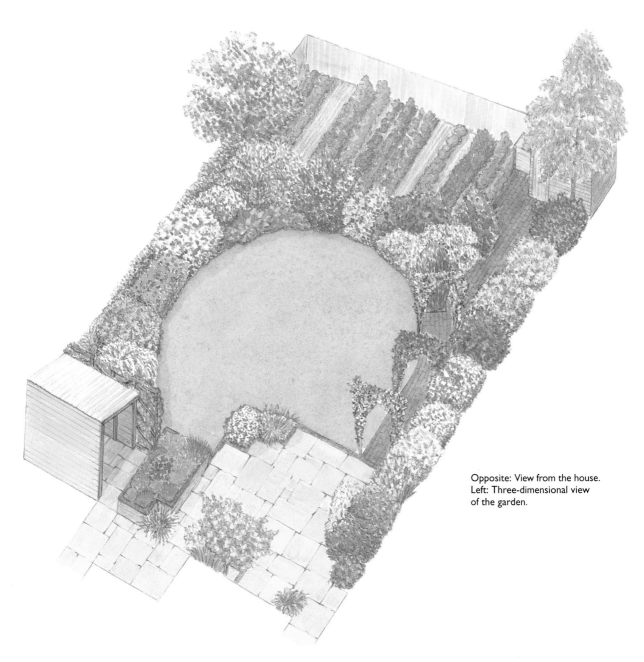

Opposite: View from the house.
Left: Three-dimensional view of the garden.

KEY TO PLANTING

1 *Nerine bowdenii*
2 *Helleborus lividus* var. *corsicus*
3 *Skimmia japonica* 'Rubella'
4 *Berberis thunbergii* f. *atropurpurea*
5 *Sisyrinchium striatum variegatum*
6 *Iris pallida* var. *dalmatica*
7 *Philadelphus* 'Manteau d'Hermine'
8 *Clematis* 'The President'
9 *Skimmia japonica* 'Foremannii'
10 *Vitis vinifera* 'Apiifolia'
11 *Rosa* 'Iceberg'
12 *Rosa* 'New Dawn'

13 *Aconitum* 'Bressingham Spire'
14 *Hemerocallis* 'Hyperion'
15 *Hydrangea serrata* 'Preziosa'
16 *Alchemilla mollis*
17 *Digitalis purpurea*
18 *Daphne laureola*
19 *Betula pendula* 'Dalecarlica'
20 *Ilex* x *altaclerensis* 'Golden King'
21 *Fuchsia magellanica* 'Versicolor'
22 *Chamaecyparis lawsoniana* 'Pembury Blue'
23 *Rudbeckia fulgida* var. *sullivantii* 'Goldsturm'
24 *Hydrangea paniculata* 'Grandiflora'

25 *Rosa* 'Queen Elizabeth'
26 *Osmanthus delavayi*
27 *Buddleia davidii* 'Nanho Blue'
28 *Prunus* x *subhirtella* 'Autumnalis Rosea'
29 *Aucuba japonica* 'Crotonifolia'
30 *Hosta* 'Frances Williams'
31 *Fuchsia magellanica* 'Aurea'
32 *Viburnum sargentii* 'Onondaga'
33 *Lonicera japonica* 'Aureoreticulata'
34 *Lilium regale*
35 *Euphorbia griffithii* 'Fireglow'
36 *Weigela florida* 'Foliis Purpureis'

37 *Jasminum* x *stephanense*
38 *Viburnum* x *burkwoodii*
39 *Clematis montana* 'Tetrarose'
40 *Spiraea nipponica* 'Snowmound'
41 *Helichrysum* 'Sulphur Light'
42 *Agapanthus* Headbourne hybrids
43 *Lavandula angustifolia*
44 *Hebe subalpina*
45 *Lavandula* angustifolia 'Hidcote'
46 *Iris germanica*
47 *Lonicera periclymenum* 'Graham Thomas'

includes varieties of plants that require lower maintenance and minimum care. There is a substantial framework of small trees and flowering and foliage shrubs mixed with reliable perennials to provide interest in the garden for much of the year. The perimeter fence and walls are used to good effect by planting them with a wide range of climbers such as clematis, jasmine (*Jasminum*) and climbing roses (*Rosa*), which add to the cottage-garden feel as well as helping to disguise the boundary. To put the final touches to the garden, traditional cottage-garden plants such as lavender (*Lavandula*), variegated sisyrinchium (*S. striatum variegatum*) and honeysuckle (*Lonicera*) are planted around the edge of the patio and against the house wall.

THE FEATURES

The patio is built from concrete slabs, which imitate riven sandstone. The slabs are of mixed sizes to give a random rectangular pattern and are staggered to create small pockets for plants to spill over on to the paving and soften the hard edges.

On one side the patio is edged in a brown clay paving brick, which is also used for building the path down to the kitchen garden. The bricks for the path are laid in a stretcher bond to minimize cutting, and the joints can be pointed with sand/cement mortar or just filled with sand. Brick paving is also used for the hardstanding outside the shed and compost heap, but because it is out of sight, it could be replaced with more economical plain, non-slip concrete slabs.

The free-standing arches across the path are made from round, peeled larch posts, with simple cross rails and braces in the same material, which is best bought ready treated against rot and decay. The wood can be left in a natural finish, which will weather down in time, or it can be stained to match the colour of the house door and window frames or even the fence panels. A similar style of construction is employed for the trellis screen, using the same size posts to make a square frame and thinner, round posts to create a vertical, horizontal or even chevron pattern within this frame.

The raised herb bed complements both the building and the paving by being constructed in the same brick as the house, finishing off with an artificial stone coping to match the patio flags, although the brown paving brick could be used instead of stone coping.

DESIGN VARIATIONS

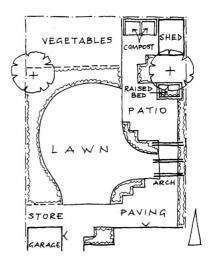

DIFFERENT ASPECT
The design is simply altered to take account of a change in aspect by moving the main patio further down the garden, while still leaving a reasonably sized paved area near the doors from the house. The raised herb bed now forms a focal point at the back of the patio, with additional plants behind it to screen the shed.

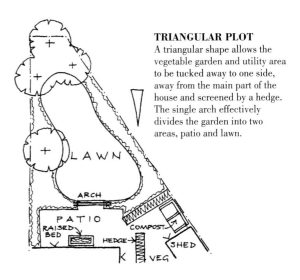

TRIANGULAR PLOT
A triangular shape allows the vegetable garden and utility area to be tucked away to one side, away from the main part of the house and screened by a hedge. The single arch effectively divides the garden into two areas, patio and lawn.

This beautifully designed bench seat is tucked into the background planting so that it does not break into the lawn area.

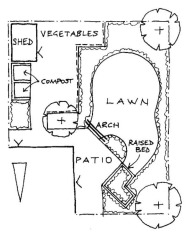

CORNER SITE

A corner site such as this lends itself well to the basic design because the utility area can be self-contained at one side. Placing the patio at an angle diverts attention across the lawn to the far corner and back around to the raised bed.

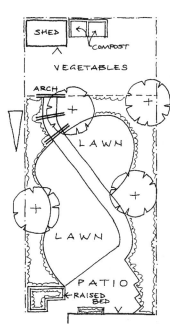

LONG, NARROW PLOT

The long, narrow shape of this garden is broken up by angling the patio and by linking the patio and vegetable area with a bold, diagonal path across the lawn. The vegetable and utility area is hidden by the border behind the lawn, while the arches make an attractive entrance to that section of the garden.

A SMALL
TOWN GARDEN

THE DESIGN

A cottage garden situated in the middle of a town or city may at first glance seem incongruous. However, many urban gardens are completely enclosed by old brick walls, cutting them off, at least visually, from neighbouring plots, and the houses to which they belong are often as charming as an old country cottage. There are, therefore, situations such as this where an old-fashioned, romantic theme is quite suitable.

In such a small space lawn is not really practical, and here its place is taken by paving, which is laid out in a very organized and angular style as a deliberate contrast to the generous areas of 'cottagey' planting. The main sitting area, or terrace, is placed towards the far end of this garden to make the best use of the available sun. Access to the terrace from the house is via a gravel path, which is enclosed by a rose arch, or via stepping stones, which meander through the planting. A gazebo, heavily planted with climbers, forms an attractive focal point at the back of the terrace when viewed from the rose arch, and in front of the French windows a tiny bubble fountain makes an eye-catching feature.

THE PLANTING

A number of large evergreen and deciduous shrubs and small trees provide a basic woody framework for the garden, infilled between and underneath with a range of smaller shrubs and perennials for

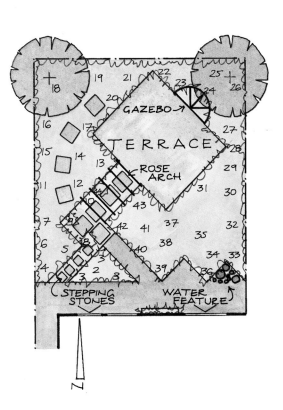

Garden 11m x 9.5m (36ft x 31ft)

24

flower and foliage colour. In such a tight area the colours of flowers in particular are carefully selected, avoiding where possible very intense, bright reds and oranges, which might otherwise destroy any feeling of depth and space. There is, therefore, a predominance of white, blue, soft pinks and pale yellows, which are complementary rather than contrasting and create a quiet, restful composition.

The warm wall at the end of the garden is used to good effect by planting relatively tender climbers and wall shrubs such as carpenteria and abutilon against it. Nearer the house, the area in front of the French windows, which is in cool shade for much of

Opposite: View from the house.
Below: Three-dimensional view
of the garden.

KEY TO PLANTING

1 *Clematis* 'Nelly Moser'
2 *Skimmia japonica* 'Foremannii'
3 *Vinca minor* 'Purpurea'
4 *Skimmia japonica* 'Rubella'
5 *Geranium ibericum*
6 *Viburnum farreri*
7 *Alcea rosea* Chater's Double Group
8 *Alchemilla mollis*
9 *Lavandula angustifolia* 'Nana Alba'
10 Climbing roses on arch: 'Zéphirine Drouhin', 'Albertine', 'Iceberg', 'New Dawn', 'Schoolgirl', 'Handel'
11 *Garrya elliptica* 'James Roof'
12 *Phlox paniculata* 'White Admiral'
13 *Caryopteris* x *clandonensis* 'Heavenly Blue'
14 *Anthemis tinctoria* 'E.C. Buxton'
15 *Agapanthus* 'Blue Giant'
16 *Syringa microphylla* 'Superba'
17 *Dicentra eximia*
18 *Sorbus aucuparia* 'Sheerwater Seedling'
19 *Mahonia* x *media* 'Charity'
20 *Aronia* x *prunifolia*
21 *Carpenteria californica*
22 *Abutilon* x *suntense*
23 *Choisya ternata*
24 Climbing roses on gazebo: 'Swan Lake', 'Golden Showers', 'Paul's Scarlet Climber'
25 *Ceanothus* 'Puget Blue'
26 *Prunus* x *subhirtella* 'Autumnalis Rosea'
27 *Lavatera* 'Barnsley'
28 *Stipa calamagrostis*
29 *Cistus ladanifer*
30 *Hibiscus syriacus* 'Woodbridge'
31 *Solidago* 'Golden Thumb'
32 *Matteuccia struthiopteris*
33 *Hosta* 'Krossa Regal'
34 *Astilbe* 'Deutschland'
35 *Daphne odora* 'Aureomarginata'
36 *Primula florindae*
37 *Aster amellus* 'King George'
38 *Iris germanica* 'Frost and Flame'
39 *Genista hispanica*
40 *Lavandula angustifolia* 'Loddon Pink'
41 *Ilex crenata* 'Golden Gem'
42 *Artemisia* 'Powis Castle'
43 *Potentilla fruticosa* 'Tilford Cream'
44 *Thymus serpyllum*

A perfect example of the art of cottage gardening in a town house.

the day, is ideal for plants such as hardy ferns, hostas and astilbes. The arch is planted with roses for scent as well as flowers.

Self-seeded plants are a typical feature of cottage-garden planting, and here this effect is simulated by deliberately placing occasional plants within the gravel areas, using low-growing varieties of thyme (**Thymus**), dwarf lavender (**Lavandula angustifolia** 'Nana Alba') and alchemilla, so as not to impede passage over the stepping stones.

THE FEATURES

Paving for the terrace is composed of old, worn, rectangular stone flags in a warm grey or buff colour, set out in a random pattern and with unpointed joints to allow plants to establish in the cracks. The same material is used for the stepping stones through the planting and also laid in gravel for the path beneath the rose arches leading to the terrace.

Around the house the paving changes to an old, yellow brick, which is laid in a herringbone pattern. It is also used as an edging to the gravel path under the rose arch. This round-topped arch is made from black-painted, wrought-iron hoops, linked together with slender horizontal matching tie-rods, and it matches in material and style the semicircular gazebo on the opposite side of the terrace.

Just off the corner of the brick paving in front of the French windows, a tiny bubble fountain uses a submersible pump to supply water from an underground sump, allowing it to spill out over small cobbles supported by a sheet of steel mesh. This attractive feature is enhanced by the adjacent shade- and moisture-loving plants, which will benefit from the extra dampness in the air from the fountain, especially in hot, dry weather.

Design Variations

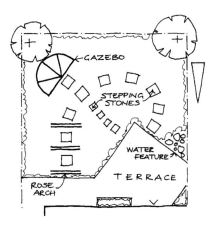

TRIANGULAR PLOT

The angle of the terrace and the meandering paths of stepping stones help to draw attention away from the tapering shape of the garden. This diversion is further helped by the deliberate placing of the gazebo part of the way down the garden, rather than at the very end, and by partly obscuring it with a tree.

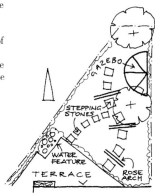

DIFFERENT ASPECT

Here the terrace is moved against the house to catch the sun, and the gazebo is positioned to create a focal point in the opposite corner. The arches and stepping stones still provide a circular route through the planting, with additional stones permitting an alternative path from the patio to the gazebo.

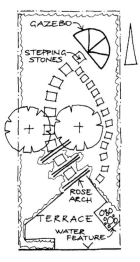

LONG, NARROW PLOT

Setting the terrace at an angle focuses attention through the rose arches in the foreground. Beyond these, two trees effectively divide the garden across its width and create a separate area. The gazebo, at the far end of the garden, is reached by two alternative stepping-stone paths.

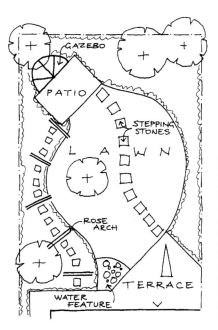

LARGER PLOT FOR FAMILY USE

The extra space that is available in this garden makes it possible to have both a generous lawn area and additional paving in front of the gazebo, which can act as an alternative patio. Having the patio and gazebo in opposite corners creates an illusion of greater space, which is further emphasized by the strong curves of the stepping-stone paths and the lawn edges.

KITCHEN GARDENS

Kitchen gardens may range in size from tiny plots, with no more than a few rows of salad crops and vegetables, to large walled gardens that keep the owner almost entirely self-sufficient in vegetables, salad, fruit and even cut flowers. What all basic kitchen gardens have in common, however, is a degree of formality and symmetry, resulting from the nature of the crop, and a limited visual appeal, especially out of season.

The first example in this chapter emphasizes this formality and symmetry by using ornamental features and planting that are carefully integrated with traditional crops. It strikes a fine balance between a purely functional, productive garden on the one hand and an ornamental one on the other.

In the second example more space is available, and the kitchen garden is retained as a separate functional unit, although incorporated within a more traditional family garden setting, which is laid out in such a way that the kitchen garden is not immediately evident.

Kitchen gardens need not be rows of vegetables. This one has been enlivened by the inclusion of globe artichokes, sweet peas and nasturtiums.

A POTAGER GARDEN

THE DESIGN

Gardens devoted entirely to growing fruit and vegetables do not necessarily need to look like allotments. In this example, a very formal design, which uses an interesting range of materials and includes several attractive features, results in a garden that is not only productive, but also eye-catching, in the manner of the traditional French ornamental kitchen garden, or *potager*.

Criss-cross paths leading from the patio break the garden down into a number of distinct areas, which can be devoted to particular types of crop, before reaching the far corners of the garden. Here are located an ornamental greenhouse (or, alternatively, a summerhouse) and an arbour, beneath which is a small bench seat. Stepping stones are used throughout for additional access.

Wrought-iron arches enclose the central square of the herb garden and provide support for both permanent and annual climbers, and on the two long boundary walls stained timber trellis is designed as a decorative feature as well as a support for climbers and trained fruit trees.

A raised bed off the edge of the patio provides ideal conditions for those herbs requiring sun and good drainage, and it is balanced by a bed for vigorous herbs such as mint, which need containing.

THE PLANTING

Although much of the garden is allocated to annual vegetable and salad crops, there is nevertheless

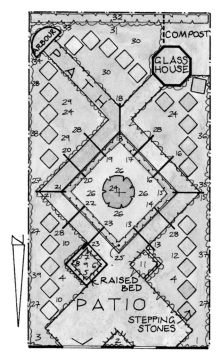

Garden 16.5m x 9m (54ft x 29ft)

some permanent planting to provide structure and, in part, an evergreen framework. The herb garden and raised bed contain many plants that are both decorative and useful, including purple and golden sage (*Salvia officinalis* 'Tricolor' and *S. o.* 'Aurea'), variegated thyme (*Thymus citriodorus* 'Silver Posie') and rosemary (*Rosmarinus officinalis* 'Miss

KEY TO PLANTING

1 *Laurus nobilis* 'Aurea'
2 *Lippia citriodora*
3 *Rosmarinus officinalis* 'Miss Jessopp's Upright'
4 *Laurus nobilis* (pyramid)
5 *Salvia officinalis* 'Tricolor'
6 *Thymus citriodorus* 'Silver Posie'
7 *Salvia officinalis* 'Aurea'
8 *Thymus vulgaris*
9 *Artemisia dracunculus*
10 Herb bed
11 *Mentha spicata*
12 Vegetables
13 *Rosa* 'Albertine'
14 Sweet peas
15 *Jasminum officinale* f. *affine*
16 Sweet peas
17 *Rosa* 'New Dawn'
18 *Clematis alpina* ssp. *sibirica* 'White Moth'
19 Sweet peas
20 *Jasminum* x *stephanense*
21 *Rosa* 'Zéphirine Drouhin'
22 *Clematis macropetala*
23 *Rosa* 'Golden Showers'
24 Ballerina apple
25 *Buxus sempervirens* 'Suffruticosa'
26 Salads
27 Cordon fruit
28 Runner beans
29 Vegetables
30 Soft fruit
31 *Ilex* x *altaclerensis* 'Golden King'
32 *Taxus baccata*
33 *Rosa* 'Seagull'
34 *Vitis vinifera* 'Purpurea'
35 Morello cherry
36 *Hedera helix* 'Tricolor'
37 *Hedera helix* 'Buttercup'
38 Aubergines
39 Tomatoes

Opposite: View from the house.
Left: Three-dimensional view of the garden.

DESIGN VARIATIONS

DIFFERENT ASPECT
Moving the patio and raised herb bed into the centre of the garden keeps them in a sunny position, but the mint bed is now contained within the smaller paved area in front of the patio doors, so retaining the symmetry of the design.

TRIANGULAR PLOT
The patio and long path are set parallel to the long boundary fence so that the axis of the plan maintains a symmetrical feel to the layout. Positioning the arbour and glasshouse at opposite ends of the garden serves to emphasize the formality of the design.

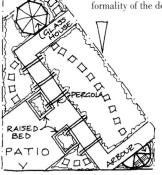

LONG, NARROW PLOT
Criss-cross paths in this narrow garden would create too many small, impractical spaces, so a single, dog-leg route is preferred, which gives a geometric rather than a symmetrical feel to the garden. The patio is set at an angle to the house to focus on the stepping-stone path through the planting and to minimize the overall narrowness of the site.

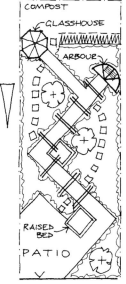

WIDE, SHALLOW PLOT
This arrangement creates a number of focal points, all of which serve to divert the eye from the shallowness of the garden – the arbour and glasshouse are in the two far corners, while an apple tree is planted at the junction of the zigzag paths and the patio. The stepping-stone paths provide the opportunity to move around the garden in a number of different ways.

Jessopp's Upright'). A hedge of dwarf box (**Buxus sempervirens** 'Suffruticosa') encloses the central herb area, and a clipped yew hedge (**Taxus baccata**) makes a beautifully neat green background along the far boundary. Height is given by columnar apple trees and bay (**Laurus nobilis**), while on the pergola several climbing roses and jasmine (**Jasminum officinale** 'Affine') add an extra dimension, mixed in with sweet peas and climbing beans.

The east-facing boundary wall is suitable for fan training a Morello cherry, with sufficient space left on either side of it for planting two variegated ivies (**Hedera** spp.) to give evergreen interest. The opposite wall is warmer, and is devoted entirely to growing cordon fruit trees, salad crops such as aubergine and tomato, and in a warmer climate possibly a grape vine or apricot.

THE FEATURES
The patio and criss-cross paths are laid in a basketweave pattern using a red paving brick, with brown bricks used to define the edges, while the stepping-stone paths are made from square, buff-coloured, imitation stone slabs to complement the red and brown bricks.

*The formality of this kitchen garden is emphasized by the
ornate path, edged on both sides by lavender hedging and
leading to the gateway in the old brick wall.*

In contrast, the raised herb bed consists of a box built from treated softwood planks set on their ends in concrete, with a narrow strip of matching timber nailed on top as a coping, and backfilled with good quality topsoil, which is improved with organic matter and sharp grit. Decorative wooden trellis panels are nailed or screwed on to horizontal softwood battens fixed to the long boundary walls, and all the timber is treated and stained in a light oak colour to match the raised bed.

The arches around the central herb garden are made from slender hoops of wrought iron or plastic-coated steel tube. These open structures cast very little shade on to the herbs themselves. Additional support for annuals such as sweet peas is provided by horizontal wires or lightweight plastic netting stretched over the whole structure. The semi-circular arbour in the far corner is made in the same style and materials as the pergola, and provides an enclosed, private area.

In the opposite corner to the arbour, and providing a balance to it, is a cedarwood green-house, which can be heated if required and is useful for propagation and for growing on plants such as beans and tomatoes before planting out as well as providing winter protection to plants in pots.

A PRODUCTIVE AND ORNAMENTAL GARDEN

THE DESIGN

To be most productive kitchen gardens are usually best laid out as square or rectangular areas. However, this can make them difficult to fit comfortably into a garden where the emphasis is on informality as well as on providing lots of space for children's play and general garden recreation.

In this example the problem is overcome by locating the area for fruit and vegetables in one corner and creating a long, diagonal view by the use of generous, sweeping borders, which also help to disguise the rectangular shape of both the kitchen garden and the rest of the plot. By emphasizing this extended view with an arch and hiding the boundaries, an impression of much greater space is created.

The simple but generous patio has provision for an outdoor clothes line, and people and activities can spill comfortably onto the lawn when things become overcrowded. Near the patio are a water feature and a herb garden, while an innocuous stepping-stone path gives easy access from the house, across the lawn to the kitchen garden, compost bin and glass-house. The grassy area extends below an arch into an orchard, which serves not only as a source of fruit for eating but also as a safe play area, and by keeping the trees well spaced, play structures for the children such as a climbing frame or slide can also be fitted in.

At the side of the house, conveniently placed near the back door, a carefully screened outdoor utility

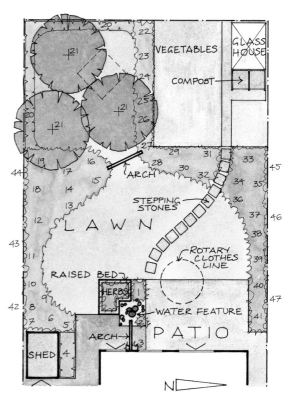

Garden 19m x 13m (62ft x 43ft)

KEY TO PLANTING
1 *Pinus mugo* 'Humpy'
2 *Iris sibirica* 'Perry's Blue'
3 *Actinidia kolomikta*
4 *Lonicera nitida* 'Baggesen's Gold'
5 *Juniperus chinensis* 'Blue Alps'
6 *Hydrangea serrata* 'Preziosa'
7 *Sinarundinaria nitida*
8 *Photinia* x *fraseri* 'Red Robin'
9 *Persicaria affinis* 'Donald Lowndes'
10 *Ligustrum ovalifolium* 'Argenteum'

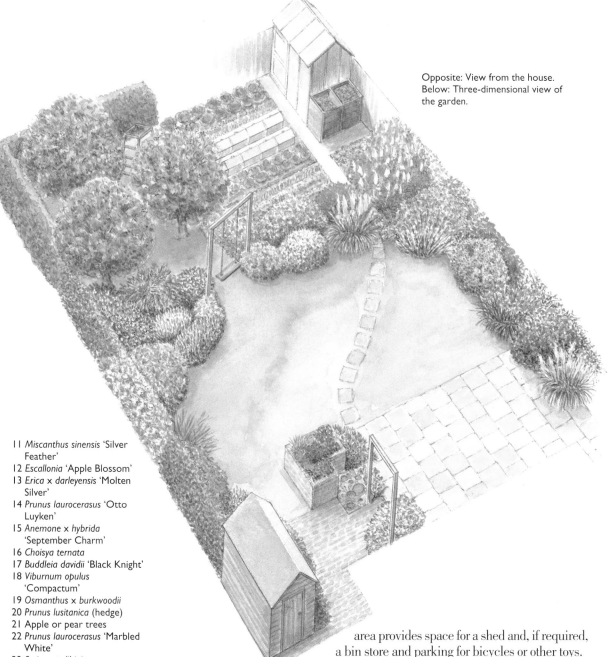

Opposite: View from the house.
Below: Three-dimensional view of the garden.

11 *Miscanthus sinensis* 'Silver Feather'
12 *Escallonia* 'Apple Blossom'
13 *Erica* x *darleyensis* 'Molten Silver'
14 *Prunus laurocerasus* 'Otto Luyken'
15 *Anemone* x *hybrida* 'September Charm'
16 *Choisya ternata*
17 *Buddleia davidii* 'Black Knight'
18 *Viburnum opulus* 'Compactum'
19 *Osmanthus* x *burkwoodii*
20 *Prunus lusitanica* (hedge)
21 Apple or pear trees
22 *Prunus laurocerasus* 'Marbled White'
23 *Syringa palibiniana*
24 *Elaeagnus* x *ebbingei* 'Limelight'
25 *Weigela florida* 'Foliis Purpureis'
26 *Cornus alba* 'Elegantissima'
27 *Philadelphus* 'Beauclerk'
28 *Monarda* 'Croftway Pink'
29 *Photinia davidiana* 'Palette'
30 *Potentilla fruticosa* 'Abbotswood'
31 *Viburnum tinus*
32 *Cortaderia selloana* 'Gold Band'
33 *Syringa vulgaris* 'Madame Lemoine'
34 *Weigela florida* 'Variegata'
35 *Cotoneaster franchetii* var. *sternianus*

36 *Geranium himalayense* 'Plenum'
37 *Viburnum* x *bodnantense* 'Dawn'
38 *Ceanothus* 'Blue Mound'
39 *Hemerocallis* 'Stafford'
40 *Choisya ternata* 'Sundance'
41 *Stipa gigantea*
42 *Parthenocissus henryana*
43 *Hydrangea anomala* ssp. *petiolaris*
44 *Lonicera* x *brownii* 'Dropmore Scarlet'
45 *Hedera helix* 'Buttercup'
46 *Akebia quinata*
47 *Jasminum officinale* 'Argenteovariegatum'

area provides space for a shed and, if required, a bin store and parking for bicycles or other toys.

THE PLANTING

The ornamental planting in the garden is deliberately kept bold yet simple, using a mix of shrubs, reliable perennials and ground-cover plants that require little more than an annual trim and top-dressing of compost or fertilizer to keep them in good shape. Accidental damage by footballs and bikes is likely in such a garden, and provision is made for this eventuality by selecting plants that are generally durable or that are able to regenerate quickly and easily.

Tall shrubs such as laurustinus (***Viburnum tinus***) are used to screen the kitchen garden from

35

the house. On the boundary with the orchard area a single row of flowering and foliage shrubs, including variegated dogwood (**Cornus alba** 'Elegantissima'), creates an attractive, informal hedge and acts as a protective buffer between the play area among the fruit trees and the more delicate rows of fruit and vegetables behind.

The fruit trees in the orchard serve two purposes: first, by creating a larger scale tree framework for the garden as a whole, and second, by providing flowers and fruit. Remember, though, that whether apples or pears are chosen, two or more compatible varieties of each must be planted to ensure good cross-pollination and cropping.

THE FEATURES

The patio is built with square, buff-coloured, reproduction stone slabs and provides ample space for dining outside, sitting and general recreation. On a corner of the patio the raised herb bed is constructed from red clay paving bricks with its coping set at a height convenient for sitting on. In the angle created by two walls of this bed, a small and perfectly safe bubble fountain sits at patio level, with the water, pumped from a hidden sump beneath, gently cascading from a selection of stones and round cobbles supported on steel mesh.

A simple, strong arch made from pressure-treated and stained softwood frames the long view into the orchard area. With the addition of two large eye bolts in the top rail, plus rope and a seat, it can be converted easily into a swing. An identical arch links the raised bed to the house wall and emphazises the distinction between the main sitting area in front of the patio doors and the more functional path of red clay paving bricks, which leads round the corner of the house to the back door and outside utility area.

The traditional French potager *or ornamental kitchen garden includes fruit and vegetables grown in geometric beds.*

DESIGN VARIATIONS

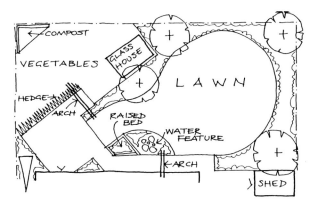

WIDE, SHALLOW PLOT
Here, the design emphasizes the long corner-to-corner diagonal, which, with the strongly curving lawn, effectively disguises the shape of the plot while at the same time creating an ideal space for the kitchen garden, which is conveniently sited just behind the patio.

DIFFERENT ASPECT
Moving the patio further down the garden means that the kitchen garden area needs to take up the whole width of the plot behind it, and this makes the rest of the garden rather square. Turning the paved areas through 45 degrees has the effect of making the garden seem larger, and an additional arch into the kitchen garden adds to this impression.

TRIANGULAR PLOT
The thin end of this wedge-shaped plot is devoted to the kitchen garden, but the rest of the garden is necessarily rather truncated. To create an illusion of greater space, the lawn edges and stepping-stone path converge at the arch at the entrance of the kitchen garden, which suggests that there is more space behind it.

LONG, NARROW PLOT
This narrow plot is broken down into three definite areas – the patio, the lawn and the kitchen garden. The raised bed, water feature and arch separate the patio from the lawn, which is circular, thus forming a strong contrast to the shape of the overall garden. Beyond, three arches follow a short, curving path round a tree to suggest another part of the garden beyond.

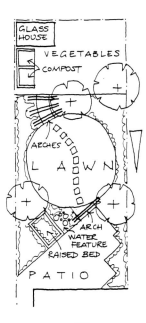

GARDENS FOR ENTERTAINING

Using your garden to its full potential makes a lot of sense,
and being able to entertain outdoors in pleasant surroundings adds
greatly to a garden's attraction.

Regardless of its size, a garden for entertaining should have as
much space as possible for sitting and general circulation, with a
large proportion of this being paved in brick, stone, flags and the
like. Adjacent lawn areas are useful for overspill in dry weather
and, for maximum convenience, patios and terraces should be
located as near to the house as possible.

The first example shows what is possible in a small town garden
in which, although half the total area is paved, the design is such
that the effect is very lush and green. This is a low-maintenance
scheme, ideally suited to someone who has little time to spare for
gardening but who wants to make the best use of the space.

The second garden is larger and has not only generous lawn
and paved areas but also a summerhouse to provide the
opportunity for year-round use. The planting is designed to
encourage minor garden tasks such as dead-heading
but avoids the need for major work.

A garden in a warm climate is perfect for entertaining and,
in the final example, a swimming pool forms the focal point around
which this takes place.

*Outdoor entertaining is made much more enjoyable where
there is ample paving, as here, to cope with all
weather conditions.*

A SMALL TOWN GARDEN

THE DESIGN

The relatively small size and narrowness of many town and city gardens need not prevent them from being turned into attractive spaces for outdoor living and entertaining. By avoiding any lawn, which is not practical for much of the year, and turning the paving at an angle to the house, this particular design makes maximum use of the limited space, yet still leaves room for some striking planting. The trees at the far end have been chosen to provide height within a small space.

The irregularly shaped paved area nearest the house can be used mainly for general circulation and sitting out, and it includes a built-in barbecue area, seat and garden store, as well as a small water feature. It leads on to a more spacious terrace, which is ideal either for organized dining out or as a rather more private and secluded area in which to sit. The two paved areas are separated by a dwarf brick wall which supports a trellis screen, and on a gently sloping site this wall would retain the ground on one side or the other according to the direction of the slope, with steps used to link the two.

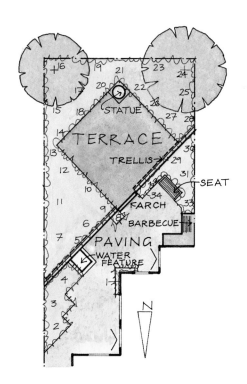

Garden 15m x 7.5m (49ft x 25ft)

THE PLANTING

The style of planting is very luxuriant and bold in order to provide a dramatic background and edging to the angular paving. A large proportion of the planting is made up of evergreen or foliage shrubs and climbers, and the effect is one of privacy and

KEY TO PLANTING
1 *Trachelospermum jasminoides* 'Variegatum'
2 *Astilbe x arendsii* 'Snowdrift'
3 *Garrya elliptica* 'James Roof'
4 *Choisya ternata* 'Sundance'
5 *Jasminum officinale* 'Aureovariegatum'
6 *Hebe* 'Marjorie'
7 *Miscanthus sacchariflorus*
8 *Clematis* 'Jackmanii Superba'
9 *Phormium* 'Sundowner'
10 *Geranium macrorrhizum* 'Album'
11 *Mahonia x media* 'Winter Sun'

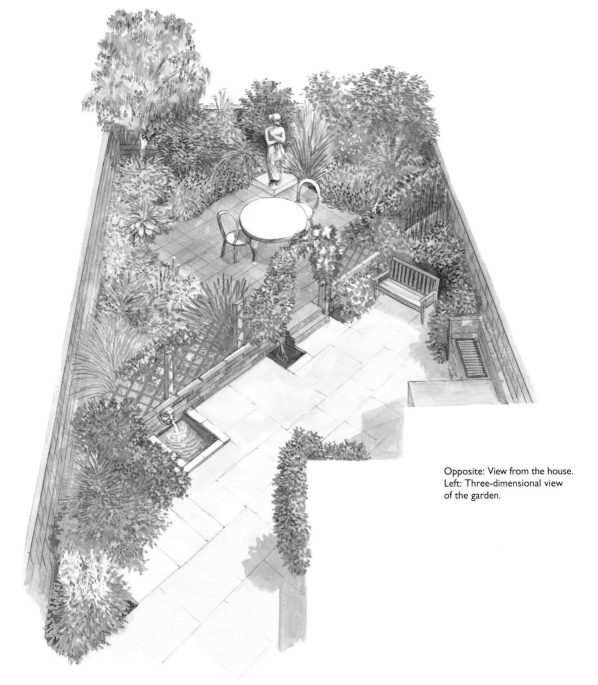

Opposite: View from the house.
Left: Three-dimensional view
of the garden.

12 *Physocarpus opulifolius* 'Dart's
Gold'
13 *Hydrangea anomala* ssp.
petiolaris
14 *Hosta fortunei* 'Picta'
15 *Hydrangea quercifolia*
16 *Betula pendula* 'Fastigiata'
17 *Acer palmatum* f.
atropurpureum
18 *Lamium maculatum* 'Aureum'
19 *Fatsia japonica*
20 *Fuchsia magellanica*
'Versicolor'
21 *Ilex aquifolium* 'J.C. van Tol'
22 *Phormium tenax* 'Purpureum'
23 *Elaeagnus* x *ebbingei*
'Limelight'

24 *Aralia elata*
25 *Buddleia* 'Lochinch'
26 *Ceanothus* 'Blue Mound'
27 *Hemerocallis* 'Catherine
Woodbery'
28 *Carpenteria californica*
29 *Hedera colchica* 'Sulphur
Heart'
30 *Sinarundinaria nitida*
31 *Cotinus coggygria* 'Royal
Purple'
32 *Geranium phaeum* 'Album'
33 *Viburnum tinus*
34 *Clematis* 'Henryi'

seclusion within the garden, albeit in a very limited
space. Perennials and ground-cover plants are chosen not only for their year-round interest but also
for their low-maintenance requirements, so that the
garden will require little in the way of upkeep,
apart perhaps from an annual spring or autumn tidy
and prune.

THE FEATURES
The paving nearest the house is laid in random,
rectangular, natural stone flags, which are chosen
to complement, rather than contrast with, the
colour of the house and garden walls. Joints

41

between the paving flags are flush pointed with mortar to provide a regular surface and to throw off surface water as quickly as possible, which is assisted by laying the paved area to a gentle slope.

The retaining wall and steps (if required) leading from this paved area to the terrace are built using the same or similar bricks as the house and boundary walls, with a natural stone coping to match the paving. Fixed on top of this low wall is a dividing trellis screen, made from standard-sized softwood panels and pressure-treated posts, the purpose of which is principally to create a division between the general paved area and formal terrace by supporting abundant climbing plants.

The terraced dining area, which is sufficiently large to take a small table and several chairs, is built in a paving brick that closely matches the garden walls. The bricks are laid in a basketweave pattern, which suits the squareness of the area, and a small statue carefully set in one corner provides a decorative finishing touch.

A mask or spout mounted on the face of the low dividing wall allows water to cascade gently into a tiny concrete-lined pool, edged on the other three sides by the stone paving. This water feature takes up little room yet provides an extremely attractive focal point, especially if picked out at night by a spotlight.

DESIGN VARIATIONS

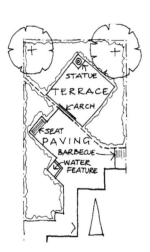

DIFFERENT ASPECT
The general paved area is reorganized to a more central part of the garden to make the best use of the available sunlight. This is helped by making the terrace wider and shallower, by altering the angle of the terrace and by moving the trellis screen. The planting that this paving replaces is moved nearer to the back door, where paving is kept to a minimum and is merely for access.

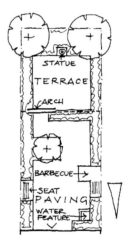

LONG, NARROW PLOT
The elements have been placed square to the boundaries of the site, although the paving has been laid in a dog-leg fashion to obstruct any long, end-to-end views. The trellis separating the paved areas forms another barrier that, although not solid, helps to create a feeling of greater space beyond it.

TRIANGULAR PLOT
The angular layout of the terrace and paved areas makes it possible to fit this garden design into a plot that is almost any shape. Here, the features are laid out to run parallel to the long boundary, which not only disguises the triangular shape of the garden but also creates an impression of greater space by emphasizing the diagonal axis.

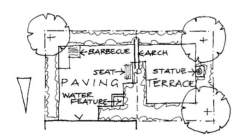

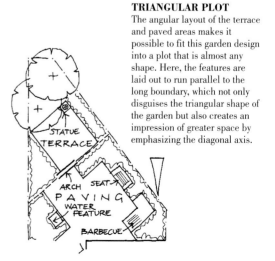

WIDE, SHALLOW PLOT
The squareness of the paving and terrace fit comfortably into this shallow site, where the trellis screen is used to divide the garden into two separate but linked halves. The features,

such as a seat, barbecue and water, make that half an irregular, geometric shape, which contrasts with the terrace in the other half, which has a rather formal, square arrangement.

*A square terrace, made with attractive old flags, is enclosed
with walls and trellis to create a secluded area within
this garden.*

A LARGE INFORMAL GARDEN

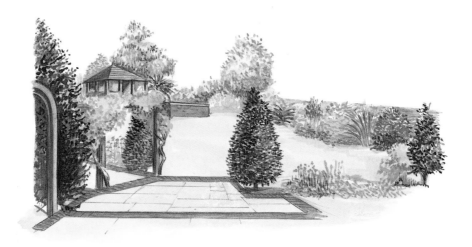

THE DESIGN

A large garden, such as the example shown here, provides plenty of scope if you like to entertain on a regular basis or spend your leisure time in the garden. With generous paving, a neat lawn, summerhouse complete with table and chairs, and a barbecue, this garden can be enjoyed to the full at almost any time of year.

The layout of paths and paving allows for easy movement, and the planting, which makes the garden into a very private and enclosed area, is carefully sited so as not to interrupt this flow. The design deliberately takes advantage of the aspect, and provides opportunities for sitting in a choice of positions which catch the sun at different times of day.

A utility area at the side of the house is separated from the rest of the garden by a trellis screen and arch, and a generously wide path leading from the house to the summerhouse passes beneath a striking pergola.

As a final decorative touch, a partially raised pool for Koi located on the corner of the summerhouse terrace creates a fascinating as well as an attractive feature.

THE PLANTING

The planting style is deliberately loose and informal, and while the garden is designed for year-round entertaining, much of this is likely to take place during the warmer months of the year, so

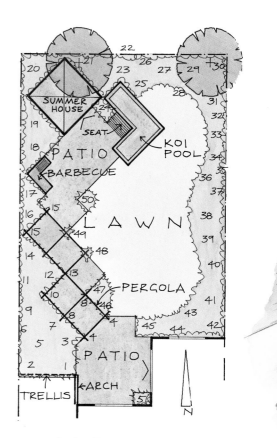

Garden 17m x 11m (56ft x 36ft)

KEY TO PLANTING

1 *Juniperus virginiana* 'Grey Owl'
2 *Viburnum opulus* 'Aureum'
3 *Geranium* x *oxonianum* 'Wargrave Pink'
4 *Clematis* 'Niobe'
5 *Miscanthus sinensis* var. *purpurascens*
6 *Lonicera* x *brownii* 'Dropmore Scarlet'
7 *Aster novi-belgii* 'Lady in Blue'
8 *Rosa* 'Golden Showers'
9 *Philadelphus* 'Avalanche'
10 *Hedera helix* 'Silver Queen'
11 *Hedera helix* 'Goldheart'
12 *Hydrangea macrophylla* 'Blue Wave'
13 *Vitis coignetiae*
14 *Camellia* 'Donation'
15 *Jasminum officinale* f. *affine*
16 *Cotinus coggygria* 'Royal Purple'
17 *Miscanthus sinensis* 'Strictus'
18 *Choisya ternata*
19 *Sinarundinaria nitida*
20 *Prunus lusitanica*
21 *Betula pendula* 'Tristis'
22 *Hedera canariensis* 'Variegata'
23 *Buddleia davidii* 'Royal Red'
24 *Euphorbia characias* ssp. *wulfenii*

25 *Potentilla fruticosa* 'Tilford Cream'
26 *Pyracantha coccinea* 'Red Column'
27 *Ligustrum* 'Vicaryi'
28 *Aster* x *thomsonii* 'Nanus'
29 *Hoheria glabrata*
30 *Sorbus aria* 'Lutescens'
31 *Photinia* x *fraseri* 'Robusta'
32 *Cotoneaster franchetii* var. *sternianus*
33 *Geranium renardii*
34 *Macleaya microcarpa* 'Kelway's Coral Plume'
35 *Actinidia kolomikta*
36 *Leucanthemum* x *superbum* 'Snowcap'
37 *Viburnum tinus* 'Eve Price'
38 *Buddleia* x *weyeriana*
39 *Stipa gigantea*
40 *Elaeagnus* x *ebbingei* 'Gilt Edge'
41 *Potentilla fruticosa* 'Abbotswood'

42 *Camellia* 'Adolphe Audusson'
43 *Coreopsis verticillata* 'Grandiflora'
44 *Aster novi-belgii* 'Little Pink Beauty'
45 *Ilex meservae* 'Blue Prince'
46 *Ilex meservae* 'Blue Angel'
47 *Achillea* 'Moonshine'
48 *Clematis orientalis* 'Bill Mackenzie'
49 *Rosa* 'New Dawn'
50 *Buxus sempervirens* 'Elegantissima'

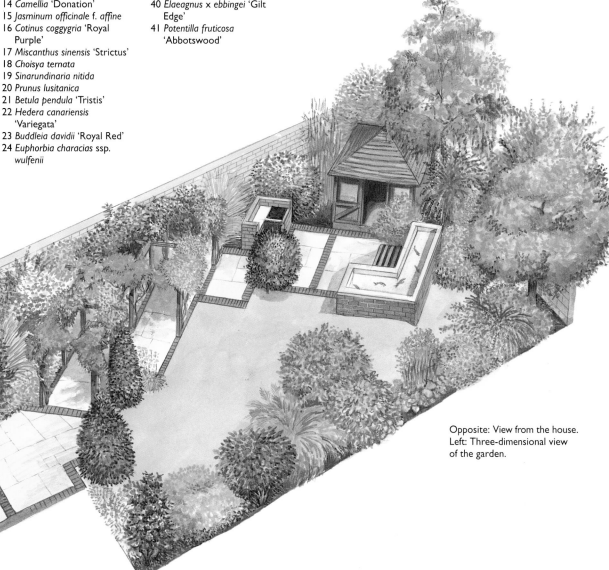

Opposite: View from the house.
Left: Three-dimensional view of the garden.

*Well-maintained lawns, sweeping around beds of shrubs
and trees, provide both sunny and shady spots in which
to sit and relax.*

there is an emphasis on plants that provide interest during this period. Herbaceous perennials and summer-flowering shrubs therefore figure strongly in the overall design, and much use is made of climbers along the boundary walls, fences and on the pergola. By restricting tree planting to the far end of the garden, extra privacy and shelter is created without casting undue shade or shadow on the rest of the garden during the day.

THE FEATURES

Paving throughout the garden is in old, rectangular sandstone flags edged in (and in places divided up by) a warm red paving brick, creating a theme running through the whole of the area. A simple built-in barbecue near the summerhouse is made from matching brick piers supporting a large sandstone paving flag.

The stained softwood pergola, which spans the dog-leg path leading from the house to the summer-house, is constructed from a modular, ready-made system using a range of moulded, grooved and planed timbers. This makes an attractive feature even without climbing plants. In the far corner of the garden a square summerhouse is built from iroko and red cedar with a shingle roof, providing a comfortable, weatherproof room large enough to accommodate several people dining around a small table, or suitable for sitting in and relaxing.

On the corner of the paved area immediately outside the summerhouse the rectangular, raised Koi pool is built from the same red brick as the barbecue, with a coping of sandstone to match the paving. The internal face of the pool is cement rendered, and at one end a simple bench seat, constructed from red cedar slats to match the summerhouse, conceals a built-in filtration system for the pool.

DESIGN VARIATIONS

DIFFERENT ASPECT

The main patio is combined with the summerhouse to make maximum use of the available sun, while the pergola provides a shady link between the house and the summerhouse. The pool for Koi carp and the seat have been retained as features in the far corner, and they are reached via a curving perimeter path, which encloses the sweeping curve of the lawn.

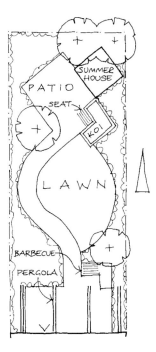

LONG, NARROW PLOT

The garden is broken down into three distinct areas, which are linked by a sweeping brick path. The main patio and barbecue areas are by the house, beneath a pergola, and leading from here, the path curves around the well-defined lawn before turning into a second patio area, which ties in with the summerhouse and pool for Koi.

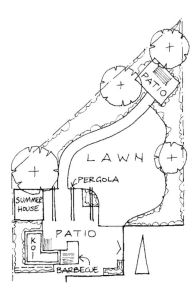

TRIANGULAR PLOT

The main area for entertaining – the summerhouse, patio and barbecue – is in the sunny half of the garden, near to the house, but the patio is divided by the barbecue to create two separate sitting areas. A curving path leads from here to a quiet spot in the far corner, where there is a small seat.

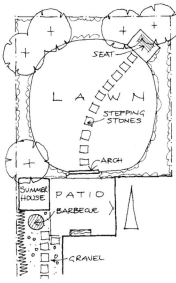

LOW-BUDGET PLOT

Cost is a major consideration in this design, and savings have been made by using gravel instead of some of the paving, by introducing a stepping-stone path and by replacing the pergola with a single arch, which marks the entrance to the lawn. The pool for Koi is replaced by a simple sitting area with a bench seat, and a small mobile barbecue is a cost-effective replacement for a built-in one.

A LARGE GARDEN IN A WARM CLIMATE

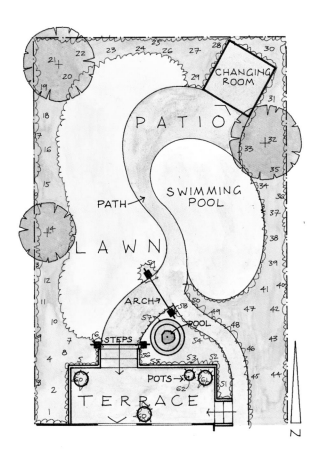

Garden 21m x 14m (69ft x 46ft)

Above: View from the house.
Right: Three-dimensional view
of the garden.

KEY TO PLANTING

1 *Citrus limon*
2 *Fuchsia* 'Madame Cornelissen'
3 *Hedera colchica* 'Sulphur Heart'
4 *Catalpa bignonioides* 'Aurea'
5 *Lantana camara*
6 *Jasminum polyanthum*
7 *Ceratostigma plumbaginoides*
8 *Cordyline australis* Purpurea Group
9 *Ceanothus* 'Italian Skies'
10 *Fuchsia* 'Tom Thumb'
11 *Olearia nummulariifolia*
12 *Photinia* x *fraseri* 'Red Robin'
13 *Jasminum officinale* 'Aureovariegatum'
14 *Eucalyptus niphophila*
15 *Hibiscus syriacus* 'Woodbridge'
16 *Juniperus chinensis* 'Aurea'
17 *Campsis* x *tagliabuana* 'Madame Galen'
18 *Euphorbia griffithii* 'Fireglow'
19 *Phormium tenax* 'Purpureum'
20 *Sedum spectabile* 'Brilliant'
21 *Cupressus arizonica*
22 *Nerium oleander*
23 *Perovskia atriplicifolia* 'Blue Spire'
24 *Phormium* 'Maori Sunrise'
25 *Fremontodendron californicum*
26 *Ozothamnus rosmarinifolius* 'Silver Jubilee'
27 *Photinia* x *fraseri* 'Rubens'
28 *Callistemon citrinus*
29 *Luma apiculata*
30 *Olea europaea*
31 *Choisya ternata*
32 *Pinus strobus*
33 *Pelargonium crispum*
34 *Santolina chamaecyparissus* var. *nana*
35 *Osmanthus decorus*
36 *Heliotropium* 'Lemoine's Giant'

THE DESIGN

In warm climates outdoor entertaining may form an important part of the social life, especially when it revolves around the use of an open-air swimming pool. Although, by their nature, pools can dominate a garden, this design carefully combines lawn, paving and planting so that the pool blends into its surroundings.

The patio and terrace are both generously sized, giving plenty of room for lounging, dining outside and barbecues, with the long, curving lawn providing extra space for these activities. Ornamental features in the garden include arches and a circular raised pool.

The garden is organized not only to take maximum advantage of sun throughout the day but also to provide alternative cool, shady spots. The warm climate allows a wide range of plants to be used to provide year-round colour and interest.

THE PLANTING

Conifers and evergreens, among others pines (*Pinus strobus*) and cypress (*Cupressus arizonica*), not only provide a framework to the garden but are carefully placed to accentuate the curves of the pool and lawn. They also create cool patches of shade at different times of the day, particularly near

37 *Hebe* x *andersonii*
38 *Phlomis fruticosa*
39 *Fatsia japonica* 'Variegata'
40 *Akebia quinata*
41 *Myrtus communis* ssp. *tarentina*
42 *Sophora tetraptera*
43 *Arbutus* x *andrachnoides*
44 *Hebe hectorii*
45 *Fuchsia magellanica* 'Aurea'
46 *Teucrium chamaedrys*

47 *Pinus strobus* 'Nana'
48 *Erica arborea* 'Albert's Gold'
49 *Pittosporum tobira* 'Nanum'
50 *Verbena peruviana*
51 *Hebe vernicosa*
52 *Lippia citriodora*
53 *Agapanthus* 'Blue Giant'
54 *Osteospermum ecklonii*
55 *Lavandula stoechas* ssp. *pendunculata*
56 *Bougainvillea* x *buttiana*
57 *Asclepias tuberosa*
58 *Trachelospermum jasminoides* 'Variegatum'
59 *Eccremocarpus scaber*
60 *Nicotiana* vars.
61 *Lilium regale*
62 *Citrus limon*

49

the changing room and patio. Climbers are allowed to scramble freely along the white painted boundary walls, supported by trellis or heavy-gauge galvanized wires. Flowering shrubs, perennials and succulents form the bulk of the border planting, with a predominance of evergreens chosen for their soft, non-spiky foliage around the immediate edge of the pool area, which will also reduce the problem of autumn leaf fall into the pool itself.

In such a warm environment, scented plants are particularly successful, and several climbers and shrubs such as myrtle (*Luma apiculata*), chosen especially for this characteristic, are thoughtfully placed near sitting areas and paths, where the pleasant perfumes can be appreciated. Other fragrant plants, such as nicotiana and lilies, could be grown in pots on the patio

THE FEATURES

The main feature in the garden is the swimming pool, which is an elongated kidney shape designed to reflect the sweeping curves of the lawn, path and patio. It is sited so that it does not dominate the gar-

DESIGN VARIATIONS

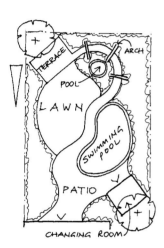

DIFFERENT ASPECT
The swimming pool remains in the same position, but the positions of the terrace and patio are changed to take account of the sun's direction. A sweep of lawn still links the terrace and swimming pool, while the strongly curving shapes throughout the garden mask its rectangular outline.

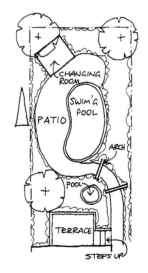

LONG, NARROW PLOT
The swimming pool has been turned slightly so that it is more centrally positioned, and the paved link from the house to the changing room sweeps from one side of the garden to the other to form a contrast with the straightness of the boundaries. With this layout, a worthwhile area of lawn is not practicable and it has been replaced with additional paving and planting.

TRIANGULAR PLOT
The swimming pool is more centrally placed here for maximum benefit, and this allows the two narrow ends of the garden to be used to accommodate the terrace and changing room. A lawn is not really practicable with this layout, and the ornamental pool is used as a focal point in the front of the patio.

WIDE, SHALLOW PLOT
The terrace has been set at an angle to focus attention through the arches and across the long dimension of the garden towards the changing room. Similarly, the patio by the pool has been turned so that it faces towards the opposite corner of the plot, thus drawing the eye away from its rather limited depth.

*Bold planting and a striking red brick path have been
deliberately combined to balance the dramatic swimming pool.*

den completely, and it is in sun for most of the day. In addition, it could be finished internally with tiles chosen to complement the colour of the surrounding paving, rather than with the more traditional light blue, to minimize its visual impact.

The paving throughout the garden is in a pale coloured sandstone with a slightly textured finish to make it non-slip when wet, which is especially important around the pool area. These randomly shaped slabs are in varying sizes and are carefully and accurately cut along both the path and pool edges to maintain the elegant curves of both.

The arches over the path leading from the house to the pool area consist of roughly sawn and sanded timber crosspieces sitting across the tops of brick piers, which are painted white. The wood is best treated with a clear preservative, but it can be left untreated so that it will bleach and weather in the warm, dry atmosphere.

At the far end of the swimming pool, and partly in the shade of a large pine, a white-painted, brick-built changing room with terracotta-tiled roof houses the plant and filtration system for the swimming pool.

At the foot of the steps leading up to the terrace is a circular, raised ornamental pool, built from a series of curved sections of cast reproduction stone, laid on a concrete base to form a circle and then rendered internally to make the whole structure waterproof. In the centre of the pool a large, dark granite boulder is drilled so that water can be pumped from beneath to flood out of the top and spill dramatically over the polished rock surface.

A low-voltage lighting system, especially designed for safe garden use, adds an extra dimension to the garden, extending its use into the evenings and highlighting individual plants or features with spot or floodlights.

FAMILY GARDENS

A garden to suit all the family is not always the easiest thing to achieve, especially when the needs of the individual family members are diverse. These needs may themselves change with time, particularly as children grow up, and the garden design therefore needs to be reasonably flexible in order to take this into account.

Where space is limited, though, this is not as easy as it sounds, and the first garden in this chapter demonstrates a simple yet effective layout for a small plot, showing how a number of different interests can be accommodated. As well as being functional, the design also pays attention to linking the various elements together to create an attractive overall view.

Cost can also be a limiting factor in achieving the ideal garden, and the second example shows how an attractive yet practical garden can be achieved for a modest outlay. It could be a permanent layout, or it might be regarded as an interim measure until such time as more money is available to spend on the garden.

This garden has plenty to offer the whole family – a lawn, paving, ornamental planting and features including a summerhouse and rose arches.

A MULTI-USE GARDEN IN A LIMITED SPACE

THE DESIGN

Many parents with young children find themselves in the situation where their garden just does not seem to be large enough to meet all their needs. The design for this typically modest plot illustrates how a compromise between play areas, flower borders, outside storage and kitchen gardening can be achieved while still allowing the garden to be visually striking.

Although this design devotes a useful area to paving and lawn for children to play on and for general relaxation, attention is also given to provision for other requirements, including a small vegetable garden with mini-glasshouse, a storage area for bicycles and garden furniture, and space for such necessities as a rotary clothes line and dustbin.

A narrow path, lined with posts to support climbing plants, is used to divide the kitchen garden from the rest of the plot, and leads underneath an arch to a small compost heap in the far corner of the garden. The large area of patio is broken up by an attractive raised bed, which is linked to the house wall by a simple pergola, and the paving continues round the corner of the house to the utility area and back door.

THE PLANTING

The main planting within the garden is in the form of a simply shaped yet effective perimeter border, in which a selection of shrubs and fruit trees, together with ground-cover perennials, provides a relatively low-maintenance yet attractive display of plants to give interest virtually all year round.

A small bed around the base of the clothes drier is planted with winter-flowering heathers (*Erica carnea* vars.) to provide interest in the late winter months, particularly for someone looking out of the

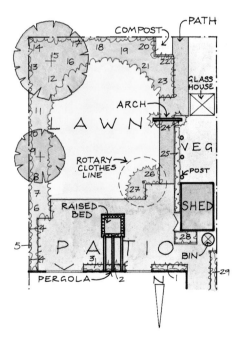

Garden 12m x 10m (39ft x 33ft)

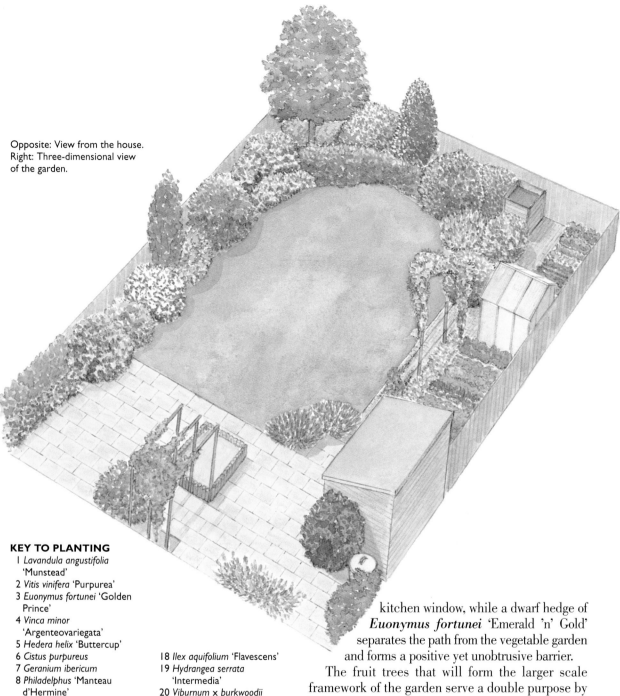

Opposite: View from the house.
Right: Three-dimensional view
of the garden.

KEY TO PLANTING

1 *Lavandula angustifolia* 'Munstead'
2 *Vitis vinifera* 'Purpurea'
3 *Euonymus fortunei* 'Golden Prince'
4 *Vinca minor* 'Argenteovariegata'
5 *Hedera helix* 'Buttercup'
6 *Cistus purpureus*
7 *Geranium ibericum*
8 *Philadelphus* 'Manteau d'Hermine'
9 Ballerina apple
10 *Hebe* 'Great Orme'
11 *Viburnum tinus* 'Variegatum'
12 *Geranium* x *oxonianum* 'Wargrave Pink'
13 *Weigela florida* 'Foliis Purpureis'
14 *Aucuba japonica* 'Maculata'
15 Apple
16 *Anemone* x *hybrida* 'Bressingham Glow'
17 *Pieris floribunda* 'Forest Flame'
18 *Ilex aquifolium* 'Flavescens'
19 *Hydrangea serrata* 'Intermedia'
20 *Viburnum* x *burkwoodii*
21 *Persicaria affinis* 'Dimity'
22 *Hypericum forrestii*
23 *Cornus alba* 'Sibirica'
24 *Clematis* 'The President'
25 *Euonymus fortunei* 'Emerald 'n' Gold'
26 *Erica carnea* 'Springwood White'
27 *Erica carnea* 'Myretoun Ruby'
28 *Ligustrum ovalifolium* 'Argenteum'
29 *Hedera helix* 'Cristata'

kitchen window, while a dwarf hedge of ***Euonymus fortunei*** 'Emerald 'n' Gold' separates the path from the vegetable garden and forms a positive yet unobtrusive barrier.

The fruit trees that will form the larger scale framework of the garden serve a double purpose by being both productive and ornamental, and the choice of varieties grown on dwarf rootstocks or that have a narrow, columnar habit ensures that they will not outgrow their allotted space and become a nuisance in the longer term.

THE FEATURES

The pergola on the patio is made from round-sectioned softwood posts and overhead rails, which are stained to match the window frames of the house. Climbers to grow up it can be planted either in a narrow border against the house wall or in the adjoining raised bed. This low box structure is built from short lengths of stained and treated, round softwood posts to match the pergola, which are set on end in concrete. It can be used for several purposes, starting out life as a sandpit, eventually developing into a raised herb garden and ultimately, perhaps, being converted into a small ornamental pool.

The arch further down the garden, leading to the vegetable plot, is similar in style to the pergola and joins on to a row of matching posts along the edge of the kitchen garden, forming a transparent screen. Incorporating several horizontal wires between these posts allows them to be used for growing crops such as runner beans as well as, or instead of, ornamental climbers.

The patio is built from a rectangular reproduction stone slab in a warm beige or honey colour, while the narrow dividing path leading down the garden to the compost heap is laid in a paving brick chosen to match closely the colour of the house walls.

This tiny family garden is made to look much larger
than it really is by the clever use of the sweeping lawn, which
disappears at the far end, where it is framed by
two old apple trees.

DESIGN VARIATIONS

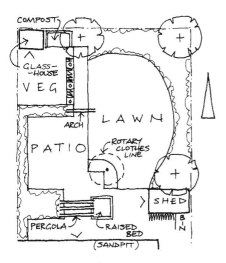

TRIANGULAR PLOT
The shape of the patio has been designed to mirror the shape of the garden, although the curve of the perimeter border effectively masks this. To keep the patio to a usable size, the sandpit has been moved to one corner, and the arch now becomes an entrance to the ornamental garden, while the vegetable plot and utility area are tucked away in the narrow corner.

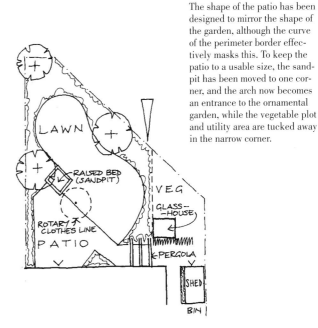

DIFFERENT ASPECT
The patio has been extended to catch as much sun as possible while at the same time keeping it fairly close to the house. The raised bed is still near the kitchen window, but the arch has been turned through 90 degrees to make an entrance on to the patio. Turning the shed provides space for extra planting behind it, and the vegetable plot is hidden from the patio by a hedge.

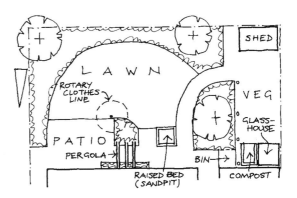

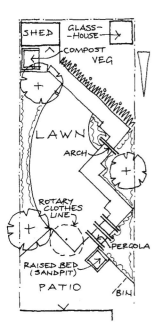

LONG, NARROW PLOT
The narrowness of this garden is countered by the zigzag path, which runs down one side, and by the strong curve of the lawn, which skirts the opposite side. Angling both the patio and the vegetable garden helps to create a feeling of space while avoiding the creation of a 'corridor' effect.

WIDE, SHALLOW PLOT
The wide rectangular shape of this garden is successfully masked by the pronounced curve of the lawn, which is echoed in the curved path. Although the patio and paved area are fairly narrow, they run across the full width of the house so that the lawn can be as large as possible. The shed and vegetable plot are screened by a well-planted mixed border.

A LARGER PLOT ON A
LIMITED BUDGET

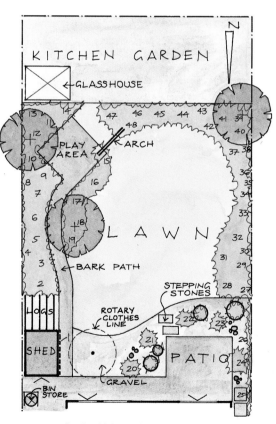

THE DESIGN

As the family grows, in both size and number, many people need to move to a larger house, which, more often than not, will be accompanied by a larger garden. It is also often the case, especially with a new house, that the funds needed to create the ideal garden are not immediately available. However, by making a number of compromises it is still possible, as this design shows, to meet the needs of all the family at the same time as creating an impressive garden.

Tree and shrub planting, together with paving using stone flags or paving bricks, tend to be the most expensive items in a garden. Here they are kept to a minimum while still providing the basic framework of an attractive layout, with a relatively low-cost, seed-produced lawn occupying a generous proportion of the garden.

At the far end of the plot a useful kitchen garden, including space for compost and a glasshouse, is screened from view by a simple hedge of mixed shrubs. It is reached by a narrow, bark-covered path, which widens near the far end of the lawn to create room for a safe play area around a climbing frame or an alternative sitting area to the patio. The small patio area of paving slabs is extended by the use of gravel, so that ornamental features such as large boulders, decorative pots and specimen plants can be displayed around it, but without getting in the way of the garden furniture.

Garden 20.5m x 12.5m (67ft x 41ft)

Opposite: View from the house.
Left: Three-dimensional view of
the garden.

KEY TO PLANTING

1 *Hedera canariensis*
  'Variegata'
2 *Mahonia* x *media* 'Charity'
3 *Abelia* x *grandiflora*
4 *Jasminum officinale*
5 *Ligustrum* 'Vicaryi'
6 *Syringa palibiniana*
7 *Achillea* 'Moonshine'
8 *Hedera canariensis*
  'Variegata'
9 *Cistus laurifolius*
10 *Rhododendron* 'Praecox'
11 *Persicaria amplexicaulis*
  'Inverleith'
12 Apple
13 *Pyracantha* 'Orange Glow'
14 *Hebe* 'Alicia Amherst'
15 *Lonicera periclymenum*
  'Serotina'
16 *Geranium* x *oxonianum* 'A.T.
  Johnson'
17 *Euonymus fortunei* 'Emerald
  Gaiety'
18 *Malus floribunda*
19 *Cotoneaster* x *suecicus* 'Coral
  Beauty'
20 *Hebe* 'Mrs Winder'
21 *Phormium* 'Yellow Wave'
22 *Helictotrichon sempervirens*
23 *Pinus mugo* var. *pumilio*
24 *Fuchsia magellanica* var.
  gracilis 'Aurea'

25 *Euonymus fortunei* 'Silver
  Queen'
26 *Hydrangea anomala* ssp.
  petiolaris
27 *Pulmonaria rubra* 'Redstart'
28 *Juniperus* x *media* 'Old Gold'
29 *Buddleia davidii* 'Nanho
  Purple'
30 *Clematis* 'Henryi'
31 *Liriope spicata* 'Alba'
32 *Viburnum tinus* 'Variegatum'
33 *Potentilla fruticosa* 'Princess'
34 *Skimmia japonica* 'Fragrans'
35 *Hedera helix* 'Silver Queen'
36 *Cornus sanguinea* 'Winter
  Flame'
37 *Vinca minor*
  'Argenteovariegata'
38 *Skimmia japonica* 'Nymans'
39 Apple
40 *Viburnum rhytidophyllum*
41 *Azalea* 'Gibralter'
42 *Astilbe* x *arendsii*
  'Bressingham Beauty'
43 *Hydrangea paniculata*
  'Kyushu'
44 *Viburnum tinus* 'Purpureum'
45 *Hypericum* 'Hidcote'
46 *Viburnum opulus*
  'Compactum'
47 *Weigela florida* 'Variegata'
48 *Hedra helix* 'Ivalace'

A simple archway with climbing plants marks the entrance to the kitchen garden, which can be secured with a gate, while at the other end of the garden a utility area incorporating a shed, an area for logs or coal and a bin store is screened from view by a very simple trellis arrangement.

THE PLANTING

The basic framework of planting around the garden is made up of long-lived shrubs and perennials that require a modest amount of annual maintenance and are selected to avoid varieties with sharp spines, poisonous berries or irritating sap. Reliable climbers such as jasmine (***Jasminum officinale***) and ivy (***Hedera canariensis*** 'Variegata') grow along the boundary fences and up the shed walls to

59

provide screening and to help to disguise the rectangular shape of the garden.

The kitchen garden is separated from the rest of the garden by a row of medium-sized evergreen and deciduous shrubs, which act as a natural barrier without giving the impression of being a formal hedge. The planting on the arch and around the entrance to the kitchen garden is carefully chosen and arranged to screen this gateway and to give the impression that the lawn continues through into another part of the garden beyond.

Around the patio, plants can be grown through the membrane and gravel mulch, both individually and in small groups to provide focal points of interest without creating solid masses of planting that will take up too much space. They can be used in combination with rocks and cobbles of varying sizes to provide sculptural groups which will give interest all the year round.

THE FEATURES

A simple, rustic arch of peeled and treated larch poles provides a link between the main recreational area of the garden and the kitchen garden behind, with durable honeysuckle (**Lonicera periclymenum** 'Serotina') and ivy (**Hedera**) providing plant interest.

All the areas of gravel and bark are laid on top of a porous, weed-suppressing membrane, which is pegged down on the levelled and compacted soil. They are separated from the lawn and planting areas by a treated, thin softwood timber edge fixed to pegs driven into the ground. By using this flexible edging it is possible to produce long, elegant curves, which are in keeping with the theme of the garden.

The basic patio and path leading to the back door are laid in very simple square, concrete slabs. If the house is new, this could well be the paving that was laid by the builder.

DESIGN VARIATIONS

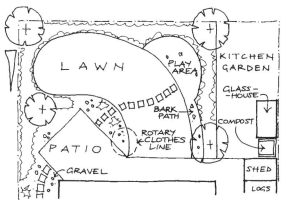

WIDE, SHALLOW PLOT
Here the play area and patio have been sited in opposite corners, with the lawn curving round in the other direction to give a greater impression of depth. This is further helped by having the kitchen garden down one side, with the mixed border in front of it, screening it from view.

TRIANGULAR PLOT
Using the corners for the kitchen garden and utility area leaves space in the centre for a worthwhile lawn, which is almost circular and helps to draw attention from the irregular shape of the plot. The play area, now sited next to the shed and fuel store, is away from the general ornamental part of the garden.

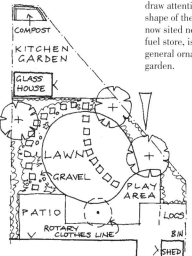

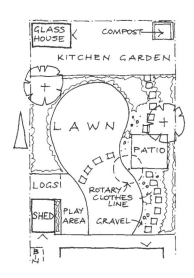

DIFFERENT ASPECT

The square patio is moved part way along one side of the garden, away from the shade, and access to it and to the kitchen garden are via a path of stepping stones laid in gravel. The play area is moved in front of the shed, so that a long sweep of attractively curved lawn leads the eye towards the far end of the garden, while stepping stones are used to link the play/utility area with the patio.

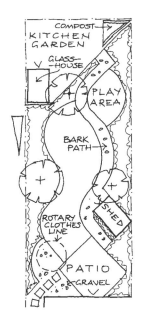

LONG, NARROW PLOT

The length of garden is accentuated by the long, sweeping curves of both the path and the borders, which serve nevertheless to disguise the straight boundaries. Placing the patio at an angle adds to the overall effect by focusing attention on the tree beyond. The play area is at the far end of the plot, in the triangular space left next to the kitchen garden.

For a modest outlay this attractive family garden has been designed to create space for play and relaxation, all within a framework of evergreen planting, lightened by splashes of bright colour.

GARDENS FOR THE DISABLED

Many otherwise attractive gardens are often inaccessible, uninviting places to those who may be handicapped in some way, sometimes simply because there are steps instead of a ramp or because the paths are not wide enough to accommodate a wheelchair. With just a little thought and care in detailing, however, these gardens can be transformed so that anyone can gain enjoyment from them.

The first design is aimed at people who have limited mobility and who may need to use a wheelchair or walking aid. Its layout of generous paved areas provides easy circulation, while the narrow borders are easily accessible for routine gardening chores such as dead-heading.

In the second garden special attention is paid to providing stimuli for someone who may have learning difficulties. The overall layout is also, however, carefully detailed so that it can be used by other family members.

At first glance the final garden appears to be an example of a good, elegant design with which many gardeners would be very happy. However, it contains a number of small, but significant, details of both construction and planting that make it also admirably suited to a blind or partially sighted person.

A raised pool, raised beds and generous, even paving make this attractive garden accessible for all.

A SMALL GARDEN WITH WHEELCHAIR ACCESS

THE DESIGN

Many gardens are designed on the basis that the people who will use them are generally able to move about the garden with comparative ease. However, this is not always the case, and if you are less mobile the pleasure of an attractive garden can often be outweighed by the difficulties encountered in moving around it and negotiating obstacles. This small, rather formal ornamental garden is therefore specifically designed to avoid the problems often encountered by people with limited mobility.

For all-year-round access in virtually any weather, paving is used in preference to a lawn, and it is laid out in generous areas to avoid dead ends and tight corners. On very hot days in summer this paving may reflect a lot of heat, so carefully positioned trees, together with a pergola and arbour, provide shady spots for such times.

The planting areas are quite narrow so that access into them for weeding or watering is easy, and yet they interlock with the paving to draw attention away from the squareness of the plot.

A circular, raised bed in the centre of the garden makes an attractive feature and is complemented on the other side of the pergola by a small pool, which provides a focal point both in the garden itself and when it is viewed through the patio doors.

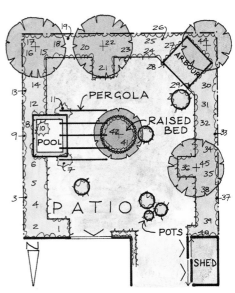

Garden 10.5m x 10m (35ft x 33ft)

KEY TO PLANTING
1 *Lavandula angustifolia* 'Hidcote'
2 *Choisya ternata* 'Sundance'
3 *Parthenocissus henryana*
4 *Stipa calamagrostis*
5 *Taxus baccata* 'Semperaurea'
6 *Hemerocallis* 'Catherine Woodbery'
7 *Ampelopsis glandulosa* var. *brevipedunculata* 'Elegans'
8 *Miscanthus sinensis* 'Strictus'
9 *Hedera helix* 'Glacier'
10 *Sagittaria sagittifolia*
11 *Jasminum* x *stephanense*
12 *Hebe* 'Midsummer Beauty'
13 *Trachelospermum jasminoides*
14 *Kerria japonica* 'Variegata'
15 *Euphorbia amygdaloides* var. *robbiae*
16 *Anemone hupehensis* 'September Charm'

Opposite: View from the house.
Right: Three-dimensional view
of the garden.

17 *Prunus* x *schmittii*
18 *Aucuba japonica*
 'Crotonifolia'
19 *Hydrangea anomala* ssp.
 petiolaris
20 *Pleioblastus auricomus*
21 *Heuchera micrantha* 'Palace
 Purple'
22 *Sorbus* 'Joseph Rock'
23 *Prunus laurocerasus* 'Otto
 Luyken'
24 *Persicaria affinis* 'Dimity'
25 *Aconitum* 'Bressingham Spire'
26 *Clematis* 'Marie Boisselot'
27 *Taxus baccata* 'Fastigiata
 Aurea'
28 *Lonicera implexa*
29 *Rosa* 'Golden Showers'
30 *Berberis thunbergii* 'Rose
 Glow'
31 *Mahonia* x *wagneri*
 'Undulata'
32 *Geranium phaeum* 'Album'
33 *Actinidia kolomikta*
34 *Fargesia murieliae* 'Simba'

35 *Digitalis* x *mertonensis*
36 *Epimedium* x *youngianum*
 'Niveum'
37 *Rubus henryi* var.
 bambusarum
38 *Hydrangea serrata* 'Preziosa'
39 *Skimmia japonica* 'Rubella'
40 *Hedera helix* 'Ivalace'
41 *Cotoneaster dammeri*
42 *Malus* x *schiedeckeri* 'Red
 Jade'
43 *Ampelopsis glandulosa* var.
 brevipedunculata 'Elegans'
44 *Betula pendula* 'Fastigiata'
45 *Prunus virginiana* 'Schubert'

THE PLANTING

Tall, privacy-creating planting is achieved within the narrow borders by the careful use of small trees, shrubs and perennials specially chosen for their upright habit of growth and tolerance to overhead shade and root competition. Over-vigorous varieties that require substantial maintenance are deliberately avoided, and in addition evergreen climbers, especially some of the smaller leaved ivies (such as **Hedera helix** 'Glacier'), are used to clothe the bare boundary walls. Ground-cover planting between and underneath the taller plants not only suppresses annual weeds but spills over the paving to soften its hard edges.

65

Annuals for summer colour can be planted in a selection of pots and planters that are carefully placed on the patio to break up some of the angles and straight lines of the paving but without creating bottlenecks or making access difficult.

The circular raised bed in the centre of the garden is planted with a weeping crab apple (**Malus** x **schiedeckeri** 'Red Jade'), which in turn is underplanted with very low ground-cover plants to trail over the edges of the bed and cascade down.

THE FEATURES

The paving, of rectangular, buff-coloured and lightly textured concrete slabs, is laid in a staggered bond, mixed in and edged with multi-coloured brick. The whole of the paved area is carefully laid to slope gently away from the house so that no water is allowed to accumulate and cause unsightly stains or dangerous icy patches in the winter.

The central circular raised bed is built from pressure-treated, round-sectioned logs set on end in concrete. The advantage of using logs in this way is that a very small diameter circle can be constructed relatively easily, allowing access from any point around the edge of the bed right into the centre.

The pergola provides an attractive frame up which climbers can be grown, and it not only links the raised bed to the ornamental pool but also frames a view through to the rest of the garden beyond. It is built very simply from square-section softwood posts and rectangular-section overhead rails, all pressure-treated and stained to match the raised bed. A matching arbour in the corner of the garden is built from four square-sectioned posts infilled with standard-sized trellis panels, to form three sides and an overhead canopy.

At the side of the house the garden store is specially constructed to be wide and shallow with sliding doors opening along the full width, allowing easy access to anything stored inside.

As a further labour-saving aid, the garden is supplied with an irrigation system consisting of flexible porous pipe buried just below the soil surface and running throughout the length of the perimeter bed. Watering is then simply a matter of connecting the system to a standpipe at the bottom of the garden or, alternatively, to a wall tap conveniently located near the back door.

DESIGN VARIATIONS

TRIANGULAR PLOT

This garden is divided in two by the pergola, which joins on to the boundary, the pool and the raised bed. The arbour fits neatly into the narrow space at the far end, while the shed is placed in the opposite corner, which would otherwise be dead space.

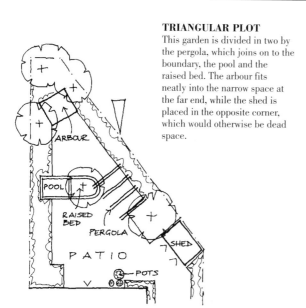

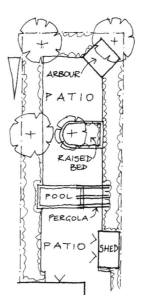

LONG, NARROW PLOT

The raised bed has been separated from the pergola and pool, and this creates a somewhat zigzag effect in the garden, breaking it into a series of interesting spaces while retaining room for access and manoeuvring.

Not only is this garden practical – with its generous paved areas, raised beds and water feature – but it is also attractive and easy to maintain.

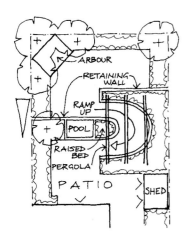

SLOPING PLOT

This garden slopes away from the house, and the design creates two level areas, one for the patio and one for the arbour, which are linked by a long, curving ramp. The pool and the raised bed are incorporated within the retaining wall, which is necessary between the two main areas.

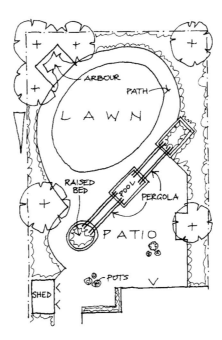

LARGER PLOT

The additional space that is available in this plot allows the garden to be split into two by the diagonal construction of the raised beds, a pool and pergolas. The rather angular patio forms a strong contrast with the smoothly elliptical lawn, which is banded on both sides by paths affording easy access to the arbour.

A GARDEN FOR PEOPLE WITH LEARNING DIFFICULTIES

THE DESIGN

It is well known that certain sounds, colours and movement, as well as tactile sensations, can both stimulate and benefit people with learning difficulties, and with some thought a garden can be created to provide all of these. This particular garden not only places a special emphasis on such stimulation but also considers the needs of the rest of the family.

In a situation such as this, time for gardening is invariably in short supply, and the garden is carefully designed, particularly with regard to planting, so that only a very modest amount of time and effort will be needed to maintain it. The simple, effective layout avoids any hidden corners, so the entire garden can be in view at all times, and areas where access might need to be limited, such as the tool store and compost bin at the bottom of the garden and the shed, fuel store and bin area outside the back door, can be secured by gates.

A slight slope down the length of the garden is easily taken into account by the gently sloping path and lawn, so avoiding any potentially difficult steps or sudden changes of level. The layout of extra-wide paths and non-slip paving allows easy movement around the garden, whether on foot or in a wheelchair. By having two patio areas in diagonally opposite corners of the garden there is the option of sitting out in the sun, or shade, at virtually any time of the day.

Above: View from the house.
Right: Three-dimensional view of the garden.

KEY TO PLANTING

1 *Photinia x fraseri* 'Rubens'
2 *Hebe* 'Margret'
3 *Crocosmia* 'Lucifer'
4 *Osteospermum ecklonii*
5 *Phygelius aequalis* 'Yellow Trumpet'
6 *Campsis radicans*
7 *Hemerocallis* 'George Cunningham'
8 *Pleioblastus auricomus*
9 *Leucanthemum x superbum* 'Snowcap'
10 *Buddleia davidii* 'Black Knight'
11 *Geum chiloense* 'Mrs J. Bradshaw'
12 *Romneya coulteri*
13 *Penstemon* 'Sour Grapes'
14 *Prunus serrula* var. *tibetica*
15 *Lonicera nitida* 'Baggesen's Gold'
16 *Hedera canariensis* 'Variegata'
17 *Geranium sanguineum*
18 *Physocarpus opulifolius* 'Dart's Gold'
19 *Cornus alba* 'Sibirica Variegata'
20 *Astilbe x arendsii* 'Snowdrift'
21 *Betula pendula* 'Tristis'
22 *Rhododendron* 'Pink Perfection'
23 *Spiraea japonica* 'Gold Mound'
24 *Deschampsia cespitosa* 'Bronzeschleier'
25 *Campanula persicifolia alba*
26 *Hydrangea serrata* 'Diadem'
27 *Fargesia murieliae* 'Simba'
28 *Clematis* 'Niobe'
29 *Acer negundo* 'Flamingo'
30 *Helleborus niger*
31 *Camellia* 'Leonard Messel'
32 *Trollius x cultorum* 'Alabaster'
33 *Daphne odora* 'Aureomarginata'
34 *Euonymus fortunei* 'Silver Queen'
35 *Lavandula angustifolia* 'Hidcote'
36 *Actinidia chinensis*
37 *Astrantia maxima*
38 *Hebe* 'Alicia Amherst'
39 *Rudbeckia fulgida* var. *speciosa*
40 *Hedera helix* 'Goldheart'
41 *Prunus x subhirtella* 'Autumnalis'
42 *Sorbus aria* 'Lutescens'

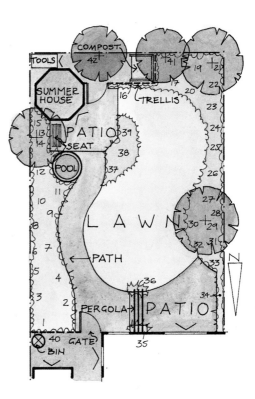

Garden 13m x 9.5m (43ft x 31ft)

69

DESIGN VARIATIONS

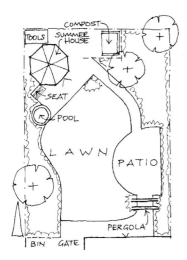

TRIANGULAR PLOT

The paved area outside the summerhouse is angled so that the path can link back to the house around an almost circular lawn, which helps to disguise the irregular shape of the plot. At the far end of the garden, the awkward space behind the summerhouse is ideal for the compost bins and tool store.

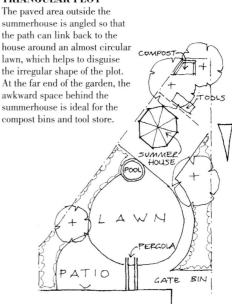

DIFFERENT ASPECT

The patio has been moved so that it is in a sunnier part of the garden and it has been given a curved edge to complement the shape of the lawn. The paved area outside the summerhouse has been altered so that it is linked to the main patio by a gently curving path.

LONG, NARROW PLOT

The sweeping path cuts across the elliptical lawn to link with the angled patio in front of the summerhouse. This helps to draw attention away from the narrowness of the garden yet avoids creating hidden corners.

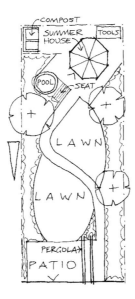

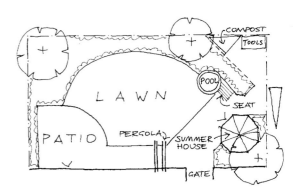

WIDE, SHALLOW PLOT

The lack of depth in this plot is not apparent because the layout is designed to concentrate on the diagonals, with the patio, summerhouse and pool located in the corners, leaving space for a practical yet attractive central lawn.

THE PLANTING

Planting in this garden is very carefully chosen to avoid plant varieties with poisonous berries, stems, leaves and sap, as well as those that might cause physical injury because of their spines, needles or stiff branches. They are also chosen for their ability to stimulate visually through bright or intensely coloured flowers and foliage, as well as for their ability to recover from damage.

A high proportion of the planting is evergreen, and much of the main border is infilled with ground-cover perennials and prostrate shrubs to prevent annual weed seeds from germinating. The trees along the far boundary act as a windbreak and also provide more distant interest and height.

The gentle curve of the brick path emphasizes the edge of the lawn, while a clear-stemmed *Acer negundo* 'Flamingo' nearer to the main patio helps to break up the straight line of the boundary fence while allowing an unrestricted view below its crown.

THE FEATURES

The two patio areas at opposite ends of the garden are constructed from creamy-yellow, rectangular reproduction stone slabs, which are slightly tex-

tured to give a non-slip finish but are not so irregular as to cause a problem when walking on them. These two patios are linked by a path made from a contrasting dark red paving brick, which is laid in a stretcher bond to emphasize the long curve and which is sufficiently textured to provide good grip when walking.

A small octagonal summerhouse in the top corner of the garden catches the sun during the middle of the day and provides a very pleasant sitting area even when the weather is unpleasant. At the junction of the patio and the path outside the summerhouse, a raised brick bed with an internal skin of flexible pond liner contains a bubble fountain. This consists of various sizes of stones and cobbles with a central, large drilled boulder through which water is pumped gently, spilling over the smooth rock surface. The coping of the raised bed is at a convenient height for sitting, allowing close examination of this safe yet stimulating water feature.

Against the house wall a small pergola structure using round, treated timber posts with rectangular-section overhead rails breaks the patio into two areas, giving a sense of seclusion to the sitting area in front of the patio doors.

Brightly coloured annuals can make a stimulating display.

A GARDEN FOR THE BLIND
OR PARTIALLY SIGHTED

THE DESIGN

When the phrase 'gardens for the blind' is mentioned, many people immediately conjure up an image of raised beds full of scented flowers with plant names imprinted in braille on a surrounding handrail. This is not only a restricted view but also one that can alienate the blind and partially sighted, who often ask for nothing more than to be accepted as normal members of society. Far better to imagine a beautiful garden where attention to a few simple details of layout, construction and planting will make it suitable for anyone, whether sighted or not.

In this particular example, the garden is primarily ornamental and slopes very gently down to the far end, so that there is no need for steps or changes of level. Separate sitting areas are located outside both the French windows and the back door for convenience, with the former being in a predominantly sunny situation and the latter lightly shaded by a pergola and trellis.

At the junction of these two areas, a path leads down one side of the garden under arches covered with climbers and around to a tiny arbour with seat in a cool, shady spot beneath small trees. Further interest is created by including two attractive raised beds in the garden, one containing herbs for both scent and culinary use, and the other forming a pool containing a fountain.

Paving throughout the garden is detailed in such a way that changes of direction and boundaries between different areas are marked by a different texture or colour, with the lawn edged in brick for further guidance.

Areas of light and shade are accentuated by the arches and pergola, as well as by carefully placed trees and tall shrubs within the perimeter border.

THE PLANTING

The style of planting is deliberately bold, using a mixture of trees, shrubs, perennials and climbers

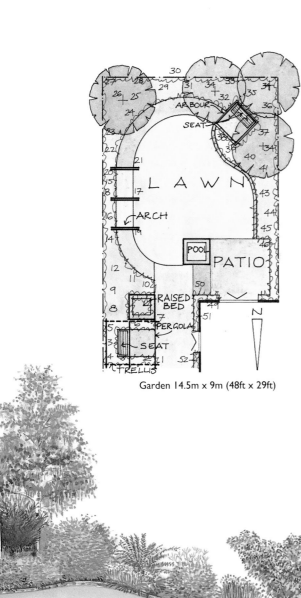

Garden 14.5m x 9m (48ft x 29ft)

KEY TO PLANTING

1 *Akebia quinata*
2 *Potentilla fruticosa* 'Tilford Cream'
3 *Hemerocallis* 'Hyperion'
4 *Wisteria floribunda* 'Alba'
5 *Azalea* 'Gibraltar'
6 *Alchemilla mollis*
7 *Lonicera periclymenum* 'Graham Thomas'
8 *Miscanthus sacchariflorus*
9 *Carpenteria californica*
10 *Hebe armstrongii*
11 *Salvia officinalis* 'Tricolor'
12 *Salix purpurea* 'Nana'
13 *Campsis x tagliabuana* 'Madame Galen'
14 *Leucanthemum x superbum* 'Wirral Supreme'
15 *Trachelospermum jasminoides*
16 *Miscanthus sinensis* 'Silver Feather'
17 *Clematis* 'Henryi'
18 *Lupinus* 'Gallery Red'
19 *Lonicera implexa*
20 *Paeonia lactiflora* 'Sarah Bernhardt'
21 *Jasminum x stephanense*
22 *Hebe brachysiphon*
23 *Viburnum x burkwoodii*
24 *Anemone x hybrida* 'Bressingham Glow'
25 *Digitalis purpurea* f. *alba*
26 *Prunus sargentii*
27 *Sinarundinaria nitida*
28 *Ribes sanguineum* 'Brocklebankii'
29 *Sarcococca confusa*
30 *Lonicera tragophylla*
31 *Hydrangea macrophylla* 'Blue Wave'
32 *Skimmia japonica* 'Foremannii'
33 *Clematis* 'Niobe'
34 *Betula pendula* 'Tristis'
35 *Fargesia murieliae*
36 *Osmanthus x burkwoodii*
37 *Buddleia davidii* 'Royal Red'
38 *Skimmia japonica* 'Rubella'
39 *Phlox paniculata* 'Mother of Pearl'
40 *Cyclamen coum*
41 *Lonicera nitida* 'Baggesen's Gold'
42 *Cotoneaster horizontalis*
43 *Dianthus* 'Doris'
44 *Ferula* 'Giant Bronze'
45 *Viburnum japonicum*
46 *Agapanthus* Headbourne hybrids
47 *Ampelopsis glandulosa* var. *brevipedunculata* 'Elegans'
48 *Lilium regale*
49 *Iris unguicularis*
50 *Cistus* 'Silver Pink'
51 *Lavandula angustifolia* 'Hidcote'
52 *Hemerocallis* 'Bonanza'

Opposite: View from the house.
Left: Three-dimensional view of the garden.

73

chosen for their scent, strong colour of flower or foliage, and interest of texture, whether in leaf or stem. Plants with obviously unsafe characteristics, such as thorns and spiky leaves, are avoided, while a number of slender-stemmed and long-leaved species, such as bamboo (*Sinarundinaria nitida*) and dwarf willow (*Salix purpurea* 'Nana'), are included to provide movement and sound in light breezes. A notable feature of the planting is the use of soft-foliaged, evergreen shrubs, such as hebes and cistus, to help denote corners and changes of direction.

In addition to these characteristics, the plants are also selected for their ground-covering qualities or minimal maintenance requirements, so that, once mature, the garden can be kept in shape with only a modest amount of work.

THE FEATURES

The two patio areas are constructed in a uniform, smooth yet non-slip concrete flag in a light colour such as beige or buff. A contrasting, dark brown paving brick is used in bands or blocks to denote points where the paving changes direction, and the same brick is also used to form the mowing strip along the lawn edge. The path leading down the garden uses the same brick for the curved sections, with the straight run below the arches in flags to match the patios.

The shallow raised bed is made from heavy timbers, such as old railway sleepers, and it is lined with a flexible pond liner to make a striking water feature on the corner of the sunny patio. A submersible pump powers a gentle fountain in the pool, creating a relaxing background noise, which is particularly refreshing on a hot day. The width and height of the timber edge makes this a pleasant place to sit and dangle fingers in the water. This timber box construction is repeated on the corner of the back door patio area, but in this case without the pond liner. It can be backfilled with topsoil and used as a raised herb bed, or alternatively can become a seat.

Three simple arches over the brick and flag path are made from pairs of square-sectioned, stained and treated softwood posts, each pair being surmounted by two matching crosspieces, up and over which climbers such as summer-flowering jasmine (*Jasminum* x *stephanense*) and honeysuckle (*Lonicera*) can scramble. The path finishes in the cool, shaded corner of the garden where a sitting area, laid out in flags to match the patio, is enclosed on three sides by a low edging of stained and treated round logs set on end in concrete.

Soft-foliaged and aromatic plants have been made accessible to blind people by being placed in this well-detailed and attractive raised bed, which does double duty as a seat.

Design Variations

TRIANGULAR PLOT

Turning the paved layout through an angle so that it matches the boundary fence allows one patio to be in the sun while the other is in the shade cast by the fence as well as by the pergola. The small sitting area and seat at the far end combine with the planting behind it to hide the narrow, awkwardly shaped corner.

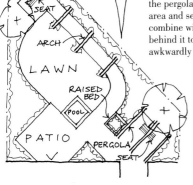

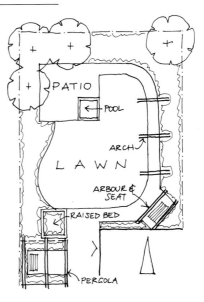

DIFFERENT ASPECT

The main patio and small area for sitting are simply reversed here to take advantage of the available sun. The raised pool, set on the corner of the patio, provides an additional focal point, while the other raised bed is moved slightly further down the garden, away from the shade of the pergola.

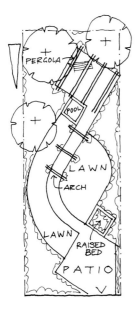

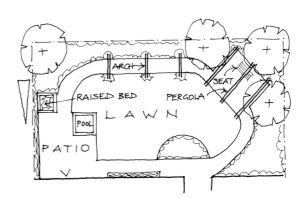

LONG, NARROW PLOT

The patio areas are sited at opposite ends of the plot, and are linked by a path, running under arches, that curves through the centre of the lawn, which can extend almost across the full width of the garden. The shapes and lines of the features have been deliberately chosen to divert attention from the corridor-like proportions of the plot.

WIDE, SHALLOW PLOT

The two patio areas are located in diagonally opposite corners, so that each forms a viewpoint for the other. The arches on the far side of the garden, with the climbers growing over and through them, help to mask the far boundary, and in order to contribute to the feeling of space the path continues around the back to the house.

PLANT ENTHUSIASTS' GARDENS

Under the heading of plant enthusiasts come those gardeners who primarily want to enjoy the benefits of plants in their gardens, whether by looking at them, growing them or cutting and picking them to bring the garden indoors. All three gardens in this chapter, therefore, place the emphasis on plants for these purposes, although the overall designs are quite different.

The first garden contains a selection of plants that can be cut for both flowers and foliage, but it is laid out in a striking way so that the overall design is as eye-catching as the individual plants themselves. Regular cutting makes this garden almost self-maintaining.

In the second example an elegant yet functional layout provides a strong framework for plants, the chief interest of which lies in the quality of their foliage rather than in their flowers. A degree of regular pruning and thinning makes this a suitable garden for someone who enjoys this type of gardening work.

The third design, which has a large area of planting in quite a tiny garden, is suited to the gardener who has an inherent interest in both the appearance and cultivation of plants, some of them unusual. The layout uses groups of plants according to their particular requirements so that a wide range of species is included.

Gardens for plant enthusiasts do not need to be large, as can be seen from this collection of tender, container-grown plants, which include agave, cyrtanthus, echeveria and dudleya.

A SMALL PLOT FOR CUT AND DRIED FLOWERS

THE DESIGN

Flower arranging using both fresh and dried plant material is an increasingly popular interest, which can sometimes prove expensive if you have to buy all the flowers, foliage and stems. Growing your own is not only economical but can also be very satisfying, and, given some thought and planning, even the smallest garden can produce a worthwhile harvest.

This tiny garden produces a surprising quantity of cut and dried flowers, stems and foliage from a limited space, and it is primarily designed to meet the needs of the regular flower arranger or the gardener who just likes to pick the occasional bunch of flowers. At the same time, the overall design is striking, and the combined effect of soft planting areas and hard surfaces is given as much consideration as the qualities of the individual plants themselves.

A small patio immediately outside the French windows makes a useful sitting-out area. This joins on to a central, circular gravel area, which can be reached directly from the patio or via a small stepping-stone path. The path leads beneath a group of rose arches and provides a link between the patio and the circular gravel area. The gravel area provides an attractive contrast to the fairly dense perimeter planting, and individual plants can be grown through it without allowing the garden to become completely taken over by vegetation, which might become claustrophobic in such a small space.

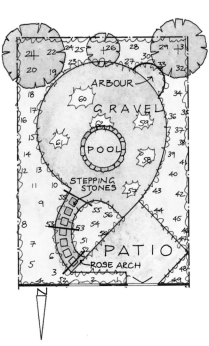

Garden 12.5m x 9m (41ft x 29ft)

THE PLANTING

A selection of medium-sized to large, predominantly evergreen shrubs, provides the basic framework for the planted areas and is supplemented in the far corners of the garden by a flowering crab apple (*Malus floribunda*) and mountain ash (*Sorbus aucuparia* 'Fastigiata'). The infill planting of perennials, dwarf shrubs and grasses is chosen to make use of the different microclimates

KEY TO PLANTING

1 *Hebe* 'Mrs Winder'
2 *Crinum x powellii*
3 *Doronicum* 'Miss Mason'
4 *Pyracantha* 'Orange Glow'
5 *Phormium* 'Sundowner'
6 *Lavandula angustifolia* 'Munstead'
7 *Delphinium* Galahad Group
8 *Hedera helix* 'Goldheart'
9 *Cornus alba* 'Sibirica Variegata'
10 *Rudbeckia fulgida* var. *sullivantii* 'Goldsturm'
11 *Miscanthus sinensis* 'Silver Feather'
12 *Chaenomeles x superba* 'Crimson and Gold'
13 *Rosa* 'The Fairy'
14 *Ilex aquifolium* 'Ferox Argentea'
15 *Aster thomsonsii* 'Nanus'
16 *Lonicera implexa*
17 *Astilbe x arendsii* 'Bressingham Beauty'
18 *Pseudosasa japonica*
19 *Hosta fortunei* 'Picta'
20 *Skimmia japonica* 'Fragrans'
21 *Malus floribunda*
22 *Elaeagnus x ebbingei* 'Gilt Edge'
23 *Skimmia japonica* 'Nymans'
24 *Vitis coignetiae*
25 *Matteuccia struthiopteris*
26 *Chamaecyparis lawsoniana* 'Chilworth Silver'
27 *Liriope muscari*

28 *Garrya elliptica* 'James Roof'
29 *Mahonia x media* 'Winter Sun'
30 *Azalea* 'Homebush'
31 *Sorbus aucuparia* 'Fastigiata'
32 *Ilex x altaclerensis* 'Golden King'
33 *Rosa* 'Albertine'
34 *Aruncus sylvester*
35 *Vitis vinifera* 'Brant'
36 *Hosta* 'Krossa Regal'
37 *Elaeagnus pungens* 'Maculata'
38 *Allium christophii*
39 *Persicaria affinis* 'Donald Lowndes'

40 *Cornus stolonifera* 'Flaviramea'
41 *Hydrangea petiolaris*
42 *Cotinus coggygria* 'Royal Purple'
43 *Helichrysum* 'Sulphur Light'
44 *Tanacetum coccineum* 'Robinson's Red'
45 *Stipa calamagrostis*
46 *Actinidia kolomikta*
47 *Agapanthus* 'Bressingham White'
48 *Choisya ternata*
49 *Ceanothus* 'Puget Blue'
50 *Briza media*

51 *Erica x darleyensis* 'Molten Silver'
52 *Rosa* 'Golden Showers'
53 *Rosa* 'Schoolgirl'
54 *Pennisetum alopecuroides*
55 *Rosa* 'New Dawn'
56 *Achillea* 'Moonshine'
57 *Daphne odora* 'Aureomarginata'
58 *Lunaria annua*
59 *Euphorbia griffithii* 'Dixter'
60 *Corylus avellana* 'Contorta'
61 *Phormium* 'Yellow Wave'
62 *Iris sibirica* 'White Swirl'

Opposite: View from the house.
Right: Three-dimensional view of the garden.

The gravel path runs under the plants, not only to set off the foliage but also to act as a mulch and, in this case, to disguise an edging rail.

within the garden, so that astilbes, hostas and hardy ferns, for example, are located predominantly in the cooler, shadier parts of the garden, while sun-loving plants such as helichrysum and lavender (**Lavandula**) are positioned in the hotter, drier areas of the garden nearer to the house.

Planted through the gravel are plants that look their best when given some space or isolation in which to develop, including phormium, euphorbia and contorted hazel (**Corylus avellana** 'Contorta'). To supplement the permanent planting in the garden, a collection of tubs or pots could also be assembled in which flowering annuals for cutting or drying can be grown.

THE FEATURES

Three free-standing, delicate, black-painted wrought-iron arches follow the curve of the stepping stone path beneath them and provide suitable support for climbing roses and other climbers such as clematis and sweet peas. In the opposite corner of the garden a semicircular arbour, in matching style and material, is an attractive complement to the arches and provides another opportunity for growing climbing roses.

At the centre of the garden a simple, circular pool is edged with small pieces of natural stone paving and, in combination with a fountain, provides a dynamic focal point. Because of the density of planting around the perimeter of the garden, the gravel is allowed to merge beneath the foliage of the surrounding plants, and the broadly circular shape of the area is maintained by judicious and regular pruning and trimming, rather than by a clearly defined timber or brick edging.

The simple patio is built from equal-sized, rectangular concrete slabs with a lightly textured finish, honey- or beige-coloured to blend in with the gravel. The same slab is also laid in the gravel to make the stepping stones beneath the rose arches.

A combination of simple trellis panels and heavy-gauge horizontal wires provides support on the boundary walls and fences for additional climbers and wall shrubs such as pyracantha and ceanothus, which can be tied back or trimmed close to provide additional cutting material.

DESIGN VARIATIONS

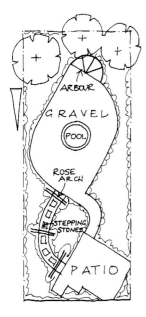

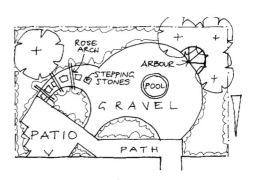

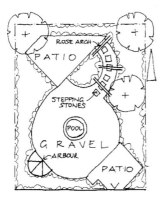

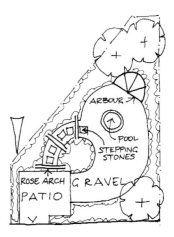

LONG, NARROW PLOT
All the features are in the same position relative to each other as in the main design, but the proportions of the gravel area have been changed to allow planting to close in at both ends and to break the garden down into separate spaces.

WIDE, SHALLOW PLOT
The layout has been turned through 90 degrees to capitalize on the diagonal dimensions of the plot and to play down the lack of depth. An additional access path has been introduced and this is separated from the gravel area by a mixed border.

DIFFERENT ASPECT
The main patio is moved to the sunny end of the garden, together with the rose arches, and this allows the arbour to be located in the opposite corner. The focus is now on the pool, while a small, additional patio area links the gravel area to the house through the French windows.

TRIANGULAR PLOT
The patio here has been turned so that it sits squarely in the corner, linking comfortably into the gravel area, whose curves draw the eye away from the triangular shape of the garden. The arbour, which now sits in the far corner, focuses back towards the pool.

A FOLIAGE GARDEN

THE DESIGN

All too often the qualities of foliage are not fully appreciated in a garden setting. Yet it is quite possible to create stunning gardens in which flowers are secondary by taking advantage of the wide range of colours, shapes and sizes of both leaves and stems. In this small garden plants chosen primarily for their foliage qualities are combined with a number of features to produce a dramatic effect.

Since the rear of the house is in shade, the principal area for sitting is located beneath a softwood pergola in the top corner of the garden, so that it catches plenty of sun. It is reached via an elegantly curving path leading from the house, under an arch, around the front of a natural-looking pool and up a series of shallow steps. The gentle slope of the garden is split into two levels by a bank of rocks, which also forms the back edge of the pond.

Nearer to the house a semicircular patio provides a spot to sit on during the early or later parts of the day, as well as being home to a rotary clothes line. A carefully screened shed is located at the rear of the garage, conveniently near the back door.

THE PLANTING

A large proportion of the planting is chosen for its evergreen foliage or interesting stems to provide winter interest, although the effects of foliage in the garden are at their peak from early spring to late autumn. However, even plants chosen primarily for their foliage, such as **Heuchera micrantha**

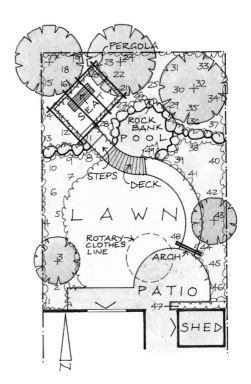

Garden 12m x 9m (39ft x 29ft)

KEY TO PLANTING

1 *Ribes sanguineum* 'Brocklebankii'
2 *Hydrangea quercifolia*
3 *Acer palmatum* f. *atropurpureum*
4 *Miscanthus sinensis* 'Strictus'
5 *Vinca minor* 'Argenteovariegata'
6 *Ilex meservae* 'Blue Angel'
7 *Geranium macrorrhizum* 'Album'
8 *Artemisia ludoviciana* 'Valerie Finnis'
9 *Yucca filamentosa* 'Bright Edge'
10 *Acanthus spinosa*
11 *Vitis vinifera* 'Purpurea'
12 *Brachyglottis greyi*
13 *Polygonatum multiflorum*
14 *Jasminum officinale* 'Aureovariegatum'
15 *Miscanthus sacchariflorus*
16 *Alchemilla mollis*

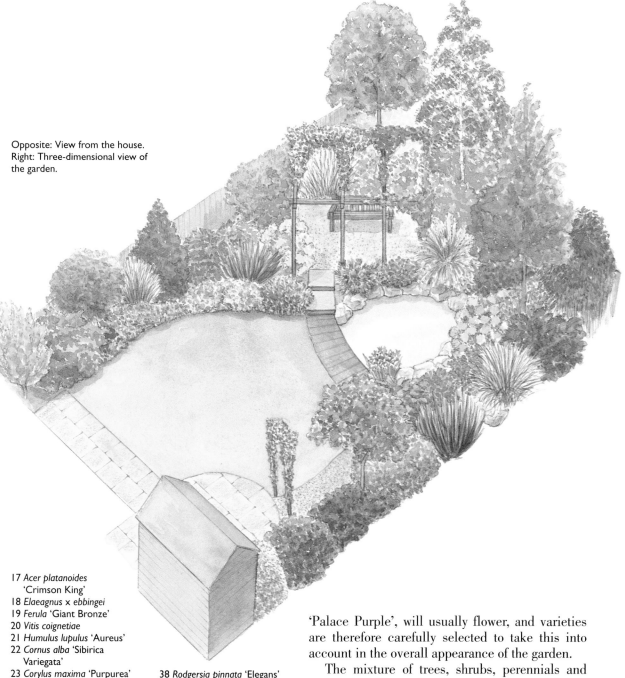

Opposite: View from the house.
Right: Three-dimensional view of the garden.

17 *Acer platanoides* 'Crimson King'
18 *Elaeagnus* x *ebbingei*
19 *Ferula* 'Giant Bronze'
20 *Vitis coignetiae*
21 *Humulus lupulus* 'Aureus'
22 *Cornus alba* 'Sibirica Variegata'
23 *Corylus maxima* 'Purpurea'
24 *Betula pendula* 'Fastigiata'
25 *Euphorbia characias* ssp. *wulfenii*
26 *Stipa calamagrostis*
27 *Tellima grandiflora* 'Purpurea'
28 *Pinus mugo* 'Ophir'
29 *Juniperus procumbens* 'Nana'
30 *Iris foetidissima* 'Variegata'
31 *Philadelphus coronarius* 'Aureus'
32 *Sorbus aria* 'Lutescens'
33 *Phyllostachys viridiglaucescens*
34 *Mahonia lomariifolia*
35 *Acer palmatum* 'Senkaki'
36 *Geranium renardii*
37 *Miscanthus sinensis* var. *purpurascens*

38 *Rodgersia pinnata* 'Elegans'
39 *Rheum* 'Ace of Hearts'
40 *Phormium tenax* 'Purpureum'
41 *Festuca glauca*
42 *Elaeagnus pungens* 'Dicksonii'
43 *Aralia elata*
44 *Heuchera micrantha* var. *diversifolia* 'Palace Purple'
45 *Hydrangea aspera* Villosa Group
46 *Lonicera nitida* 'Baggesen's Gold'
47 *Osmanthus heterophyllus* 'Variegatus'
48 *Trachelospermum jasminoides* 'Variegatum'
49 *Iris laevigata*

'Palace Purple', will usually flower, and varieties are therefore carefully selected to take this into account in the overall appearance of the garden.

The mixture of trees, shrubs, perennials and grasses is deliberately planted densely to produce a luxuriant and weed-suppressing effect. The garden will therefore require periodic thinning, cutting back and feeding to maintain the best quality of foliage, especially in plants such as **Cornus alba** 'Sibirica Variegata', which produces larger, more highly coloured leaves and stems after hard pruning in early spring.

THE FEATURES
The paving in front of the patio doors is constructed from pale, sandstone-effect concrete flags, which are carefully cut to produce a neatly curving

arc running along the edge of the semicircular patio.

A simple yet striking arch, made from black-stained softwood posts and crosspieces, forms a gateway from which a narrow, timber-edged gravel path leads to the pond. Here the path changes to a timber deck, built from oak planks and forming a pleasant spot at which to stop and view the pond.

The pond is built from a flexible liner, concealed along its edges partly by the deck and partly by a rock bank on the opposite side, which continues across the width of the garden and creates, in effect, an informal retaining wall. From the deck, shallow timber-edged steps lead to a covered gravel sitting area, below a handsome pergola designed and built to match the arch.

DESIGN VARIATIONS

TRIANGULAR PLOT
The main patio and pergola have been turned so that they focus on the pool, while the utility area, patio and clothes drier are moved to one side, into the corner of the plot, separated from the path by the arch. The pool is brought forwards slightly so that it meets the lawn, and the path runs behind it.

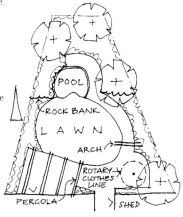

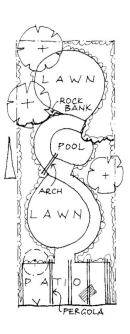

DIFFERENT ASPECT
The pergola has been moved on to the main patio, which has been extended and still has room for the clothes drier. The decking is moved behind the pool to form a small sitting area, and the arch is moved up the garden to the side of the pool.

LONG, NARROW PLOT
Here, the main elements are used to divide the garden into a series of spaces, with the lawn, which is now in two sections, separated by the centrally placed pool. The patio is allowed to take up the full width of the garden, while the path sweeps up the garden in a serpentine fashion, contrasting with the straightness of the boundaries.

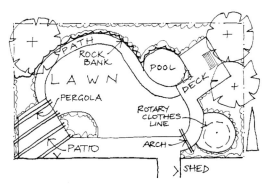

WIDE, SHALLOW PLOT
The main patio and pergola have been turned to focus on the pool and decking in the diagonally opposite corner. A small bed in the foreground provides additional interest, while the utility area is enclosed by planting and hidden from the patio by the arch.

The flowers of Alchemilla mollis *are here of secondary importance to the elegant foliage, which is used to contrast with the hostas,* polygonatum *and* Athyrium niponicum *var.* pictum.

A GARDEN FOR
YEAR-ROUND INTEREST

THE DESIGN

This really is a garden for a plant enthusiast, since, apart from a narrow, winding path leading from a tiny patio to an equally small lawn and summerhouse, the entire plot is devoted to plants to provide year-round interest.

The design breaks the garden down into several areas where plants are either grown to suit particular conditions or are used to create a specific effect. It includes a pool with a boggy area, a rockery and scree garden, and a sunny mixed border.

Wires and trellis panels are used to support a wide range of climbers and wall shrubs on the boundary fences, with simple rustic arches over the path, and the summerhouse in one corner provides an opportunity to grow additional climbing plants.

An informal patio is just large enough to take a table and chairs, and the similarly sized lawn is transformed into a private, secluded spot by the planting around it.

THE PLANTING

The transition between the various planting areas is gradual, so that the overall effect of the design is not fragmented and, for example, a Westonbirt dogwood (**Cornus alba** 'Sibirica') provides a logical link between the winter bed near the house and the adjoining mixed border.

A number of small trees and tall shrubs such as crab apple (**Malus** x **zumi** 'Golden Hornet') and

Above: View from the house.
Opposite: Three-dimensional view of the garden.

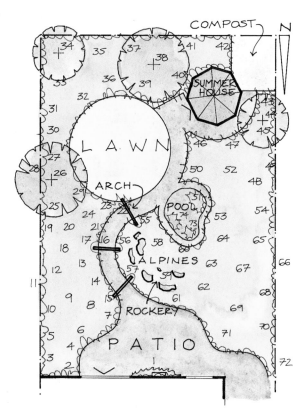

Garden 16.5m x 11.5m (54ft x 38ft)

KEY TO PLANTING

1 *Ampelopsis glandulosa* var.
  brevipedunculata 'Elegans'
2 *Hebe* 'Great Orme'
3 *Mahonia* x *media* 'Charity'
4 *Taxus baccata* 'Semperaurea'
5 *Daphne mezereum*
6 *Erica* x *darleyensis* 'Molten
  Silver'
7 *Erica carnea* 'Myretoun
  Ruby'
8 *Euonymus* 'Emerald Gaiety'
9 *Cornus alba* 'Sibirica'
10 *Garrya elliptica* 'James Roof'
11 *Clematis orientalis*
12 *Ilex aquifolium* 'Ferox
  Argentea'
13 *Aster* x *thomsonii* 'Nanus'
14 *Doronicum* 'Miss Mason'
15 *Clematis cirrhosa* var.
  balearica
16 *Clematis* 'Marie Boisselot'
17 *Ceratostigma plumbaginoides*
18 *Potentilla* 'Primrose Beauty'
19 *Viburnum farreri*
20 *Miscanthus sinensis*
  'Gracillimus'
21 *Euphorbia polychroma*
  'Purpurea'

22 *Hedera helix*
  'Buttercup'
23 *Achillea* 'Moonshine'
24 *Aster amellus* 'King George'
25 *Pyracantha* 'Orange Glow'
26 *Sorbus hupehensis*
27 *Polygonatum odoratum*
  'Variegatum'
28 *Parthenocissus henryana*
29 *Dicentra* 'Luxuriant'
30 *Aronia* x *prunifolia*
31 *Ilex aquifolium* 'J.C. Van Tol'
32 *Ceratostigma willmottianum*
33 *Cotinus coggygria* 'Foliis
  Purpureis'
34 *Cupressus macrocarpa*
  'Goldcrest'
35 *Philadelphus* 'Virginal'
36 *Potentilla fruticosa* 'Princess'
37 *Osmanthus* x *burkwoodii*
38 *Betula utilis*

39 *Sarcococca confusa*
40 *Skimmia japonica* 'Rubella'
41 *Chaenomeles* x *superba*
  'Crimson and Gold'
42 *Phyllostachys aurea*
43 *Elaeagnus* x *ebbingei*
44 *Malus* x *zumi* 'Golden
  Hornet'
45 *Viburnum japonicum*
46 *Hosta* 'Frances Williams'
47 *Skimmia laureola*
48 *Ribes sanguineum*
  'Brocklebankii'
49 *Lonicera implexa*
50 *Astilbe* x *arendsii* 'Snowdrift'
51 *Iris laevigata*
52 *Ligularia* 'The Rocket'
53 *Primula japonica*
54 *Viburnum tinus* 'Purpureum'

55 *Jasminum* x *stephanense*
56 *Rosa* 'Schoolgirl'
57 *Vitis vinifera* 'Purpurea'
58 *Pinus mugo* 'Ophir'
59 *Juniperus communis*
  'Compressa'
60 *Salix* 'Boydii'
61 *Iris unguicularis*
62 *Hebe armstrongii*
63 *Caryopteris* x *clandonensis*
  'Kew Blue'
64 *Magnolia stellata*
65 *Rosa* 'Pink Grootendorst'
66 *Actinidia kolomikta*
67 *Phormium* 'Sundowner'
68 *Pyracantha* 'Soleil d'Or'
69 *Helleborus lividus* var. *corsicus*
70 *Weigela florida* 'Foliis
  Purpureis'
71 *Juniperus* x *media* 'Gold
  Coast'
72 *Jasminum nudiflorum*
  'Aureum'
73 *Schoenoplectus lacustris* ssp.
  tabernaemontani 'Zebrinus'
74 *Nymphaea* 'Graziella'

Even a small part of a plant enthusiast's garden can be used to demonstrate wonderful contrasts and harmonies, made all the more dramtic by a mulch of pea shingle.

winter-flowering viburnum (***V. farreri***) give height to the garden and provide scale to the smaller shrubs, perennials and bulbs planted between and beneath them.

Although the planting scheme for the garden gives interest for all seasons, the bed immediately in front of the French windows places a special emphasis on late winter and early spring colour with plants such as ***Daphne mezereum***, winter-flowering heathers (***Erica carnea*** and ***E. darleyensis***) and Algerian iris (***Iris unguicularis***).

THE FEATURES

Random, broken pieces of old sandstone paving are laid in 'crazy-paving' style to create the small, informal patio, and some of the larger joints between the slabs are left unpointed so that creeping plants, such as thyme (***Thymus serpyllum***) and stonecrop (***Sedum acre***), can establish themselves in them.

Built in the same material as the patio, the narrow path leads to a small area of matching crazy paving in front of the door to an octagonal wooden summerhouse, which is just large enough to accommodate a couple of chairs and a table. Using a very natural, pale stain, such as light oak or walnut, to treat the summerhouse will help it to merge into, rather than contrast with, the background planting.

The pool with its adjoining bog garden is made from a single sheet of flexible pond liner, held in place with an edging of sandstone paving on a mortar bed. At 45cm (18in) it is not excessively deep, since its main purpose is to grow aquatic and marginal plants rather than to provide a place in which to keep fish, and among the varieties to be found in this pool are iris (***Iris laevigata***), variegated rush (***Schoenoplectus lacustris*** ssp. ***tabernaemontani*** 'Zebrinus') and dwarf water lilies (***Nymphaea*** spp.)

Design Variations

DIFFERENT ASPECT
The patio has been moved to the centre of the garden so that it is in the sun and lies behind the pool, which is now nearer the house. The raised bed is in the shadow of the house, while a path of stepping stones links the side gate to the small paved area outside the patio doors.

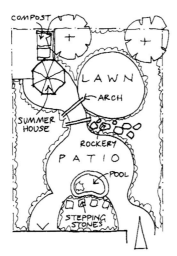

TRIANGULAR PLOT
The rock garden has been moved to one side of the patio, creating a division between the patio and the side access. The compost area is now tucked away into the far corner of the plot, which would otherwise be unused. The summerhouse is moved to the opposite far corner, in front of the compost area, while the circular lawn combines with the curving path to draw attention away from the angular boundary.

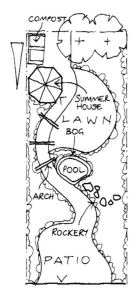

LONG, NARROW PLOT
Within this restricted width, the patio is now deeper and the shape of the lawn has been changed so that the emphasis is on the long, sinuous curves on both sides, with the bog garden now lying between the pool and the lawn.

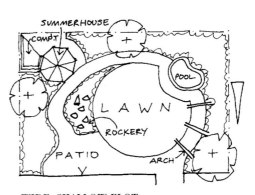

WIDE, SHALLOW PLOT
The patio, summerhouse, pool and arches have been moved into the four corners of the plot to create diagonal views that give an impression of greater depth. This is further emphasized by the pronounced curves of the path, which now forms a complete circuit around the garden, and the lawn.

89

WATER GARDENS

Water features in various forms are always an added attraction in a garden, where both their sound and appearance can add an extra dimension. Usually they are used more as cosmetic features, perhaps playing a minor role in the overall garden design. In the two examples in this chapter, however, water forms the major element of the design.

The first garden uses rectangular shapes and precisely finished materials to create a series of architectural raised pools running down to a very formal, timber-decked patio area, and it is perhaps suited to someone who wants a rather controlled, organized feature.

The second example, in contrast, is built around two pools, which are linked by a meandering stream, with planting and other natural materials creating a natural, informal feel, suited to gardeners looking for a soft, rather old-fashioned style.

This garden successfully incorporates a formal raised pool, a waterfall, a pond with aquatic subjects and a bog garden – all within a space that is not much larger than the average patio.

A SPLIT-LEVEL GARDEN WITH DECKING

THE DESIGN

A water feature in a garden may be large or small, formal or informal, and it can, quite often, be secondary in importance to other elements of a design. Here, however, the main centrepiece of a small garden is created by two rectangular, raised pools, linked by cascades to a larger pool, which forms the foreground to a timber-decked sitting area. The natural slope of the ground, which falls from the top of the garden down to the house, adds extra emphasis to the changes in level from one pool to the next.

Access around and over the water is encouraged by the provision of a bridge, additional decking and stepping stones, which can also be used to gain access to the perimeter planting areas for maintenance and pruning when necessary. The pools and the main patio decking are set at an angle to the house, providing interesting views across the garden while at the same time helping, in combination with some dramatic planting, to disguise the rectangular nature of the plot. A series of timber overheads provides a degree of shade and enclosure above the main deck area by the patio doors, complementing in both colour and style the other timber work in the garden.

Although it is shown here as a complete garden, this striking water feature could easily be included as a special corner in a much larger garden.

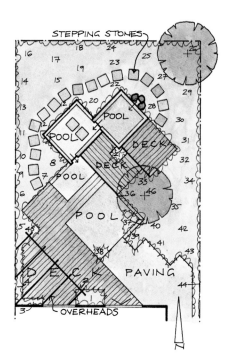

Garden 14m x 10m (46ft x 33ft)

KEY TO PLANTING
1 *Carpenteria californica*
2 *Vitis vinifera* 'Purpurea'
3 *Euonymus fortunei* 'Sheridan Gold'
4 *Parthenocissus henryana*
5 *Choisya* 'Aztec Pearl'
6 *Ceratostigma willmottianum*
7 *Hebe armstrongii*
8 *Iris sibirica* 'White Swirl'
9 *Filipendula ulmaria* 'Variegata'
10 *Taxus baccata* 'Fastigiata Robusta'

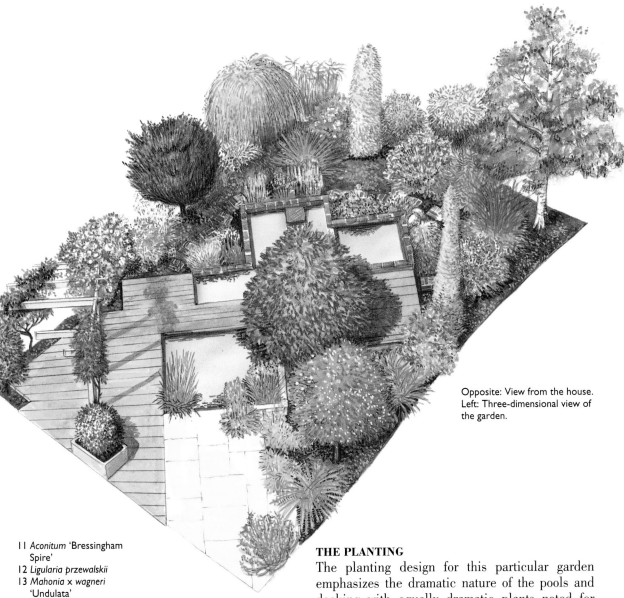

Opposite: View from the house.
Left: Three-dimensional view of the garden.

11 *Aconitum* 'Bressingham Spire'
12 *Ligularia przewalskii*
13 *Mahonia x wagneri* 'Undulata'
14 *Salix purpurea* 'Nana'
15 *Phormium cookianum* ssp. *hookeri* 'Tricolor'
16 *Pseudosasa japonica*
17 *Philadelphus coronarius* 'Aureus'
18 *Thalictrum delavayi* 'Hewitt's Double'
19 *Juniperus chinensis* 'Kaizuka'
20 *Pinus mugo* 'Ophir'
21 *Panicum virgatum* 'Rubrum'
22 *Erica erigena* 'Irish Salmon'
23 *Aruncus sylvester*
24 *Prunus lusitanica* 'Variegata'
25 *Hydrangea aspera* Villosa Group
26 *Betula pendula* 'Youngii'
27 *Dryopteris filix-mas*
28 *Ilex crenata* 'Golden Gem'
29 *Arundo donax*
30 *Astilbe x thunbergii* 'Ostrich Plume'
31 *Juniperus chinensis* 'Aurea'
32 *Cotinus* 'Grace'
33 *Hosta* 'Halcyon'
34 *Pleioblastus auricomus*
35 *Rodgersia pinnata* 'Elegans'
36 *Luzula sylvatica* 'Marginata'
37 *Iris laevigata*
38 *Schoenoplectus lacustris* ssp. *tabernaemontani* 'Zebrinus'
39 *Rheum alexandrae*
40 *Skimmia japonica* 'Rubella'
41 *Pulmonaria saccharata* Argentea Group
42 *Sorbus koehneana*
43 *Polystichum polyblepharum*
44 *Chaenomeles x superba* 'Pink Lady'
45 *Akebia quinata*
46 *Acer palmatum* 'Bloodgood'

THE PLANTING

The planting design for this particular garden emphasizes the dramatic nature of the pools and decking with equally dramatic plants noted for their bold foliage (such as hostas and ligularias) or striking habit (such as **Arundo donax** and phormium). This style of planting is not only visually effective, but it requires little in the way of maintenance once mature, apart from a once- or twice-yearly thinning and pruning. Its rather lush nature also helps to hide the rectangular boundary, giving the impression of being in a secluded space within a much larger garden.

THE FEATURES

The two smaller, upper pools are constructed from brick walls laid on reinforced concrete base foundations and rendered internally with waterproof mortar, although to save time and money concrete blocks could be used for the lower pool instead of

bricks since it is not raised and no outer wall faces are visible. The coping to the brick or block walls can be partly in a matching brick and partly in timber where the decking meets the pool edges.

A 'spring' emerging between rocks set in the planting provides the source of water to the top pool, and is supplied via a submersible pump and connecting hose from the largest pool. All the timber decking, including the bridge over this pool, is constructed from carefully selected, seasoned and treated softwood, which is prepared by removing any splinters or excessively rough spots. Alternatively, hardwood obtained from sustainable forestry resources can be used and will require less long-term maintenance, being more durable than softwood.

The stepping stones across the middle pool, which are built from the same frostproof brick as the walls and coping, are laid on top of concrete block piers, which are, in turn, bedded onto the concrete base foundation. A similar detail is also used for the stepping stones through the planting, although here the bricks are bedded directly onto square concrete pads.

The timber overheads, built from the same wood and in the same style as the decking, are fitted with additional wires to support the growth of deciduous climbers, giving shade during the heat of summer but allowing plenty of light to penetrate in winter. The entire structure is supported by two posts at the front edge near the large pool and by the house and boundary walls at the back.

DESIGN VARIATIONS

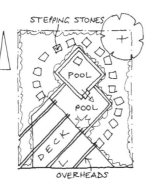

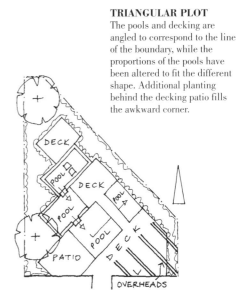

TRIANGULAR PLOT
The pools and decking are angled to correspond to the line of the boundary, while the proportions of the pools have been altered to fit the different shape. Additional planting behind the decking patio fills the awkward corner.

SMALL PLOT
The water feature is here reduced to two overlapping pools, with a path of stepping stones running through the planting around the garden. The decking and pools are angled to match the diagonal of the garden, and the timber overheads extend to the edge of the lower pool.

A crisply constructed deck is set off by the bold planting and, of course, by the beautiful Koi carp and golden orfe in the pool.

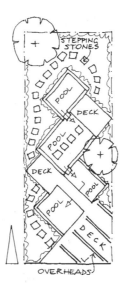

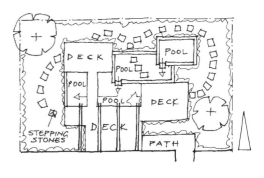

LONG, NARROW PLOT
The centres of the pools lie along the central axis of the garden, and the pools themselves are turned at a sharper angle than before so that the decking and planting do not appear too mean. The main patio can be smaller because of the additional sitting areas further up the garden.

WIDE, SHALLOW PLOT
Here, the pools are long and narrow to permit sufficient change of level in the restricted space. For the same reason, they also overlap. Planting at the sides and back of the garden is generous to hide the boundaries, while additional stepping stones are introduced for access.

95

A STREAM GARDEN

THE DESIGN

Few people are fortunate enough to have a rippling natural stream or babbling brook running through their garden, yet there is a certain indefinable quality about such a feature that makes it very attractive. Using modern water-garden techniques, it is possible to create your own water course, especially, but not necessarily, on a natural slope. Both of these features are utilized to the full in this design, which is based around two informal pools, one at each end of the garden, linked by a natural-looking stream.

The meandering path of the stream is emphasized by the two elliptical lawn areas where they meet the main perimeter border, creating strongly sweeping curves, which add to the informal atmosphere. Immediately in front of the house an irregularly shaped patio wraps interestingly around the edge of the larger pool and catches both late evening and early morning sun, while in the opposite corner of the garden, and linked to it by a stepping-stone path, is a smaller sitting area partly enclosed by a circular gazebo, adjoining the upper pool. The natural feel of the garden is reflected in the careful choice of sympathetic paving materials, including stone flags and bark chippings, as well as by the generous, lush planting throughout.

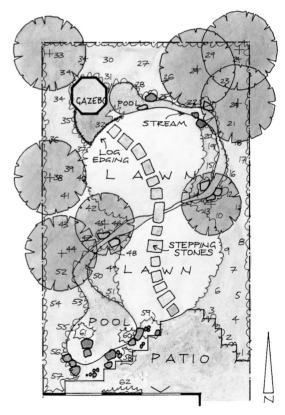

Garden 18.5m x 11m (61ft x 36ft)

96

Opposite: View from the house.
Left: Three-dimensional view
of the garden.

KEY TO PLANTING

1 *Spiraea japonica* 'Gold Mound'
2 *Azalea* 'Homebush'
3 *Carex hachijoensis* 'Evergold'
4 *Lupinus* 'Gallery White'
5 *Hydrangea serrata* 'Preziosa'
6 *Geranium sanguineum* 'Album'
7 *Cotinus coggygria* 'Foliis Purpureis'
8 *Viburnum tinus* 'Eve Price'
9 *Achillea* 'Moonshine'
10 *Rhododendron* 'Praecox'
11 *Stipa gigantea*
12 *Prunus laurocerasus* 'Otto Luyken'
13 *Prunus* x *subhirtella* 'Autumnalis'
14 *Trollius* x *cultorum* 'Canary Bird'
15 *Persicaria bistorta* 'Superba'

16 *Asplenium scolopendrium*
17 *Chaenomeles speciosa* 'Nivalis'
18 *Cornus alba* 'Sibirica Variegata'
19 *Osmunda regalis*
20 *Caltha palustris* var. *palustris* 'Plena'
21 *Prunus laurocerasus* 'Rotundifolia'
22 *Iris pseudacorus*
23 *Viburnum lantana*
24 *Betula pendula*
25 *Filipendula ulmaria*
26 *Cornus sanguinea*
27 *Viburnum opulus*
28 *Daphne mezereum*
29 *Clematis vitalba*
30 *Lonicera periclymenum*
31 *Daphne laureola*
32 *Ligularia* 'The Rocket'
33 *Alnus incana*

34 *Corylus avellana*
35 *Digitalis purpurea*
36 *Rosa canina*
37 *Cytisus* x *praecox* 'Albus'
38 *Malus* 'John Downie'
39 *Mahonia aquifolium*
40 *Geranium* 'Johnson's Blue'
41 *Cornus alba* 'Sibirica'
42 *Astilbe* x *arendsii* 'Bressingham Beauty'
43 *Aucuba japonica* 'Variegata'
44 *Prunus padus* 'Watereri'
45 *Betula utilis*
46 *Geranium* x *cantabrigiense* 'Biokovo'
47 *Ligularia dentata* 'Desdemona'
48 *Astilbe* x *arendsii* 'Snowdrift'
49 *Rheum* 'Ace of Hearts'
50 *Rodgersia pinnata* 'Superba'
51 *Iris laevigata* 'Variegata'
52 *Berberis* x *ottawensis* 'Superba'

53 *Persicaria amplexicaulis* 'Inverleith'
54 *Choisya ternata* 'Sundance'
55 *Miscanthus sinensis* 'Variegatus'
56 *Osmanthus heterophyllus* 'Purpureus'
57 *Hydrangea serrata* 'Grayswood'
58 *Hosta* 'Golden Prayers'
59 *Juniperus squamata* 'Blue Swede'
60 *Sagittaria sagittifolia*
61 *Butomus umbellatus*
62 *Chaenomeles* x *superba* 'Crimson and Gold'

In this case, the shady aspect of the rear of the house is an advantage. The garden slopes slightly towards the house and path of the sun, so not only is sunlight attractively reflected by the running water, but the soil is warmed up earlier in spring and cools down that bit later in autumn, thereby extending the growing season.

THE PLANTING
The planting is designed to progress from ornamental varieties such as spiraea (*S. japonica* 'Gold Mound') and juniper (**Juniperus squamata** 'Blue Swede') near the house and around the main patio, through to less ornamental and native species including birch (**Betula pendula**) and **Viburnum opulus**, creating a relatively natural woodland edge effect at the furthest extreme of the garden. A wide range of trees, shrubs and perennials is utilized, and provision is made for the inclusion of both aquatic and bog planting. The garden is effectively divided into two by using groups of trees and tall, under-storey shrub planting to narrow down the lawn on either side of the garden where the stepping-stone path crosses the stream.

DESIGN VARIATIONS

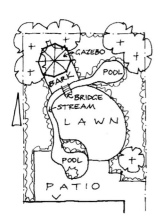

SMALL PLOT
The upper pool is moved away from the gazebo, while the stream runs in front of it, curving down one side of the garden, and the lawn curves gently on the other side. The lower pool is more enclosed by the patio and is in a more central position, as it is now the focal point from the windows of the house.

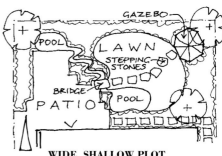

WIDE, SHALLOW PLOT
This garden is divided into two by the pools and the stream, which is much more tortuous to give as great a length of water as possible over the short distance from the back to the front of the garden. The gazebo, which is reached by a path of stepping stones, forms a separate focal point in the far corner.

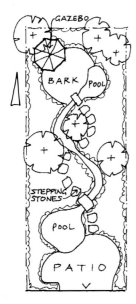

LONG, NARROW PLOT
Here, the lawn has been replaced by additional planting and by an increased bark area in front of the gazebo. The stream takes a more central path, and the lower pool is moved nearer to the patio where it becomes a foreground feature. The stepping stones are arranged through the planting to mirror the path of the stream.

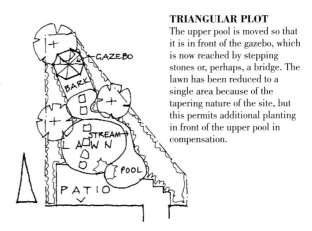

TRIANGULAR PLOT
The upper pool is moved so that it is in front of the gazebo, which is now reached by stepping stones or, perhaps, a bridge. The lawn has been reduced to a single area because of the tapering nature of the site, but this permits additional planting in front of the upper pool in compensation.

A slow-moving stream provides the ideal habitat for aquatic, marginal and bog plants.

THE FEATURES

The patio nearest the house is constructed from old, random-sized, rectangular stone flags, and to emphasize the informality of the design the edge is staggered, allowing plants to spill over and soften it. Some of the joints in this paving are left unpointed and are backfilled with gritty topsoil to allow creeping plants and mosses to become established in the cracks.

At the opposite end of the garden a small sitting area partially surrounds the upper pool, catching most of the midday sun. It is separated from the planting by a low, flexible log edging and is surfaced with ornamental bark chippings lying on top of a porous membrane, which allows surface water to drain through yet prevents the bark from becoming contaminated by the underlying soil. A simple, octagonal gazebo constructed from sawn and stained softwood encloses part of the sitting area and not only provides a pleasant location in which to relax but also makes a striking feature when viewed from different parts of the garden.

Carefully spaced stepping stones, matching the patio flags, provide a gently curving and natural path up the garden, linking the two sitting areas and crossing the stream via a larger flagstone bridge.

The pools and stream are constructed from overlapping sections of flexible pond liner, the edges of which are carefully concealed by a combination of rocks, cobbles, grass and planting. In places the liner is extended sideways and backfilled with fertile soil to create areas for bog planting. A powerful submersible pump concealed in the lower pool recirculates the water and feeds the whole system. The lower pool is designed to hold considerably more water than the stream and upper pool, so that when the pump is switched on, the pool level is not substantially reduced while the stream is filling up. Both the pools are constructed with gently sloping sides, which can be covered with gravel and stones to help disguise the liner when fluctuations in water levels occur, and also to allow access to the water for all sorts of wildlife.

JAPANESE-STYLE GARDENS

The style of Japanese gardens is well known and is frequently copied or used for inspiration in many gardens throughout the world.

In the first example, the garden is laid out very much along traditional lines, using simple materials and a limited range of plants in a quiet, controlled way. This design is well suited to the gardener who wishes simply to sit and enjoy either the overall effect or the beauty of one particular feature, such as a moss-covered rock.

The second garden uses a Japanese theme as inspiration, but puts it into a more modern context so that it takes into account practical as well as visual needs and by so doing makes the design suitable for a family.

Traditional Japanese gardens place equal emphasis on the hard and the soft landscape features, and great attention is always paid to the smallest details.

A GARDEN FOR CONTEMPLATION

THE DESIGN

One of the most attractive aspects of a Japanese garden is the way in which a few simple elements of plants, water, rocks and wood, with the occasional discreetly placed ornament, can be brought together carefully to create a garden that is at the same time both stimulating and relaxing.

This particular garden, intended for passive recreation and quiet enjoyment, uses natural materials and restrained planting in a sympathetic and controlled way to create just such an atmosphere, and the elements of the design revolve around a central pool, with variations in paving materials giving added interest to the overall effect.

The size and layout of the various paved areas allow for easy movement around the garden as well as space to sit out and relax, at the same time providing the opportunity to enjoy the changing views.

The calm, peaceful effect of the garden is further enhanced by the careful selection of plants, and varieties are chosen for their interesting foliage, habit of growth, and delicate flower colours. With nearly half the space taken up by different types of paving, rocks and water, coupled with a planting scheme in which foliage is dominant, this particular garden is very economical in terms of time needed for its upkeep.

THE PLANTING

Planting in the Japanese style relies as much on the effect of form and texture as on flower colour, and both

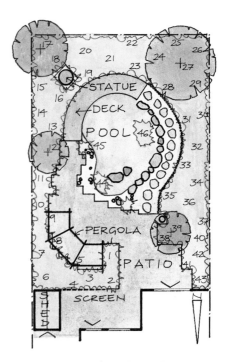

Garden 13.5m x 9.5m (44ft x 31ft)

KEY TO PLANTING

1 *Pinus densiflora* 'Oculus Draconis'
2 *Lamium maculatum* 'White Nancy'
3 *Philadelphus* 'Silver Showers'
4 *Clematis alpina*
5 *Lonicera implexa*
6 *Phyllostachys nigra*
7 *Azalea* 'Gibraltar'
8 *Vitis vinifera* 'Apiifolia'
9 *Clematis cirrhosa*
10 *Matteuccia struthiopteris*
11 *Sasa veitchii*
12 *Acer palmatum* 'Senkaki'
13 *Ophiopogon planiscapus* 'Nigrescens'
14 *Euphorbia amygdaloides* var. *robbiae*
15 *Miscanthus sacchariflorus*

102

Opposite: View from the house.
Above: Three-dimensional view
of the garden.

16 *Carex comans* Bronze form
17 *Acer saccharinum* f. *lutescens*
18 *Aucuba japonica* 'Variegata'
19 *Pulmonaria saccharata*
   Argentea Group
20 *Digitalis* x *mertonensis*
21 *Acer palmatum* Dissectum
   Viride Group
22 *Polygonatum multiflorum*
23 *Hosta* 'Thomas Hogg'

24 *Rhododendron yakushimanum*
25 *Pseudosasa japonica*
26 *Osmanthus* x *burkwoodii*
27 *Betula albosinensis*
28 *Astilbe* x *simplicifolia* 'Sprite'
29 *Hydrangea quercifolia*
30 *Miscanthus sinensis*
   'Gracillimus'
31 *Geranium macrorrhizum*
   'Ingwersen's Variety'

32 *Azalea* 'Hino-mayo'
33 *Taxus baccata* 'Repens
   Aurea'
34 *Pinus heldreichii* var.
   leucodermis 'Compact Gem'
35 *Iris sibirica* 'Tropic Night'
36 *Geranium phaeum*
37 *Jasminum nudiflorum*
38 *Waldsteinia ternata*
39 *Acer palmatum* 'Osakazuki'

40 *Hosta* 'Krossa Regal'
41 *Juniperus virginana* 'Sulphur
   Spray'
42 *Pleioblastus auricomus*
43 *Choisya* 'Aztec Pearl'
44 *Iris kaempferi*
45 *Ligularia dentata*
   'Desdemona'
46 *Nymphaea alba*

individual plants and plant groupings are chosen to avoid strident colours and an over-abundance of flowers. A strong degree of control is always evident in such planting, in dramatic contrast perhaps to the rather more fluid and easy-going manner of a traditional cottage garden. The plant design in this garden emulates that style and relies very much on dwarf or slow-growing pines, bamboos, azaleas and other ground-cover subjects, particularly foliage plants such as hostas and ornamental grasses such as bronze sedge (*Carex comans*). Japanese maples (*Acer palmatum* vars.) underplanted with low perennials are used as striking focal points, and a limited range of small-flowered clematis and a vine, such as *Vitis vinifera* 'Apiifolia', clothe the fences and pergola.

In the pool margins and shallows, irises, such as *Iris kaempferi*, and other water-loving plants are carefully placed to provide a soft green contrast to the hard stones and rocks.

THE FEATURES
Four arches, made of sawn oak posts with overhanging crossrails, are linked across their tops with narrow softwood laths to form a simple yet elegant pergola along the back edge of the main sitting area. This is built of old, well-worn sandstone flags laid in a random pattern, the open joints backfilled with grit or fine gravel on top of

soil to allow tiny creeping plants and mosses to become established.

The path around the side of the pool uses the same material to form stepping stones set among flat pebbles or 'paddlestones' of varying sizes. This path is separated from the planting by a low edging of log sections set on end in the ground, while on the far side of the pool the path leads to a deck of oak planks, which match the pergola. This deck overhangs the pool by only a few centimetres, yet in doing so it creates a dark, crisp shadow, which gives the impression that the water goes right underneath.

A flexible pond liner forms the basis of the central pool, with rocks set along part of the margin creating interesting reflections as well as retaining the stepping-stone path. The sitting area leads towards the shallow edge of the pool, where the paved surface changes from flags to a mixture of cobbles and pebbles, which spill into the water down the gently sloping sides and in doing so hide the liner from view.

The more practical features of this garden, such as a shed and bin store, are located at the side of the house, conveniently placed for access to the back door, and this area is separated and hidden from the rest of the garden by a lightweight screen made from thick bamboo canes fixed vertically to a timber post and rail framework.

DESIGN VARIATIONS

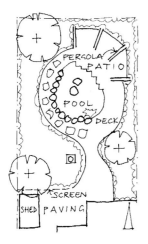

DIFFERENT ASPECT
The pergola and main patio are moved to the diagonally opposite side of the pool so that they are still in a sunny position. A small amount of additional paving provides a link from the patio doors of the house into the garden.

TRIANGULAR PLOT
The pool is moved rather closer to the house, with the patio and pergola in the corner focusing on it. The bamboo screen and some additional planting are positioned to hide the shed, and an extra path of stepping stones is used to explore the new planting space in the far corner of the garden.

*This tiny garden is a good example of a western interpretation
of the Japanese style, with the carefully detailed wood, stone
and water features enhanced by restrained planting.*

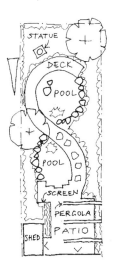

LONG, NARROW PLOT

In view of the narrowness of the
plot, the patio and pergola are
squarer, leaving space for the
shed to one side. The pool is
divided into two by the path,
which crosses the water by
means of a bridge before
reaching the decking beyond.

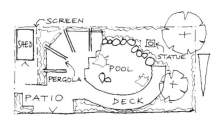

WIDE, SHALLOW PLOT

Access to the pool is via one
side only so that there is room
for a reasonable depth of
planting at the opposite side.
The pergola and patio are
brought across the garden to
create a space behind for the
shed and the other utilities.

A FAMILY GARDEN

THE DESIGN

Although a traditional Japanese-style design lends itself well to a garden for passive recreation and relaxation, it is not so well suited to more active pursuits, such as children's play. This design re-creates as closely as possible the general feeling of a Japanese garden, while at the same time taking into account the more practical and everyday needs of an active family. As a result, a relatively large part of the garden is taken up by a generous patio, which spills over to a central lawn with a bold, curving edge, forming a very adequate area for both general play and relaxation.

Other more basic garden requirements, such as storage for tools and bicycles, a compost heap, rotary clothes line and even a small glasshouse, are all carefully accommodated within the design without detracting from its obvious Oriental influence. This is also evident in the simple, natural materials that are chosen for the paving and structures such as the pergola, as well as in the style, choice and composition of the planting. Other features in the garden include a rock grouping and an area of timber decking, both of which contribute to the overall Japanese effect.

THE PLANTING

Although the general theme of the planting relies very much on traditional varieties, such as dwarf pine (**Pinus**), maple (**Acer**) and azalea, some additional trees, shrubs and perennials have been

Above: View from the house.
Right: Three-dimensional view of the garden.

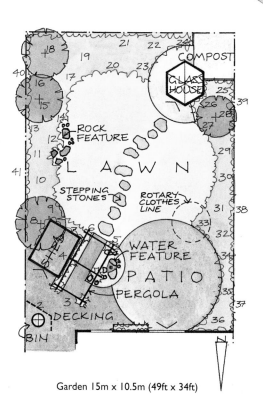

Garden 15m x 10.5m (49ft x 34ft)

introduced to extend both the colour range and the season of interest but without detracting from the overall style. Wherever possible, varieties are chosen for their controlled growth rates or distinctive habit as well as for their ability to act as ground cover, so that garden maintenance does not become a major chore.

The small trees and larger deciduous shrubs are underplanted with low-growing perennials and ground cover, not only creating a number of satisfying plant associations but also allowing their individual forms to be better appreciated.

KEY TO PLANTING

1 *Actinidia kolomikta*
2 *Hedera colchica* 'Sulphur Heart'
3 *Clematis macropetala*
4 *Clematis montana* 'Tetrarose'
5 *Akebia quinata*
6 *Lonicera periclymenum* 'Serotina'
7 *Ceanothus* 'Puget Blue'
8 *Sorbus aucuparia* 'Sheerwater Seedling'
9 *Mahonia* x *media* 'Winter Sun'
10 *Euphorbia characias* ssp. *wulfenii*
11 *Rhododendron* 'Elizabeth'

12 *Pinus mugo* 'Ophir'
13 *Hosta sieboldiana* var. *elegans*
14 *Aster amellus* 'King George'
15 *Acer palmatum* 'Katsura'
16 *Azalea* 'Homebush'
17 *Pulmonaria officinalis* 'Sissinghurst White'
18 *Pinus parviflora*
19 *Viburnum opulus* 'Xanthocarpum'
20 *Ligularia* 'The Rocket'
21 *Pyracantha* 'Orange Glow'
22 *Cotinus coggygria* 'Foliis Purpureis'
23 *Geranium macrorrhizum* 'Album'
24 *Fargesia murieliae*

25 *Rhododendron* 'Cunningham's Blush'
26 *Miscanthus sinensis* 'Silver Feather'
27 *Lamium maculatum* 'Beacon Silver'
28 *Acer palmatum* 'Senkaki'
29 *Pinus mugo* var. *pumilio*
30 *Geranium cantabrigiense* 'Biokovo'
31 *Physocarpus opulifolius* 'Dart's Gold'
32 *Vinca minor* 'Atropurpurea'
33 *Helictotrichon sempervirens*
34 *Phormium tenax*
35 *Helleborus lividus* var. *corsicus*
36 *Cistus laurifolius*

37 *Jasminum officinale* f. *affine*
38 *Parthenocissus henryana*
39 *Hedera helix* 'Green Ripple'
40 *Actinidia deliciosa*
41 *Parthenocissus tricuspidata* 'Veitchii'

THE FEATURES

The broadly circular patio is made from randomly shaped slabs of warm yellow sandstone, relieved here and there with small areas of tiny pebbles set in mortar. Linking this patio to the back door is a ground-level timber deck made from sawn and treated softwood planks, with closely spaced joints for comfort and safety, which is laid at an angle to the house, helping to disguise the relative squareness of the plot.

At the junction of the deck and patio is a geyser fountain, consisting of an area of stones, boulders and gravel, which conceals an underground plastic sump. Water is pumped up through the stones, which are supported on rigid steel mesh, before trickling back into the sump, making this not only an attractive but also a safe feature. To one side of

the fountain, running across this area of stones, a narrow extension of the timber decking simulates a bridge joining the deck to the lawn beyond, where a stepping-stone path made of random pieces of stone leads to a small, hexagonal glasshouse with a compost heap tucked away behind it.

The bridge passes under a pergola, which is built in the same wood as the decking. The pergola posts nearest the utility area are infilled with matching trellis panels which also continue around the corner, forming an immediate screen to the shed and providing support for climbing plants.

Across the lawn from the patio a small group of rocks is carefully laid in a gravel bed creating a setting for a dwarf golden pine (*Pinus mugo* 'Ophir') and providing a complementary feature to the geyser water feature.

DESIGN VARIATIONS

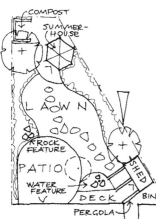

TRIANGULAR PLOT
The narrow corners at each end are usefully filled with the compost area and the shed. The circular patio and curving edge of the lawn help to minimize the angular shape of the plot.

LONG, NARROW PLOT
The circular patio is immediately in front of the house, with the water feature, pergola and shed beyond. The lawn area now forms a longer sweep, and at the point where the stepping-stone path crosses the lawn, the rock feature has been sited to create a focal point.

DIFFERENT ASPECT
The circular patio is moved up the garden into a sunnier position. The decking is extended across the doors opening from the house and up the garden towards the patio, which it joins. The glasshouse and compost area are moved to the other far corner to make sufficient room for an attractive and usable lawn.

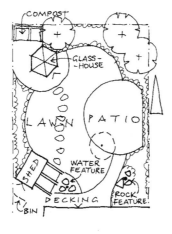

WIDE, SHALLOW PLOT
The glasshouse is located in the diagonally opposite corner to the patio to make a focal point away from the shed, which is in the other far corner, masked by the pergola. The rock feature has been brought to the corner of the patio as foreground interest.

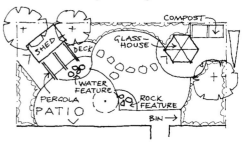

Although this overall scheme follows the Japanese style, more consideration has been given to the inclusion of practical features such as a generous lawn area.

ENCLOSED GARDENS

Enclosure in gardens can be looked at from two opposing viewpoints. On one hand, there is the garden that is surrounded, possibly hemmed-in, by walls, fences, buildings or hedges, and the challenge here is to try to disguise and draw attention away from these boundaries. On the other hand is the garden that is completely open to the elements, and possibly the neighbours, where there are no solid boundaries or other features to give any degree of privacy and where some form of enclosure is very desirable.

The first garden design is for a long, narrow, enclosed plot, of a kind often found in towns and cities, where the gardener wishes to create a feeling of greater space, at the same time as including a number of garden features that will look good together.

In the second example, the design deliberately sets out to create enclosure and privacy by using garden features and planting, and it is perhaps well suited to a new house with a completely blank small garden overlooked by adjoining properties.

The third example is for a courtyard garden with its own particular characteristics of climate and growing conditions. In this instance, the enclosing walls form a square, geometric space, which is emphasized, rather than disguised, by the design of both paving and planting.

Trellis that is made to clothe high boundary walls need not be used simply as a support for climbing plants. Here, for example, shrubs – a pyracantha and Rubus 'Beneden' – *have been trained up the trellis.*

A LONG, NARROW, WALLED PLOT

THE DESIGN

Long, narrow gardens can present quite a challenge, as it is often difficult to know how to fit everything in and at the same time how to disguise the rather claustrophobic 'corridor' effect that such a garden may produce, especially when it is enclosed by high walls or fences.

The primary purpose of the design in this particular garden is to create a feeling of greater space by developing the garden into separate areas or 'rooms', each one different in character yet all linked together, and by disguising the garden boundaries with planting and other features.

The design begins with a rather geometric and very ornamental patio, which joins a path passing under a luxuriantly planted pergola. Beyond this, an old, curving brick path weaves in and around the planting, before finally emerging from a group of trees and shrubs into an informal and secluded sitting area complete with an arbour and a small, natural-looking pond.

THE PLANTING

Near the house and around the patio the choice of planting is restricted to tall, upright-growing wall shrubs and climbers in quite narrow borders so that space for the paving is as generous as possible, allowing room for garden furniture and a barbecue. This area is discreetly separated from the more utilitarian paved area around the back door by a specimen Japanese maple (*Acer palmatum*

Above: View from the house.
Right: Three-dimensional view of the garden.

'Bloodgood'), which is underplanted with ground cover and dwarf bulbs, such as snowdrop and crocus. Beyond the patio area, a combination of dense shrub planting across the width of the garden and climbers on the pergola screens the view beyond and gives a feeling of enclosure and privacy.

On the far side of the pergola planting is a mixture of shrubs and perennials, which become increasingly natural and informal in appearance as you progress down the garden, with a centrally placed group of small trees hiding the furthest area of the garden from view. Ground-covering perennials and shrubs that require only modest or occasional pruning, coupled with the use of bark mulch on the beds, ensure that maintenance of the garden, once mature, is kept to a minimum, apart from an annual thin and prune and occasional dead-heading.

KEY TO PLANTING

1 *Euonymus fortunei* 'Silver Queen'
2 *Hedera helix* 'Ivalace'
3 *Laurus nobilis* 'Aurea'
4 *Chaenomeles x superba* 'Knap Hill Scarlet'
5 *Persicaria affinis* 'Donald Lowndes'
6 *Choisya ternata*
7 *Berberis thunbergii* 'Silver Beauty'
8 *Weigela florida* 'Foliis Purpureis'
9 *Sasa veitchii*
10 *Hydrangea serrata* 'Bluebird'
11 *Hypericum x moserianum* 'Tricolor'
12 *Acer palmatum* 'Bloodgood'
13 *Vinca minor* 'La Grave'
14 *Pyracantha* 'Soleil d'Or'
15 *Geranium renardii*
16 *Miscanthus sacchariflorus*
17 *Clematis alpina*
18 *Rosa* 'New Dawn'
19 *Jasminum officinale* 'Argenteovariegatum'
20 *Viburnum x bodnantense* 'Dawn'
21 *Fatsia japonica*
22 *Delphinium* Black Knight Group
23 *Hibiscus syriacus* 'Woodbridge'
24 *Fargesia nitida*
25 *Spiraea x vanhouttei*
26 *Iris sibirica* 'Tropic Night'
27 *Crambe cordifolia*
28 *Cornus alba* 'Spaethii'
29 *Astilbe x japonica* 'Deutschland'
30 *Hosta fortunei* var. *aureomarginata*
31 *Hebe salicifolia*
32 *Ceanothus impressus*
33 *Betula albosinensis*
34 *Viburnum* 'Pragense'
35 *Diervilla x splendens*
36 *Anemone x hupehensis* 'September Charm'
37 *Digitalis purpurea* Excelsior hybrids
38 *Amelanchier lamarckii*
39 *Macleaya microcarpa* 'Kelway's Coral Plume'
40 *Aconitum* 'Ivorine'
41 *Syringa microphylla* 'Superba'
42 *Ilex x koehneana* 'Chestnut Leaf'
43 *Miscanthus sinensis* 'Variegatus'
44 *Lonicera periclymenum* 'Graham Thomas'
45 *Humulus lupulus* 'Aureus'
46 *Exochorda x macrantha* 'The Bride'
47 *Hedera helix* 'Green Ripple'
48 *Kerria japonica* 'Pleniflora'

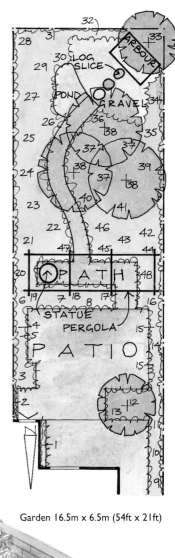

Garden 16.5m x 6.5m (54ft x 21ft)

DESIGN VARIATIONS

TRIANGULAR PLOT

The patio and pergola are turned so that they align with the long boundary, and the path crosses from one side of the garden to the other. The arbour is brought down the garden, nearer to the house, and is hidden behind the central group of trees. The pool is now beyond the area of gravel.

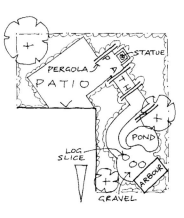

CORNER PLOT

Here, the main patio allows the statue to become the chief focus of attention, and the pergola is set to one side to create an enclosed walkway. The arbour, which is set in the far corner, is separated from the rest of the garden by the pool and planting and forms a third, distinct area.

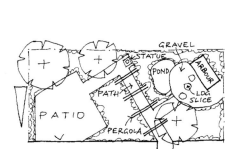

WIDE, SHALLOW PLOT

The patio, paving and arbour are all set at angles along the diagonal axis of the garden to divert attention from the proportions of the plot and to give an impression of greater space in the garden.

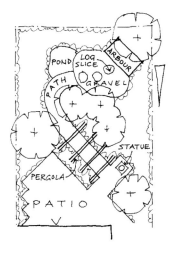

RECTANGULAR PLOT

The patio is set at an angle, while the path leads off from the corner nearest to the house, creating a meandering route around to the arbour, which is positioned in the far corner.

THE FEATURES

Square concrete flags, with an exposed aggregate finish in warm brown and cream, are butted together to form the main patio, creating an interesting texture on an otherwise plain surface. A warm red paving brick is used to define the edge of the patio and is also mixed with the flags to create a contrast in both colour and texture. The same brick is laid in herringbone style for the path from the patio, which passes beneath the pergola and down the garden to the sitting area in the far corner. At this point it joins a gravel-covered area in front of the arbour, which is reached via stepping stones made from sawn slices of softwood logs, well treated with preservative.

Both the arbour and pergola are built from ready-to-assemble modules of pressure-treated softwood and are treated on completion with a natural-

coloured wood stain, such as oak or teak, to complement the planting and other materials.

At the junction of the brick path and gravel area
the simple pond is made using a flexible liner and,
by using a thin strip of treated plywood or other
easy-to-bend material to support the edge of the
liner, the planting can be brought right up to the
water's edge, creating a natural-looking margin and
softening the edges of the pond.

*A text-book example of the
way in which a long, narrow
garden can be disguised by
the skilful positioning of
meandering lawns and
paths, which curve and curl
around the tall shrubs and
trees.*

115

A PRIVATE GARDEN

THE DESIGN

Seclusion is often one of the main requirements in a garden, but it is especially important in a small garden that is overlooked on all sides or with a new house where the plot may be completely bare.

The aim in this modestly sized garden is to create enclosure where none existed before, and this is achieved through a combination of trellis, arches and pergola, which will provide some immediate effect, and tree and shrub planting, which will provide screening and privacy in the longer term.

With the back of the house facing the sunrise, the main patio area will receive sun during the early part of the day, so a small lawn area further down the garden, reached by a simple gravel path, and a circular arbour in the far corner of the plot, provide alternative sunny sitting areas for later in the day when the patio is in shade.

THE PLANTING

In such a modest plot, tree planting is carefully thought out, using only small, compact types, such as crab apple (*Malus* x *robusta* 'Red Sentinel') and mountain ash (*Sorbus hupehensis*), with one group planted in the top left corner of the garden and another, smaller group just off the patio. This breaks up the general view into the garden without causing excessive shade or shadow on the sitting areas. Tall, upright-growing evergreen and deciduous shrubs, such as *Viburnum farreri*, predominate in the main perimeter border, while deciduous

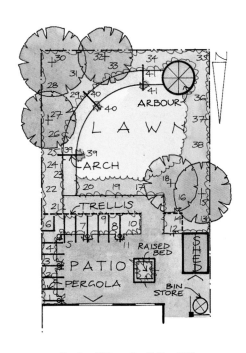

Garden 13.5m x 9m (44ft x 29ft)

KEY TO PLANTING
1 *Trachelospermum jasminoides*
2 *Osmanthus delavayi*
3 *Clematis armandii*
4 *Phygelius* x *recta* 'African Queen'
5 *Clematis* 'Henryi'
6 *Photinia* x *fraseri* 'Rubens'
7 *Hebe* 'Veitchii'
8 *Juniperus virginiana* 'Grey Owl'
9 *Clematis macropetala*
10 *Spiraea japonica* 'Gold Mound'
11 *Vitis vinifera* 'Purpurea'
12 *Ribes laurifolium*
13 *Photinia davidiana* 'Palette'
14 *Anemone* x *hupehensis* 'September Charm'
15 *Alnus incana* 'Aurea'
16 *Hydrangea serrata* 'Grayswood'
17 *Viburnum plicatum* 'Pink Beauty'

116

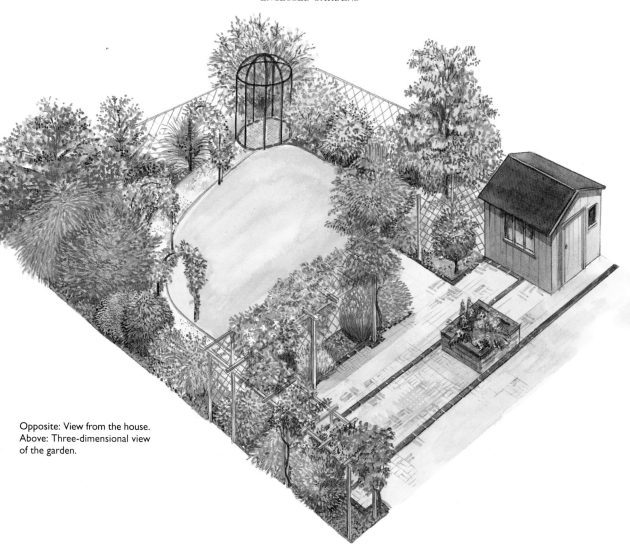

Opposite: View from the house.
Above: Three-dimensional view
of the garden.

18 *Malus* x *robusta* 'Red
   Sentinel'
19 *Viburnum farreri*
20 *Geranium* x *oxonianum*
   'Wargrave Pink'
21 *Liriope spicata* 'Alba'
22 *Cotoneaster sternianus*
23 *Potentilla fruticosa* 'Tilford
   Cream'
24 *Hibiscus syriacus* 'Blue Bird'
25 *Penstemon* 'Snow Storm'
26 *Berberis* x *ottawensis*
   'Superba'
27 *Acer negundo* 'Flamingo'
28 *Buddleia* 'Lochinch'
29 *Aster amellus* 'Pink Zenith'

30 *Prunus* x *schmittii*
31 *Leycesteria formosa*
32 *Sorbus hupehensis*
33 *Persicaria amplexicaulis*
   'Inverleith'
34 *Miscanthus sinensis*
   'Variegatus'
35 *Prunus laurocerasus*
   'Camelliifolia'
36 *Forsythia* x *intermedia*
   'Lynwood'
37 *Rosa glauca*
38 *Ligularia* 'The Rocket'
39 *Rosa* 'Schoolgirl'
40 *Rosa* 'New Dawn'
41 *Rosa* 'Iceberg'

climbers, including **Vitis vinifera** 'Purpurea', are used in abundance over the pergola, arbour and trellis work, creating extra cover in the summer when the garden is most used while letting in more light during the short, dark days of winter. Evergreen climbers and wall shrubs that are able to withstand quite close trimming are also planted around the boundaries of the main patio area, giving maximum screening while taking up a relatively small amount of ground space.

THE FEATURES

The patio is constructed from buff-coloured paving brick laid basketweave style, with a contrasting dark brown brick along the edges and also in narrow bands across the main body of the paving. Leading from the patio a timber-edged path, made from hard-packed and rolled binding gravel laid on

Tall, upright plants, such as bamboo, and evergreen shrubs that can be clipped and trimmed into shape, such as elaeagnus, are ideal for creating enclosed, secluded areas.

top of blinded hardcore, leads to the arbour, which encloses a tiny paved area built from the same buff and brown patio bricks.

A simple timber pergola screens the patio from above along two sides, and is constructed from relatively lightweight sections of softwood, treated with a clear or pale stain so that it does not appear top h eavy or overpowering. The overhead rails of the pergola can be supplemented with heavy-gauge galvanized wire, allowing climbers to cover the top of the structure completely and create a very effective canopy in summer. On the far side of the pergola standard-sized, ready-made trellis panels are slotted between the pergola uprights, giving additional privacy to the patio area without creating a solid barrier, which might cast too much shade.

Beyond the patio, the gravel path is spanned at intervals by delicate wrought-iron rose arches, which are purchased ready to assemble and are painted black, and leads finally to a little circular arbour, again purchased in kit form and painted black to match the arches.

In front of the kitchen window a small raised bed, built in buff brick with brown brick coping to match the patio materials, is backfilled with topsoil and planted with dwarf conifers and with winter-flowering heathers to make an attractive foreground feature. It also acts as a physical divider between the patio and a utility area near the back door, where there is space for a shed and bin store.

DESIGN VARIATIONS

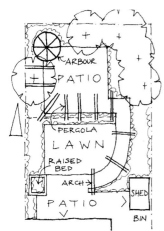

DIFFERENT ASPECT
The patio is moved to the far end of the garden, where it is combined with the arbour. It is enclosed by a trellis and pergola and is linked to the curving path that leads back to a small, practical patio in front of the house. The raised bed at this end of the garden is a point of interest when viewed from the house windows.

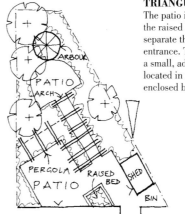

TRIANGULAR PLOT
The patio is set at an angle, and the raised bed is moved to separate the patio from the side entrance. There is no lawn, but a small, additional patio area, located in front of the arbour, is enclosed by arches.

LONG, NARROW PLOT
The proportions of the patio have been altered to take account of the limited width that is available, and the raised bed has been moved away from the general paved area. The arbour is placed more centrally, with the path and arches sweeping from one side of the garden to the other, around a circular lawn and up to the arbour.

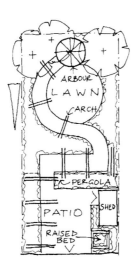

CORNER PLOT
This garden is divided into three distinct areas – the main patio, enclosed by a pergola and trellis, the semicircular lawn and the arbour, which is now separated by the curving path with arches. The raised bed is moved into a corner near the house, while an additional narrow path gives access back to the patio.

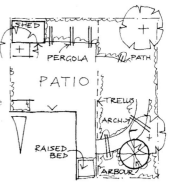

A SMALL COURTYARD
GARDEN

THE DESIGN

The concept of courtyard gardens, enclosed by high walls and buildings to give shade and privacy, goes back many centuries to the times of the Moors and the Persians, but today the term is generally applied to any small, enclosed area that is predominantly paved.

This particular courtyard is enclosed by a group of low buildings to form a square, and it is entered from one corner, giving access to both a kitchen and a sitting room. Because the buildings are only single storey a reasonable amount of sun and light can reach the courtyard, and so the garden is designed very much for practical outside use as well as for decoration.

An angular ground pattern is used to provide a theme complementing the squareness of the garden, with planting used for contrasting textural effect as well as to soften bare walls and hard paving edges. Allowing space for sitting out and access to and from doors and windows means that the area available for planting is fairly small, but it is carefully planned to produce a striking overall effect.

The patio is partly separated from the path to the kitchen door by two raised beds, one containing a water feature, and the other planted with shrubs and ground cover, with a small pergola linking them. Pots on the patio can be planted with annuals to provide summer colour or can be used for growing a variety of culinary herbs.

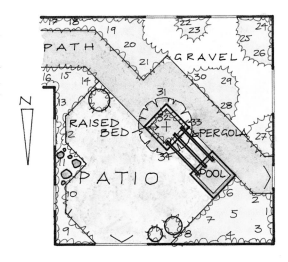

Garden 10m x 10m (33ft x 33ft)

THE PLANTING

The garden is almost completely enclosed, and although on occasions the wind will cause eddies, the microclimate in general is suited to a wide range of plants, including those that are not reliably hardy or that might be damaged by late spring frosts. Planting in the centre of the space is largely avoided to allow plenty of light and sun to penetrate, with the exception of a single Japanese maple (*Acer palmatum*), which forms a striking feature in a raised bed. Around the perimeter of the garden, wall shrubs and climbers form the basic planting framework, with particularly choice and

Opposite: View from the house.
Right: Three-dimensional view of
the garden.

KEY TO PLANTING

1 Abutilon megapotamicum
2 Achillea 'Moonshine'
3 Myrtus communis 'Variegata'
4 Campsis x tagliabuana 'Madame Galen'
5 Stipa gigantea
6 Hydrangea paniculata 'Kyushu'
7 Hebe 'Mrs Winder'
8 Convolvulus cneorum
9 Carpenteria californica
10 Lavandula stoechas ssp. pedunculata
11 Phormium 'Yellow Wave'
12 Nerine bowdenii
13 Perovskia atriplicifolia 'Blue Spire'
14 Dicentra formosa
15 Viburnum x carlcephalum
16 Clematis orientalis
17 Lonicera henryi
18 Euonymus fortunei 'Emerald 'n' Gold'
19 Daphne odora 'Aureomarginata'
20 Hydrangea arborescens 'Annabelle'
21 Potentilla fruticosa 'Princess'
22 Matteuccia struthiopteris
23 Crinodendron hookerianum
24 Hydrangea aspera Villosa Group
25 Lamium maculatum 'Aureum'
26 Phormium tenax 'Purpureum'
27 Photinia x fraseri 'Rubens'
28 Artemisia 'Powis Castle'
29 Miscanthus sinensis var. purpurascens
30 Spiraea betulifolia var. aemeliana
31 Acer palmatum f. atropurpureum
32 Small-leaved ivies
33 Eccremocarpus scaber
34 Clematis macropetala

interesting plants such as campsis and carpenteria used on the warmer walls. Lower planting of dwarf shrubs and compact perennials softens the paving edges, with individually striking plants such as phormium used as focal points and to give vertical interest.

Lightly foliaged and easily managed climbers, including **Clematis macropetala**, are trained up the pergola, creating a pleasantly shaded area on the patio in which to sit or relax away from the heat of the sun.

THE FEATURES

The principal sitting area immediately outside the patio doors consists of old, rectangular, buff sandstone flags laid at an angle to the building, and is sufficiently large to accommodate a table, chairs and a small, portable barbecue. A path in brindled paving bricks gives access from the side passage

121

The strong, angular paved design contrasts with the interesting selection of plants to give this small courtyard real character.

both to this patio area and diagonally across the courtyard to the kitchen door.

Towards the centre of the garden, two raised, square brick beds linked by a simple, lightweight timber pergola form an archway between the patio and the brick path. The more centrally placed of the beds contains a purple-leaved Japanese maple (*Acer palmatum* f. *atropurpureum*) underplanted with small-leaved ivies, while on the other side of the archway the second bed is fitted with a flexible pond liner to make an attractive pool complete with bubble fountain.

Access to ground-level windows for cleaning and maintenance is made easy by areas of gravel immediately in front of them, spreading under the foliage of surrounding plants and setting off the colour and texture of the foliage, while at the same time helping to suppress weeds and conserve moisture.

Design Variations

LONG, NARROW PLOT

The patio takes up the full width of the courtyard, and the raised bed and pool have been moved to maintain the balance in the new arrangement. The pergola provides the only access to the patio, and the path to the back door is realigned to suit the larger space that is available.

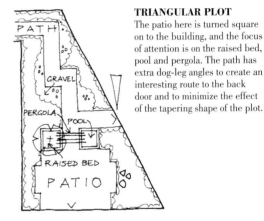

TRIANGULAR PLOT

The patio here is turned square on to the building, and the focus of attention is on the raised bed, pool and pergola. The path has extra dog-leg angles to create an interesting route to the back door and to minimize the effect of the tapering shape of the plot.

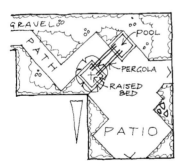

CORNER PLOT

In this corner or dog-leg plot the courtyard is still divided into two main areas, but the path comes through the pergola into the patio area before it reaches the back door. The diagonally set pergola, raised bed and pool form a focal point when viewed from both directions.

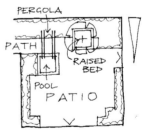

VERY SMALL PLOT

Most of the available space is taken up by the patio, and the planting is largely confined to wall shrubs and climbers. The raised bed and pool are offset to allow access through to the back door, and the pergola creates an entrance to the space by the raised bed.

FORMAL GARDENS

Formal gardens are traditionally characterized by their strong degree of symmetry and, more often than not, by the use of a relatively small number of plant varieties. Although the origins of such gardens go back for hundreds if not thousands of years, some of the seventeenth-century gardens of France are most likely to be thought of as typical examples.

The first garden in this chapter follows these principles of symmetry, but it also takes into account the practical needs of a modern lifestyle, with an emphasis on usable space. It suits those gardeners who like a strong, organized style, with little labour required for maintenance, and is a design that works best when associated with a house with its own symmetry, which can be reflected or emphasized in the garden.

The second garden uses the same strong lines and curves but in an abstract way, and it might therefore suit those who favour geometrical shapes in the garden without the severity of symmetry. Planting in this garden both emphasizes these shapes and also provides a soft foil, giving a striking garden that requires little upkeep.

The formality of this small garden is emphasized by the squareness of the paving and the shaping of the box hedging into neat, geometric forms.

A FORMAL LAYOUT FOR
MODERN USE

THE DESIGN

Traditionally, formal gardens were designed and laid out in a precise, ornamental style, with a strong degree of symmetry, and in Britain and France especially they frequently formed part of a much larger garden or estate where there was plenty of space to carry this out. However, today's smaller gardens and different lifestyles call for a more practical approach.

This formal garden design is both complementary to, and influenced by, the symmetrical rear façade of the house to which it belongs, but unlike some traditional designs it is thoughtfully laid out so that the amount of space available for lawn and terrace is far more useful to a modern-day family.

Essentially, the garden is split into two distinct halves: a rectangular paved terrace near the house and a circular lawn linked to the terrace by a central rose arch. The formality of the design is emphasized by the strong central axis and symmetry of planting on either side of the garden as well as by such details as the regular joints and bond of the paving flags on the terrace. It is also, however, a practical garden, with a generous area of paving, which is in sun for much of the day, and an uncluttered lawn area for play and recreation in drier weather. A utility area for outside storage, bins and a rotary clothes line is located at the side of the house and does not encroach on the formal layout to the rear.

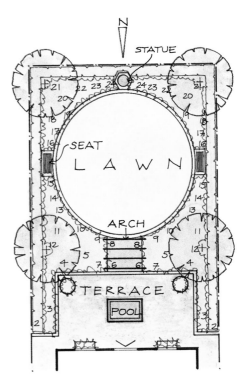

Garden 15m x 10m (49ft x 33ft)

126

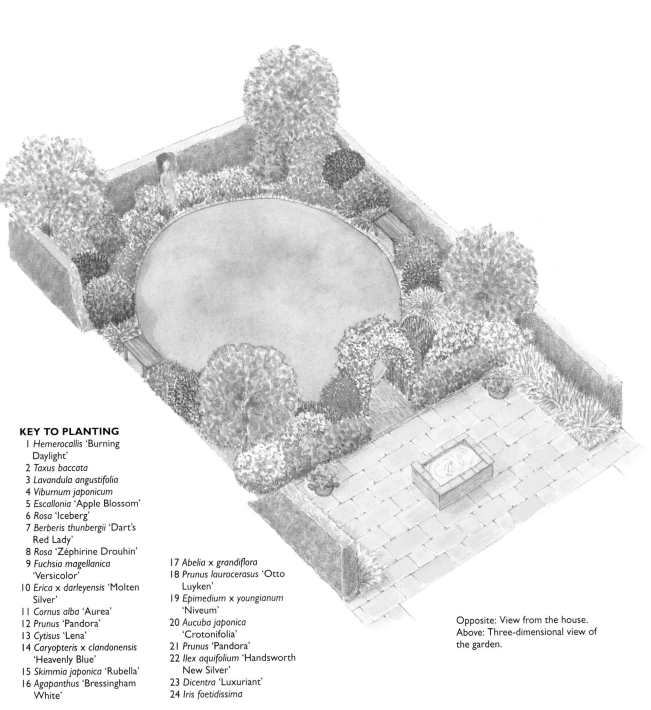

Opposite: View from the house.
Above: Three-dimensional view of the garden.

THE PLANTING

To emphasize the formal layout, planting on either side of the central axis of the garden is identical and consists of a mixture of trees, shrubs and perennials. The boundary is planted with a hedge of clipped yew (**Taxus baccata**), although thuja (**Thuja plicata** 'Atrovirens') will produce a quicker growing hedge with similar effect and is also safer to use, especially if there are small children in the garden, as it is not poisonous.

Trees planted symmetrically in the four corners of the perimeter border accentuate the squareness of the garden, with the two nearer the house also helping to create a greater sense of division between the terrace and the lawn. Planting on either side of the patio is very restrained and is limited to traditional lavender edging (**Lavandula angustifolia**), with geranium (**Pelargonium** vars.) planted in stone urns for hot spots of summer colour and climbing roses on the central arch.

THE FEATURES

The terrace consists of rows of rectangular and square sandstone flags, laid alternately, and is edged in a blue-grey paving brick, which also forms the paving directly underneath the rose arch. A common link between the two halves of the garden is created by using the same brick to form a mowing edge around the circular lawn, which at the same time emphasizes its geometric nature.

Two sitting areas on opposite sides of the lawn, complete with ornamental benches, are paved with the same flagstones as the terrace, and at the far end of the garden a statue placed in a carefully trimmed niche in the hedge forms a striking focal point when seen through the rose arch. This is made from wrought-iron hoops linked together with matching horizontal tie-rods, providing lots of support for the climbing roses.

In the centre of the terrace a rectangular pool, containing a simple jet fountain, is constructed from a flexible pond liner laid inside a raised brick bed with a stone coping to match the patio flags.

DESIGN VARIATIONS

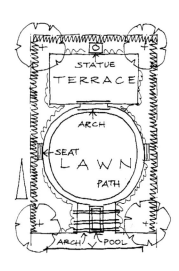

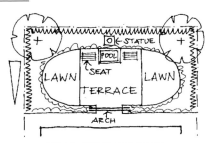

DIFFERENT ASPECT

The terrace is moved to the far end of the garden, bringing the lawn nearer to the house. The narrow perimeter path allows all-weather access. The pool is turned through 90 degrees and combines with the arch to form an entrance to the lawn, while the amount of paving near to the house itself is kept to a minimum.

WIDE, SHALLOW PLOT

The arch has been brought forwards to frame the entrance to the terrace, which is now in the centre of the garden, with the additional features of a pool and statue beyond it. The lawn is divided into two matching semicircles, and only two trees are used, one in each of the corners furthest from the house.

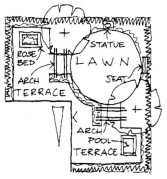

LONG, NARROW PLOT

The terrace is squarer here and is allowed to extend to the hedge at both sides, with the pool now set outside the main paved area. A path on each side leads to the arch. In a garden with these proportions the oval lawn provides more usable space than a circular one of the same width.

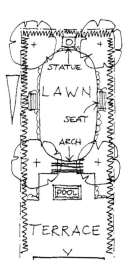

CORNER PLOT

Symmetry is maintained by placing matching terraces on either side of the circular lawn, which is placed on the diagonal axis of the plot. Both terraces have arched entrances onto the lawn, and the pool on one terrace is balanced by a rose border on the other.

*Although it is unmistakably formal in principle, this garden is
also practical, with plenty of space for sitting and relaxing.*

A SIMPLE GEOMETRIC DESIGN

THE DESIGN

By definition, formality implies a sense of symmetry and organization as displayed in the parterres of seventeenth-century French chateaux. However, today the term formal has been extended to include many gardens whose design relies on well-defined geometric shapes, such as circles, squares and rectangles as well as straight lines.

In that sense, the basic ground plan for this modest town garden is formal because it uses simple overlapping geometric shapes to define the various parts of the garden. Although uniform individually, the various shapes are carefully overlaid to create bold and interesting areas of planting so that the overall effect completely disguises the rectangular boundaries of the garden. The simple composition of the ground pattern is emphasized and contrasted by the soft masses of planting, and by defining the hard paved areas and the lawn with a brick edging.

The main sitting areas on the lawn and patio are located away from the house to make best use of the aspect by catching maximum sunlight. A combination of dense planting, trellis work and a gate separates a general utility area from the rest of the garden, and access to this is from the side passage or back door.

A formal, rectangular pool with stepping stones is linked across the garden to the utility area by a pergola, and separates the lawn and patio area from the paving immediately in front of the French windows.

THE PLANTING

A group of three trees in the far corner of the garden makes an attractive backdrop to the lower planting in front. These trees have distinct, regular crown shapes, ranging from globular to conical, and are chosen to emphasize the two-dimensional geometry of the ground pattern.

Elsewhere in the garden, planting consists of a mixture of shrubs, perennials and ground-covering

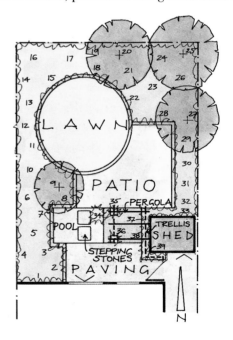

Garden 12.5m x 9.5m (41ft x 31ft)

130

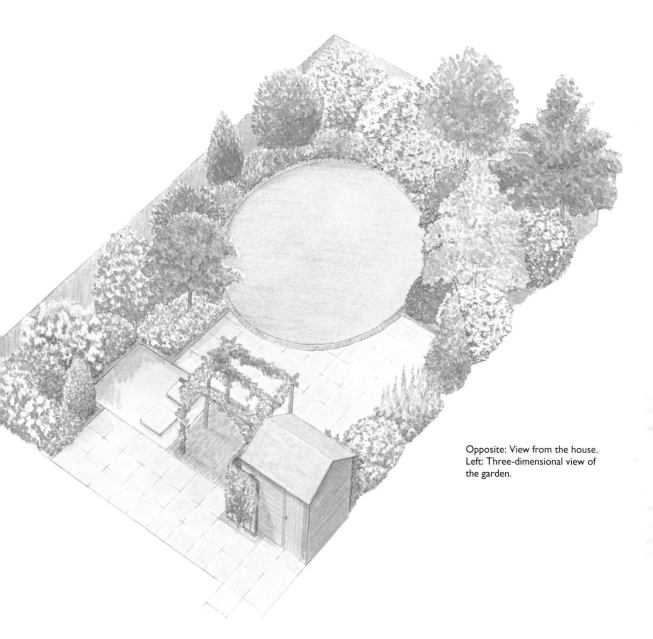

Opposite: View from the house.
Left: Three-dimensional view of
the garden.

KEY TO PLANTING

1 *Hydrangea anomala* ssp.
   petiolaris
2 *Hosta* 'Shade Fanfare'
3 *Juniperus* x *media* 'Gold
   Coast'
4 *Cornus alba* 'Elegantissima'
5 *Viburnum* 'Pragense'
6 *Weigela* 'Victoria'
7 *Epimedium* x *rubrum*
8 *Geranium macrorrhizum*
   'Ingwersen's Variety'
9 *Acer palmatum* 'Senkaki'
10 *Osmanthus heterophyllus*
   'Variegatus'
11 *Aster* x *thomsonii* 'Nanus'
12 *Juniperus chinensis*
   'Pyramidalis'

13 *Erica erigena* 'Irish Salmon'
14 *Hibiscus syriacus* 'Hamabo'
15 *Linum narbonense*
16 *Berberis julianae*
17 *Hebe salicifolia*
18 *Rudbeckia fulgida* var.
   sullivantii 'Goldsturm'
19 *Ceanothus* 'Italian Skies'
20 *Corylus colurna*
21 *Cotoneaster conspicuus*
   'Decorus'
22 *Heuchera micrantha* var.
   diversifolia 'Palace Purple'
23 *Aruncus sylvester*
24 *Prunus lusitanica*
25 *Sorbus aria* 'Lutescens'
26 *Viburnum opulus*
   'Xanthocarpum'

27 *Betula pendula* 'Fastigiata'
28 *Juniperus virginiana* 'Sulphur
   Spray'
29 *Kolkwitzia amabilis* 'Pink
   Cloud'
30 *Pittosporum tenuifolium* 'Silver
   Queen'
31 *Ligularia* 'The Rocket'
32 *Viburnum sargentii*
   'Onondaga'
33 *Pyracantha* 'Orange Glow'
34 *Iris laevigata* 'Alba'
35 *Vitis vinifera* 'Purpurea'
36 *Akebia quinata*
37 *Cotoneaster horizontalis*
38 *Clematis montana* 'Tetrarose'
39 *Lonicera nitida* 'Baggesen's
   Gold'

conifers to give year-round interest while at the same time acting as a soft foil to the brick edging and requiring only limited maintenance, once established.

In the pool a single group of white-flowered Iris (*Iris laevigata* 'Alba') makes a very striking feature, reflecting in the water, while in the bed immediately behind the pool a red-stemmed Japanese maple (*Acer palmatum* 'Senkaki') catches the early morning sun to equally dramatic effect.

THE FEATURES

The paving in front of the house and the patio is constructed from square, exposed-aggregate concrete slabs chosen for their pale buff or beige colour, with butted joints to emphasize the line and shape of the area.

Beneath the pergola, a rectangular panel of brindled or multi-coloured paving bricks continues the geometric theme and provides a contrast to the colour and texture of the slabs. This same brick is used to edge the pool, lawn and patio areas, effectively tying them all together.

In front of the French windows a formal rectangular pool of rendered brick and concrete construction makes an eye-catching focal point. Two slabs on top of brick piers built up from the bottom of the pool act as stepping stones and make an attractive alternative route across to the patio and the lawn beyond, and in the far corner of the pool a shallow marginal shelf provides a small space for planting.

A dark brown, stained timber pergola, made from square-sectioned posts and rectangular-sectioned overhead rails with square ends, provides a support for leafy climbers including *Vitis vinifera* 'Purpurea'. Together with the pool, it creates not only a sense of division between the paving near the house and the rest of the garden, but also acts as a gateway to the area beyond.

DESIGN VARIATIONS

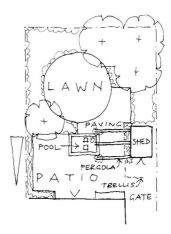

DIFFERENT ASPECT

The pool is moved away from the house and across to one side to allow the patio to be larger. The shed has been turned through 90 degrees for the same reason.

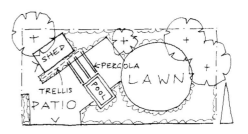

WIDE, SHALLOW PLOT

Turning the basic design through 45 degrees allows the wide, shallow proportions of the plot to be disguised, and attention is drawn away from the far boundary and focused instead on the circular lawn.

Circles can make strong geometric features in a garden.

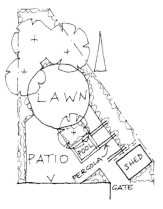

TRIANGULAR PLOT
The shed is now in the corner, with the pergola running end on to it. The patio is angled and now links directly on to the lawn or via the pergola and path on the far side. A triangular bed next to the house screens the gate from view.

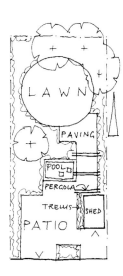

LONG, NARROW PLOT
The patio is now longer and narrower, and the pergola is moved beyond the shed to make room for this. There is planting behind the full width of the pool, which is now away from the main patio area. The stepping stones run diagonally across the corner.

133

COASTAL GARDENS

Gardens located near the sea have their own particular
advantages and disadvantages. On the one hand, they are exposed
to prevailing winds, which are not only potentially damaging in
themselves but are also salt-laden. On the other hand, the
proximity of the water reduces the incidence of frost and extremes
of temperature, with the result that some choice plants can be
grown if a sheltered spot can be found for them.

The first design suits a larger garden that takes the full force of
the on-shore wind, and the principal aim is to provide shelter for
both plants and people by using wind-resistant trees and
man-made structures.

The second garden could be slightly further inland or sheltered
from the main force of the wind by nearby buildings and trees. In
this example, smaller trees and shrubs are used to create
favourable spots in the garden, not only for people but for some
very special and unusual plants.

The final example shows a tiny seaside garden in a warm climate,
which is designed to suit weekend or holiday use, with the
planting being virtually self-maintaining.

*▴ Many gardens that are near the sea enjoy a relatively
temperate climate. This garden, for example, which is on the
west coast of Scotland, is mild enough for a Chusan palm
and a cordyline.*

A LARGE, EXPOSED GARDEN

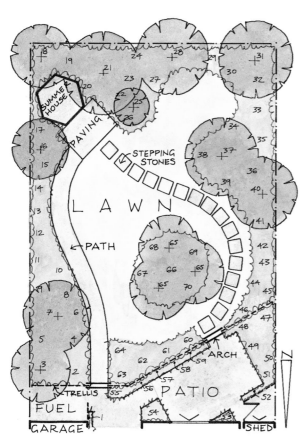

Garden 19.5m x 13m (64ft x 43ft)

THE DESIGN

Building a successful garden on a coastline in the teeth of strong winds and salt spray may at first glance appear to present quite a challenge. The relatively mild climate experienced in many coastal areas means that there are, however, many plants that positively thrive in such a situation, and some of the most dramatic and interesting gardens are to be found by the sea.

The design of this garden uses carefully selected trees and large shrubs to provide a balance between long-term shelter from the prevailing wind while retaining views out of the garden over the sea and coast-line beyond. This long-term planting is also used to create sheltered areas within the garden where conditions are ideal for growing some choice and comparatively tender plants as well as making pleasant spots for outdoor relaxation.

Additional shelter and enclosure are provided by trellis screens and overhead beams supporting quick-growing climbers around and over the patio area so that the garden can be enjoyed even in the short term while the trees and larger shrubs are developing.

KEY TO PLANTING

1 Hedera helix 'Goldheart'
2 Elaeagnus × ebbingei 'Limelight'
3 Carpinus betulus 'Fastigiata'
4 Escallonia 'Red Elf'
5 Garrya elliptica
6 Aster amellus 'Nocturne'
7 Sorbus aucuparia
8 Hebe armstrongii
9 Photinia × fraseri 'Red Robin'
10 Osteospermum ecklonii
11 Miscanthus sacchariflorus
12 Viburnum tinus 'Variegatum'
13 Euphorbia griffithii 'Dixter'
14 Stipa arundinacea
15 Potentilla fruticosa 'Abbotswood'
16 Prunus avium 'Plena'
17 Pittosporum tenuifolium
18 Pinus nigra ssp. maritima
19 Elaeagnus commutata
20 Olearia × macrodonta
21 Populus alba 'Richardii'
22 Hebe 'Alicia Amherst'
23 Tamarix pentandra
24 Griselinia littoralis 'Dixon's Cream'
25 Eucalyptus gunnii
26 Hemerocallis 'Hyperion'

27 Fuchsia 'Mrs Popple'
28 Sorbus aria 'Majestica'
29 Hippophae rhamnoides
30 Sarcococca hookeriana var. digyna
31 Cupressus macrocarpa
32 Escallonia rubra var. macrantha
33 Buddleia 'Lochinch'
34 Geranium ibericum
35 Ceanothus dentatus
36 Ilex aquifolium 'Flavescens'
37 Cupressus macrocarpa 'Goldcrest'
38 Potentilla fruticosa 'Princess'
39 Brachyglottis greyi
40 Arbutus unedo f. rubra
41 Viburnum × burkwoodii
42 Kerria japonica 'Pleniflora'
43 Hebe salicifolia

44 Leucanthemum × superbum 'Snowcap'
45 Elaeagnus × ebbingei 'Gilt Edge'
46 Phygelius capensis
47 Fatsia japonica
48 Fuchsia magellanica var. gracilis 'Variegata'
49 Helianthemum 'Rhodanthe Carneum'
50 Carpenteria californica
51 Olearia nummulariifolia
52 Hedera helix 'Tricolor'
53 Abutilon × suntense
54 Lonicera nitida 'Baggesen's Gold'

55 Pittosporum
56 Euonymus fortunei 'Gold Tip'
57 Geranium macrorrhizum
58 Clematis montana 'Tetrarose'
59 Agapanthus 'Bressingham White'
60 Fuchsia magellanica 'Versicolor'
61 Hebe 'Marjorie'
62 Helichrysum angustifolium
63 Yucca filamentosa 'Variegata'
64 Lavandula angustifolia 'Hidcote'
65 Betula pendula
66 Elaeagnus pungens 'Maculata'
67 Abelia × grandiflora
68 Genista hispanica 'Compacta'
69 Cytisus × praecox 'Albus'
70 Rosa 'Pink Grootendoorst'

Opposite: View from the house.
Left: Three-dimensional view of the garden.

In the far corner of the garden a summerhouse and an additional paved area can be reached either by an elegantly curving path or by stepping stones across the lawn, providing a pleasant, alternative recreation area regardless of the weather and inviting further exploration of the garden.

THE PLANTING

The principal shelter planting is of trees and larger conifers such as pine (*Pinus nigra* ssp. *maritima*) and cypress (*Cupressus macrocarpa*), selected for their tolerance of exposed maritime conditions. They are carefully grouped to form a series of windbreaks and baffles, thereby helping to create a number of relatively sheltered areas throughout the garden. The island bed of trees and shrubs in the lawn provides both shelter and vertical interest.

Large, equally wind- and salt-tolerant shrubs, especially evergreens such as elaeagnus and griselinia, are interplanted fairly closely with these trees in order to maintain shelter right down to ground level, as the tree crowns gradually increase in height and lose their lower branches over the years.

Ideally, these trees and shrubs should be planted during the early stages of constructing the garden, and to help them become established a temporary man-made windbreak of split chestnut-paling fencing, netting or even brushwood can be used. As these plants begin to establish, the remainder of the planting can be carried out over the next few years, with smaller, choicer plants being put in the ground only when sufficient shelter is achieved.

A number of large evergreen shrubs, including pittosporum, is planted around the fringes of the patio to provide a really strong sense of enclosure and localized shelter.

DESIGN VARIATIONS

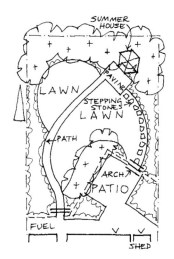

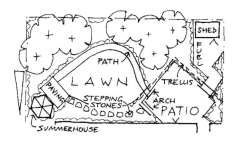

WIDE, SHALLOW PLOT
The extra width of the garden is used by placing the utility area behind the main patio and screening it from view with a trellis. The paths from the patio start from the same point, then diverge to opposite sides of the plot, enclosing a small, central lawn, before reaching the summerhouse.

DIFFERENT ASPECT
The patio is moved away from the house and an additional block of planting provides shelter along its southwest edge. The central planting area now wraps around the patio for shelter, and the summerhouse, now moved into the far corner, is reached from the patio via stepping stones and from the house via the path, which now cuts across the lawn.

TRIANGULAR PLOT
This garden is split into two by the diagonal trellis screen. Only a single path is used to reach the summerhouse, which is in the far corner, and there is a smaller, simplified lawn area in front of it. The path from the back gate to the patio is staggered through the planting to provide additional protection from the wind.

THE FEATURES

The patio is built from matching rectangular stone flags laid in running bond at an angle to the house, forming a strong geometrical pattern, and focusing on a view of a large central island bed through a narrow archway.

Near the back door the paving material changes to an old brick, again laid in a running bond, and this ultimately links into a long, narrow, curving path leading down the garden to the small hexagonal summerhouse and paved area suitable for late-afternoon and early-evening relaxation.

The summerhouse is constructed from inexpensive, pressure-treated softwood with a roof covering of artificial shingles. Maintenance consists of treating it with a transparent or pale coloured preservative, which will retain the natural tone of the wood and help it to blend in with its surroundings.

The trellis screen sheltering the patio, which runs across almost the full width of the garden, is made from vertical laths fixed to a post-and-rail fence construction, giving more effective shelter than traditional open-square trellis panels, as well as being an attractive design feature. The wood for this should also be pressure treated before purchase and subsequently maintained to preserve its natural colour.

Access to the lawn and the meandering brick path is through arches in the screen, which can be closed off with gates made in the same style, using matching vertical laths. At the end of the garage, this trellis screen encloses an area for placing rubbish bins as well as for storing fuel such as coal or logs, while in the otherwise dead space on the opposite side of the house, a gateway leads to a small covered store or shed for garden furniture.

Pines can be used to provide shelter in exposed seaside gardens, and additional protection is afforded here by a wall built from the local beach stones. The wall is enhanced by ornamental seagulls.

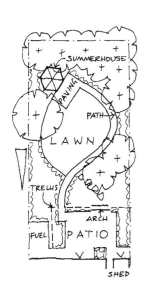

LONG, NARROW PLOT

The patio area is square on to the house, and there is planting on three sides. The stepping-stone path is shortened and now links with the solid path, which is strongly curved to contrast with the straight lines of the boundaries and which, in turn, is balanced by the equally strong curve of the lawn on the other side.

A SMALL, SHELTERED GARDEN

THE DESIGN

Not all gardens near the sea are directly exposed to the prevailing wind, and where shelter is provided it is possible to create quite striking gardens using plants that thrive in the relatively mild climate to be found along many coastlines.

In this small coastal garden some protection from the main prevailing wind blast is given by adjacent buildings and existing trees. However, these features in themselves often create swirling eddies, which can be unpleasant for people using the garden and damaging to the plants within it. The design, therefore, still provides some additional shelter within the garden by the use of planting and trellis, and offers alternative sitting areas both on the lawn and in an enclosed patio garden, so that there is always a sheltered spot regardless of wind direction. Small trees and large shrubs, especially evergreens, are used to filter the wind and reduce turbulence, as well as to create a very attractive backdrop to the lawn and patio areas.

THE PLANTING

The trees and shrubs providing the extra shelter are chosen principally for their tolerance of salt-laden wind but also include some, such as eucalyptus (**E. gunnii**) and strawberry tree (**Arbutus unedo** f. **rubra**), that may be less hardy in a garden situated away from the mild maritime influence. Planting is deliberately dense, primarily to help achieve a quicker screen, but also because plants

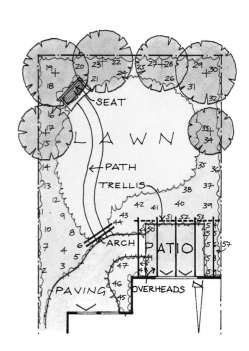

Garden 13m x 9.5m (43ft x 31ft)

KEY TO PLANTING

1 *Daphne x burkwoodii*
2 *Fatsia japonica*
3 *Artemisia schmidtiana* 'Nana'
4 *Cordyline australis* Purpurea Group
5 *Santolina rosmarinifolia* ssp. *rosmarinifolia*
6 *Jasminum mesnyi*
7 *Griselinia littoralis* 'Dixon's Cream'
8 *Convolvulus cneorum*
9 *Abelia schumannii*
10 *Cytisus battandieri*
11 *Abutilon x suntense*
12 *Teucrium chamaedrys*
13 *Pittosporum tenuifolium* 'Irene Paterson'

Opposite: View from the house.
Left: Three-dimensional view of the garden.

grown closer together have a mutually beneficial shelter effect on each other, with a subsequent improvement in growth rates. Where these larger plants create calm, sheltered microclimates, some choice or less hardy dwarf shrubs and perennials can be used. Climbers and evergreen wall shrubs are trained up the trellis and on to the overheads above the main patio area to give extra shelter and are also planted on the boundary walls.

THE FEATURES

The main patio outside the French windows is in a brick-red, non-slip tile, which makes a striking contrast with the white-painted house and boundary walls. From the patio to the back door and down the side of the house, a more robust paved area makes use of local sandstone. This is laid in a crazy-paving pattern with flush-pointed joints, and the crazy paving continues in a narrow, curving path across the lawn to a sitting area nestling in the shelter of a group of small trees and large evergreen shrubs.

Providing additional screening to the patio is a white-painted, diamond trellis fence. Although the upkeep of this style of screen is fairly demanding, it does provide a light, airy and effective foil and support for climbers and other plants. A series of overhead beams in the same finish and supported on posts above the patio area creates a greater feeling of enclosure without seriously affecting the amount of sun and light reaching the ground below.

14 *Spiraea japonica* 'Shirobana'
15 *Fuchsia magellanica* 'Versicolor'
16 *Hebe* 'Midsummer Beauty'
17 *Populus alba* 'Richardii'
18 *Elaeagnus* x *ebbingei*
19 *Eucalyptus gunnii*
20 *Hydrangea macrophylla* 'Quadricolor'
21 *Anemone nemorosa*
22 *Hebe brachysiphon*
23 *Sorbus aucuparia*
24 *Pleioblastus auricomus*
25 *Escallonia* 'C.F. Ball'
26 *Viola* 'Clementina'
27 *Miscanthus sacchariflorus*
28 *Ilex aquifolium* 'Pyramidalis'
29 *Rhamnus alaternus* 'Argenteovariegatus'
30 *Sorbus aria* 'Majestica'
31 *Hypericum moserianum* 'Tricolor'
32 *Fuchsia* 'Riccartonii'
33 *Arbutus unedo* f. *rubra*
34 *Sasa veitchii*
35 *Rosa rugosa* 'Alba'
36 *Lapageria rosea*
37 *Phormium tenax* 'Variegatum'

38 *Verbena peruviana*
39 *Carpenteria californica*
40 *Fuchsia magellanica* var. *gracilis* 'Aurea'
41 *Yucca gloriosa* 'Variegata'
42 *Halimium ocymoides*
43 *Crinodendron hookerianum*
44 *Rosa* 'Paul's Scarlet Climber'
45 *Cistus* 'Silver Pink'
46 *Phormium* 'Maori Sunrise'
47 *Callistemon citrinus* 'Splendens'
48 *Clematis armandii*
49 *Agapanthus* 'Blue Giant'
50 *Passiflora caerulea*
51 *Nandina domestica* 'Richmond'
52 *Rubus henryi* var. *bambusarum*
53 *Leptospermum scoparium* var. *nanum*
54 *Trachelospermum jasminoides*
55 *Azara dentata*
56 *Phlomis russeliana*
57 *Campsis radicans*
58 *Myrtus communis* ssp. *tarentina*
59 *Araujia sericifera*

*If shelter can be provided in a seaside garden, it is often
possible to grow successfully many succulent plants that may
be less hardy elsewhere, such as the* Yucca gloriosa *'Variegata'
and variegated pelargonium shown here.*

DESIGN VARIATIONS

DIFFERENT ASPECT

The patio is moved part way up the garden and turned through 90 degrees, with a bed of shrubs on its west side. Paving has been kept near to the house to provide access, but it is reduced in scale, permitting additional planting between the house and the patio. The path leads from the patio around the far edge of the lawn, which would otherwise be too fragmented.

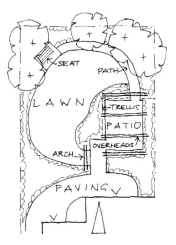

TRIANGULAR PLOT

The patio sits squarely across the garden, with dense planting on either side. The lawn is circular, which fits in well with the angular shape of the plot, and the seat is brought forwards to permit greater depth of planting, especially trees, in the distant corner.

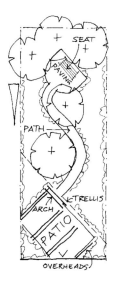

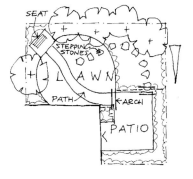

LONG, NARROW PLOT

The shape of this garden is disguised by the deliberate angling of the patio and the pronounced changes in the direction of the central path. The lawn is omitted, and the extra planting that is now possible is used to accentuate the changes in direction and to create hidden corners.

CORNER PLOT

The rectangular patio links directly to the circular lawn by means of an arch or indirectly by means of a path of stepping stones through the corner planting, which forms the main part of the windbreak. The lawn is in strong contrast to the square space in which it is positioned.

A SMALL, EASY-CARE
GARDEN IN A
WARMER CLIMATE

THE DESIGN

In warmer climates many houses and apartments situated on the coast are used only at weekends or by holiday visitors.

This tiny seaside garden is laid out in a very easy-care, low-maintenance style to suit this type of use, although it is also ideal if you have little time to spare for gardening but nevertheless enjoy being outside. Maximum use is made of the limited space to allow for sitting out and general relaxation at all times of the day, with the added option of being able to choose to be in either sun or shade. The relatively high boundary wall makes this a sheltered spot, so large areas of windbreak planting are unnecessary.

Despite its size, the garden incorporates several interesting features, which contribute to the secluded and relaxed atmosphere. Planting, which is limited both in extent and in the choice of plants, is largely confined to a simple perimeter border, leaving the central part of the garden as mostly open space, covered with gravel and small stones.

THE PLANTING

Bearing in mind the need to keep maintenance to a minimum, the planting concentrates on a basic framework of shrubs and climbers that require little more than an annual pruning, with a strong emphasis on year-round effect. In such a small space the use of trees requires great thought, and only three are used here, creating a well-balanced group and giving a choice of shady positions in which to sit on a hot day.

The central, gravel-covered portion of the garden is planted with a few compact or slow-growing plants chosen for their striking habit, which will thrive in this type of sunny, dry situation.

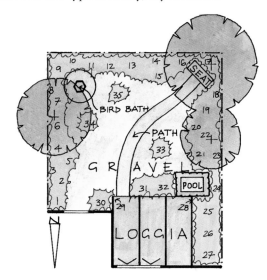

Garden 10m x 8m (33ft x 26ft)

144

Opposite: View from the house.
Above: Three-dimensional view of
the garden.

KEY TO PLANTING

1 *Pittosporum tenuifolium* 'Irene
 Paterson'
2 *Verbena venosa*
3 *Bougainvillea* x *buttiana* 'Mrs
 Butt'
4 *Citrus limon*
5 *Lavandula* 'Alba'
6 *Olea europaea*
7 *Hebe* 'Autumn Glory'
8 *Vitis vinifera* 'Purpurea'
9 *Phillyrea decora*
10 *Jasminum mesnyi*
11 *Myrtus communis* 'Variegata'
12 *Ozothamnus rosmarinifolius*
 'Silver Jubilee'
13 *Hebe* 'Macewanii'
14 *Cissus antarctica*
15 *Photinia* x *fraseri* 'Rubens'
16 *Ilex aquifolium* 'Maderensis
 Variegata'
17 *Pinus pinea*
18 *Lapageria rosea*
19 *Nerium oleander*
20 *Cordyline australis* Purpurea
 Group
21 *Abelia floribunda*
22 *Arbutus andrachne*
23 *Campsis radicans*
24 *Olearia* x *scilloniensis*
25 *Heliotropium* 'Marguerite'
26 *Abutilon megapotamicum*
27 *Phormium cookianum* ssp.
 hookeri 'Tricolor'
28 *Jasminum polyanthum*
29 *Passiflora caerulea*
30 *Phlomis russeliana*
31 *Fuchsia magellanica*
 'Versicolor'
32 *Santolina rosmarinifolia* ssp.
 rosmarinifolia
33 *Agave americana* 'Marginata'
34 *Yucca filamentosa* 'Bright
 Edge'
35 *Fuchsia fulgens*

THE FEATURES

The French windows open on to a timber-decked sitting area beneath a loggia, which is formed by a pitched roof of terracotta pantiles. Steps drop down from here to a simple stone-flagged path with wide, unpointed joints filled with fine gravel, and this leads to a small wooden bench beneath the largest of the three trees.

Immediately in front of the loggia is a slightly raised, stone-walled ornamental pool. It is fitted with a flexible pond liner and in the centre is a low, single-jet fountain powered by a submersible pump, giving movement to the water and adding to its cooling, refreshing effect.

In the opposite corner of the garden, a stone bird bath sits on a circular plinth built from small, square granite setts as a contrast to the stone. This striking feature not only complements the raised pool but also provides a welcome source of drinking and bathing water for the local bird population.

DESIGN VARIATIONS

This tiny seaside garden benefits not only from a warmer climate but also from the simple yet effective low-maintenance planting.

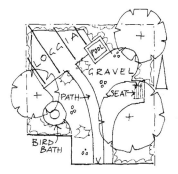

DIFFERENT ASPECT

The loggia and paving are located in a sunny corner, with the paving near to the French windows reduced to a series of steps. The bird bath is moved into the corner of the garden opposite to the seat, which is tucked away behind a bed of planting, itself in the shade of a tree moved to the south side of the seat.

TRIANGULAR PLOT

The pool is combined with the loggia to make room for a usable area of gravel beyond it. The curving borders draw attention away from the oddly shaped boundaries and focus it instead on the seat in the far corner, while the bird bath is moved to provide a second point of interest when viewed from the loggia.

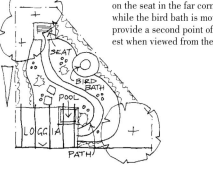

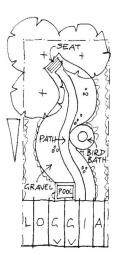

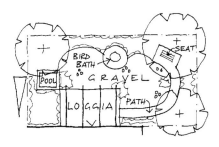

WIDE, SHALLOW PLOT

The loggia is moved away from the side boundary, which permits additional planting, and the pool, bird bath and seat are deliberately sited to create a succession of focal points to divert attention from the straight boundary. This effect is furthered by a strongly curving path, which forms an alternative route to the seat.

LONG, NARROW PLOT

The loggia takes up the full width of the garden, with the pool positioned in front of it to create foreground interest. The borders sweep in exaggerated curves around the bird bath in the middle distance and towards the seat, which is tucked away in the shade of three trees in the opposite corner.

WILDLIFE GARDENS

With the constant erosion of native wildlife habitats, gardens increasingly provide a valuable source of food and shelter for a wide range of creatures. Wildlife can be catered for and encouraged into gardens in many ways, ranging from a simple bird table to a large natural pond with bog garden and damp meadow area fringed by native woodland.

The first garden is essentially practical and its overall design is geared to the needs of a family. A number of details within the garden, however, coupled with a careful choice of plants, makes this garden far more acceptable to birds, insects, amphibians and even small mammals.

In the second example, any practical considerations such as large play areas or vegetable plots are abandoned in favour of planting and features to attract and hold wildlife. This garden is obviously suited to gardeners whose principal interest is wildlife and, perhaps, where there are no young children.

Gardens are invariably more attractive to wildlife when they are densely planted, especially if the plants are selected to provide pollen, nectar, seeds and berries.

A FAMILY GARDEN

THE DESIGN

Encouraging wildlife to visit or stay in a garden does not necessarily mean having to copy nature by trying to create broadleaf woodland or damp meadows. Any garden can be made more wildlife-friendly by paying attention to a few apparently small, yet important aspects of construction and planting, and this example demonstrates how to achieve this while still catering for the everyday needs of a family.

The overall layout includes a generous patio area across the full width of the garden, allowing plenty of space for a range of outside activities and giving good access to the shed, rotary clothes line, garage and small glasshouse.

A well-planted perimeter border encloses the attractively curving lawn, which, although modest in size, provides an additional area for play and relaxation as well as a soft green edge to the square paving. Other features include an arch and a pool which are not only decorative but also add to the wildlife-attracting qualities of the garden.

THE PLANTING

The planting consists of a carefully chosen selection of plants, which, although normally considered to be ornamental, are nevertheless also valuable for their pollen, nectar, fruits or other attributes, such as providing nesting and hibernation sites. The perimeter border is quite generous for such a limited space, giving plenty of cover and creating a

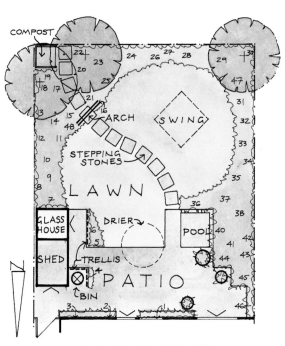

Garden 14m x 12m (46ft x 39ft)

KEY TO PLANTING

1 Euonymus fortunei 'Sheridan Gold'
2 Hedera helix 'Tricolor'
3 Hedera colchica 'Sulphur Heart'
4 Clematis alpina
5 Lavandula angustifolia
6 Lonicera periclymenum 'Graham Thomas'
7 Rosa glauca
8 Cotoneaster horizontalis
9 Osmanthus delavayi
10 Ilex aquifolium 'J.C. van Tol'
11 Rhododendron 'Praecox'
12 Miscanthus sinensis 'Silver Feather'
13 Rosa 'Zéphirine Drouhin'
14 Pyracantha 'Orange Glow'
15 Erica erigena 'Golden Lady'
16 Lonicera periclymenum 'Serotina'

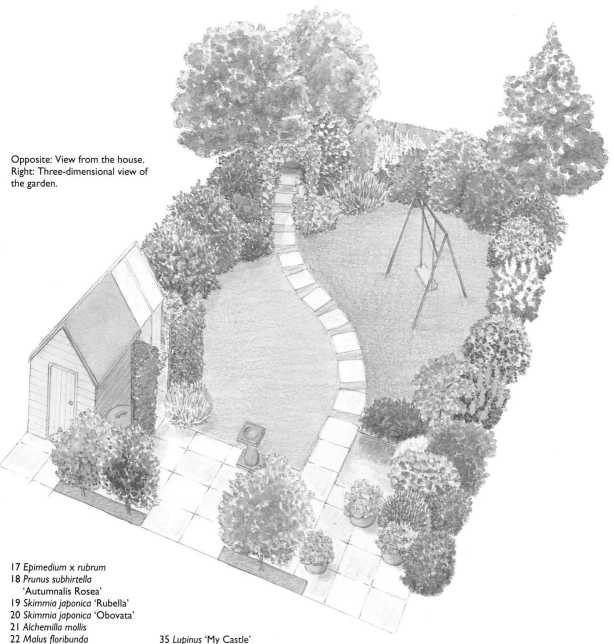

Opposite: View from the house.
Right: Three-dimensional view of the garden.

17 *Epimedium* x *rubrum*
18 *Prunus subhirtella* 'Autumnalis Rosea'
19 *Skimmia japonica* 'Rubella'
20 *Skimmia japonica* 'Obovata'
21 *Alchemilla mollis*
22 *Malus floribunda*
23 *Ilex aquifolium* 'Silver Queen'
24 *Digitalis purpurea*
25 *Lavandula angustifolia* 'Munstead'
26 *Daphne laureola*
27 *Clematis montana* var. *alba*
28 *Cornus alba* 'Elegantissima'
29 *Camellia* 'Donation'
30 *Sorbus aucuparia* 'Sheerwater Seedling'
31 *Hypericum* 'Rowallane'
32 *Astilbe* 'Snowdrift'
33 *Weigela florida* 'Foliis Purpureis'
34 *Clematis orientalis* 'Bill Mackenzie'

35 *Lupinus* 'My Castle'
36 *Caltha palustris* var. *alba*
37 *Magnolia stellata*
38 *Choisya ternata* 'Sundance'
39 *Lonicera fragrantissima*
40 *Iris laevigata* 'Variegata'
41 *Doronicum* 'Miss Mason'
42 *Lonicera japonica* 'Halliana'
43 *Aster amellus* 'Pink Zenith'
44 *Erica carnea* 'Myretoun Ruby'
45 *Mahonia repens*
46 *Jasminum nudiflorum* 'Aureum'
47 *Cotoneaster conspicuus* 'Decorus'
48 *Rosa* 'Schoolgirl'

solid mass of plants, which links with the planting in neighbouring gardens. A limited number of trees, chosen for their modest size and vigour, give height and add a further dimension to the garden. They are also selected for the amount of fruit and flower they provide, with the holly (***Ilex aquifolium*** 'J.C. van Tol') in particular acting as a useful nesting site and giving year-round cover.

All suitable vertical surfaces such as walls and fences are used to support climbers, by means of

151

trellis on solid walls and horizontal, heavy-gauge galvanized wires on fence panels.

While the bulk of the planting provides food of various kinds during the main growing season, there is a particular emphasis on plants that supply early- and late-season nourishment for wildlife, when it might otherwise be scarce.

Finally, and equally importantly, no chemical herbicides or insecticides are used in the garden, which might mean a little extra work but ensures that there is no risk to visiting wildlife.

THE FEATURES
Simple prefabricated trellis panels are nailed or screwed to horizontal timber battens fixed to the house walls, creating a support for climbers and a gap behind for nesting and foraging birds or insects. The same principle is followed for fixing horizontal wires on the fence.

The patio is built from simple, square concrete slabs, and it is large enough to accommodate various features such as a bird bath, bird table and containers of nectar-rich annuals, while leaving enough room for garden furniture and a barbecue.

In the far corner of the garden, a compost bin is reached by way of a stepping-stone path of patio flags across the lawn, and provides a rich supply of food for both plants and creatures. The base and

sides of this bin are made from pressure-treated timber planks, with the whole structure raised on bricks, creating a cosy hiding space beneath.

The simple home-made timber arch over the stepping-stone path is made from peeled and treated larch poles, supporting a late-flowering honeysuckle and a climbing rose.

On the edge of the patio a shallow, square, pool is made using a flexible pond liner edged with paving flags, and is planted with a variety of aquatic plants. The gently sloping sides of the pool allow various creatures to migrate easily in and out of the water. By planting the border right up to the pond edge, the shyer wildlife is given access to the water under cover of the overhanging foliage. For the safety of small children, the pool can be enclosed with a low fence of black-painted, hooped railings; alternatively, a sheet of galvanized steel mesh can be fixed across the pool from edge to edge.

If the lawn on the near side of the stepping-stone path is mown on a regular basis, the closely cropped grass will act as an ornamental feature. On the opposite side of the path, it can be mown infrequently, with the mower blades set high, and the resulting longer grass will give more ground-level cover for small creatures, as well as improving resistance to wear and tear around the base of the swing or climbing frame.

DESIGN VARIATIONS

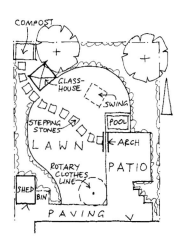

DIFFERENT ASPECT
The patio is turned through 90 degrees and moved part way up the garden so that it catches more sun. This leaves a smaller area of paving for access around the house. The arch is moved to the near end of the stepping-stone path, and the glasshouse takes its place at the other end.

TRIANGULAR PLOT
The widest part of the triangle is used to accommodate the patio and all the utility areas. The lawn is divided into two roughly circular areas by a centrally placed arch, with the swing and play area on the rougher grass of the further lawn.

*A well-planted, generous border enclosing a tiny pond is
well suited to many forms of wildlife, yet it does not encroach
on the rest of the garden.*

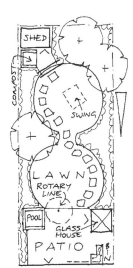

LONG, NARROW PLOT

Because of the limited width,
the patio is squarer, with only
the glasshouse and the bin store
to one side. The lawn is divided
into two equal circles, with
access around the perimeter
being by means of a path of
stepping stones, which leads to
an arch in the far corner, behind
which are the compost heap and
the shed.

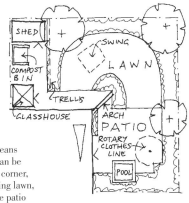

CORNER PLOT

The shape of this plot means
that all the utility area can be
tucked away around the corner,
leaving space for a curving lawn,
which sweeps around the patio
and draws attention away from
the angular boundary. The pool
is now at the back of the plot,
partially set into the border that
runs right around the perimeter.

A NATURAL GARDEN

THE DESIGN

Where wildlife is given priority over other more usual garden needs, over a period of time one can reasonably expect to have a wide range of creatures visiting the garden or even taking up residence. In this longer plot, where the only concessions to a more traditional garden style are a small informal patio, a modest lawn and a tiny adjacent rock garden, wildlife interest is the main requirement.

The garden is densely planted, and consideration is given throughout to simulating a number of individual habitats or areas of different character, which link together, providing continuous planting around the garden in which wildlife can move around in relative safety.

There is an element of the cottage garden in this design, with many biennials and annuals being allowed to seed and regenerate naturally. Although the aim is to produce as natural-looking a garden as possible, a degree of regular maintenance will be needed in order to prevent the various areas from losing the distinctive characteristics that make them attractive to wildlife in the first place.

THE PLANTING

In the immediate vicinity of the patio, a mixture of perennials and shrubs provides foreground colour and interest. Although these are certainly ornamental, they have also been selected for such benefits to wildlife as nectar, pollen and berries.

KEY TO PLANTING

1 *Pyracantha* 'Alexander Pendula'
2 *Cotoneaster procumbens*
3 *Acaena* 'Blue Haze'
4 *Erica vagans* 'Mrs D.F. Maxwell'
5 *Aster amellus* 'King George'
6 *Saponaria ocymoides*
7 *Hebe armstrongii*
8 *Helianthemum* 'The Bride'
9 *Juniperus procumbens* 'Nana'
10 *Dianthus* 'Little Jock'
11 *Pinus mugo* 'Ophir'
12 *Erica arborea* var. *alpina*
13 *Clematis cirrhosa*
14 *Daphne odora* 'Aureomarginata'
15 *Erica carnea* 'Ruby Glow'
16 *Berberis thunbergii* 'Dart's Red Lady'
17 *Lonicera periclymenum*
18 *Anthemis punctata* ssp. *cupaniana*
19 *Elaeagnus* x *ebbingei*
20 *Cornus alba* 'Elegantissima'
21 *Ligularia* 'The Rocket'
22 *Luzula sylvatica* 'Marginata'
23 *Skimmia japonica* 'Rubella'
24 *Crateagus laevigata*
25 *Ilex aquifolium* 'Handsworth New Silver'
26 *Clematis vitalba*
27 *Viola rivinlana* Purpurea Group
28 *Anemone nemorosa*
29 *Viburnum lantana*
30 *Taxus baccata*
31 *Vinca minor*
32 *Digitalis purpurea*
33 *Hedera helix* 'Chicago'
34 *Skimmia laureola*
35 *Rubus idaeus*
36 *Ilex aquifolium* 'Pyramidalis'
37 *Viburnum opulus* 'Compactum'
38 *Cornus sanguinea*
39 *Filipendula ulmaria*
40 *Caltha palustris*
41 *Mentha aquatica*
42 *Iris pseudoacorus*
43 *Hosta plantaginea*

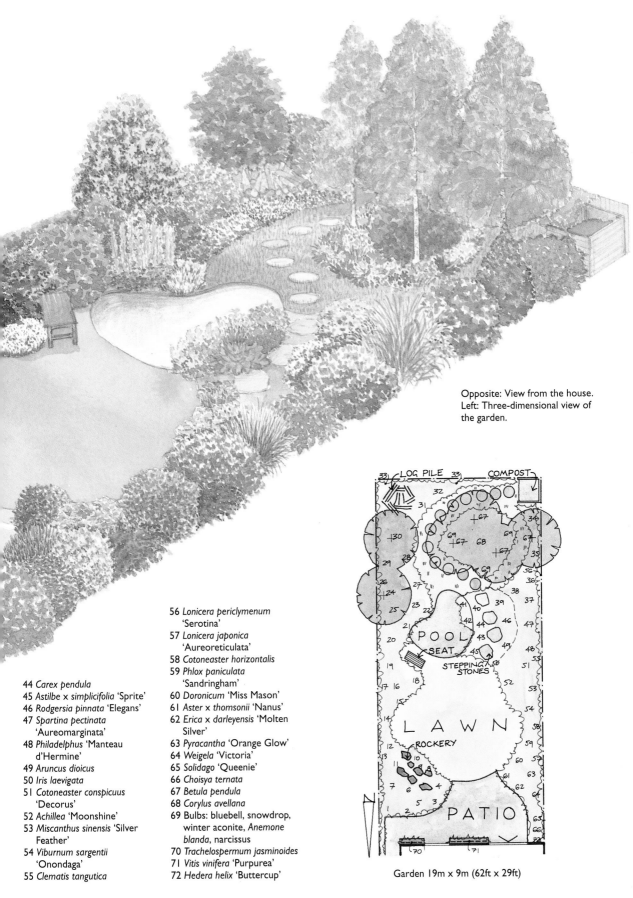

Opposite: View from the house.
Left: Three-dimensional view of the garden.

44 *Carex pendula*
45 *Astilbe* x *simplicifolia* 'Sprite'
46 *Rodgersia pinnata* 'Elegans'
47 *Spartina pectinata* 'Aureomarginata'
48 *Philadelphus* 'Manteau d'Hermine'
49 *Aruncus dioicus*
50 *Iris laevigata*
51 *Cotoneaster conspicuus* 'Decorus'
52 *Achillea* 'Moonshine'
53 *Miscanthus sinensis* 'Silver Feather'
54 *Viburnum sargentii* 'Onondaga'
55 *Clematis tangutica*

56 *Lonicera periclymenum* 'Serotina'
57 *Lonicera japonica* 'Aureoreticulata'
58 *Cotoneaster horizontalis*
59 *Phlox paniculata* 'Sandringham'
60 *Doronicum* 'Miss Mason'
61 *Aster* x *thomsonii* 'Nanus'
62 *Erica* x *darleyensis* 'Molten Silver'
63 *Pyracantha* 'Orange Glow'
64 *Weigela* 'Victoria'
65 *Solidago* 'Queenie'
66 *Choisya ternata*
67 *Betula pendula*
68 *Corylus avellana*
69 Bulbs: bluebell, snowdrop, winter aconite, *Anemone blanda*, narcissus
70 *Trachelospermum jasminoides*
71 *Vitis vinifera* 'Purpurea'
72 *Hedera helix* 'Buttercup'

Garden 19m x 9m (62ft x 29ft)

155

DESIGN VARIATIONS

DIFFERENT ASPECT
The lawn and patio areas have been switched so that the patio is now in the sun. The seat is behind the pool but just in front of the rock garden. The patio is joined to the paving near the house by a narrow, curving path, which complements the shape of the pool, lawn and patio.

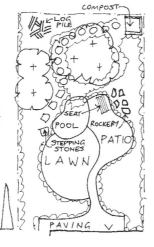

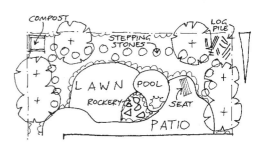

WIDE, SHALLOW PLOT
The patio is much wider but is almost divided by the rock garden. A path of stepping stones leads from one end of the patio to the other, through the planting, which is generous because the pool, lawn and rock garden are centrally placed. The copse is replaced by groups of trees at each end of the plot.

TRIANGULAR PLOT
Although the basic layout is practically unchanged, the compost heap and log pile are combined in the furthest corner, which is now reached by a single path of stepping stones through the woodland area, which is not wide enough to create a central copse.

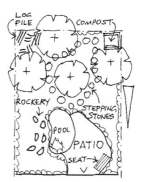

SMALL PLOT
Here the lawn is omitted entirely, and the patio adjoins directly on to one side of the pool, with the seat now positioned at the back of the patio. The rock garden forms the other side of the pool, with the bog planting now at the far end of the garden, near the boundary of the woodland area.

Beyond the patio area the style of planting gradually changes, with plants becoming less ornamental the further one travels down the garden, so that the far end is essentially a collection of native trees and shrubs with a natural understorey of herbaceous planting, including bulbs such as winter aconites and bluebells.

Apart from space devoted to the patio, lawn and pool, the remainder of the garden is taken up entirely by planting, providing generous cover both around and across the garden.

Although much of the general activity in the garden can be viewed from the patio and house, the planting has also been organized to create one or two additional small and secluded sitting areas where the wildlife can be observed at much closer quarters,

especially near the pool, where hostas, irises and other moisture-loving species are planted.

THE FEATURES
Trellis panels fixed to horizontal timber battens provide support for climbers on the walls, creating a space behind for nesting birds and hibernating insects, while on the boundary fences heavy-gauge horizontal wires to support climbers are held a similar distance away from the fence boards, for the same reason.

The patio is constructed from old, broken pieces of sandstone flags laid as crazy paving, creating a very informal feel in keeping with the remainder of the garden. At one side of this, a small rockery and scree garden is planted with winter-flowering

This beautiful example of a wildlife pond has both aquatic and marginal plants, and there are boggy areas and a damp 'meadow' in the foreground.

heathers (***Erica*** spp.), dwarf conifers (***Juniperus*** and ***Pinus*** spp.) and alpines for very late and early season interest.

A generously sized though relatively shallow pool, approximately 600mm (24in) deep, is created with a flexible pond liner. The sides of this pool slope gently to the bottom, which is covered with a layer of inverted turves on top of heavy clay sub-soil. This provides a growing medium for aquatic plants that is not too high in nutrients, which might otherwise cause algal problems in sunny weather.

The pond liner is extended into an immediately adjacent hollow and is backfilled with topsoil to create a bog garden, which effectively separates the lawn from the wilder area of the garden beyond. A narrow path of sandstone flags, each laid on a con-crete base for support, provides access across this boggy area, and the path continues into the 'meadow' and 'woodland' areas, where the stone flags are replaced by log slices.

In one corner of the garden a large compost area provides a home and source of food for many crea-tures as well as plants, while in the opposite corner there is space to deposit any large woody prunings, including logs, in a random heap. This will provide not only an ideal location for hibernating creatures, but also suitable conditions for the establishment of fungi.

Bird boxes on the north side of trees and bat boxes on the house walls, under the eaves, will add to the attraction of the garden, although these need not, of course, be restricted purely to wildlife gardens.

WOODLAND GARDENS

Gardens dominated by trees may or may not be a blessing depending upon your viewpoint. On dry or poor soils, large, dense trees such as beech (**Fagus sylvatica**) and sycamore (**Acer pseudoplatanus**) cast heavy shade and demand huge amounts of moisture and nutrients from the ground, making the establishment of a worthwhile garden quite a challenge. Alternatively on damp, rich soils, less robust trees such as bird cherry (**Prunus padus**) and rowan (**Sorbus aucuparia**) allow you to underplant successfully with a range of shrubs, perennials and bulbs.

The first garden described shows one approach to dealing with established trees by indicating how to make best use of the space unaffected by them and suggesting suitable plants for the difficult areas.

The second design, which is perhaps suited to a new or sparsely planted garden, illustrates how to establish a small woodland area with all of the benefits and none of the drawbacks.

Spring on the woodland floor. Snowdrops, arums, hellebores and periwinkle provide good ground cover while in the background and yet to flower are Anemone nemorosa *and symphytum.*

A SMALL GARDEN WITH EXISTING TREES

THE DESIGN

A small garden with existing trees can sometimes prove to be a bit of a headache, especially if they not only occupy the sunnier areas of the garden but also cast shade and compete with other plants for moisture and nutrients. In this garden, therefore, in which there are lime, oak and wild cherry, to make the best use of the sun at different times of the day paving is extensively used in the more open section of the garden. There is a centrally located arbour on the edge of the tree canopy catching the midday summer sun. A small, circular lawn provides an additional sitting or play area for drier weather, and is carefully placed to avoid immediate overhead shade and competition from the trees.

A narrow woodland path leads from the patio to the arbour, passing through an arch as it does so, and a compost area tucked into one corner is reached by a stepping-stone path.

THE PLANTING

Throughout the garden, plants are selected to suit the varying degrees of sun, shade and soil moisture found in different locations. Immediately below the deciduous tree canopy, planting is predominantly spring-flowering bulbs mixed with shade-tolerant perennials and evergreen shrubs such as skimmia or dwarf laurel (**Prunus laurocerasus** 'Otto Luyken'). On an acid soil where moisture is not a

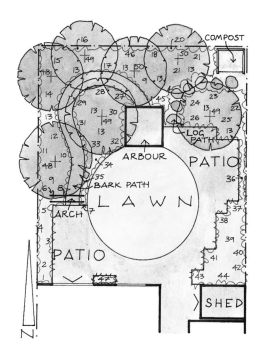

Garden 12m x 11m (39ft x 36ft)

problem, the selection of plants could be extended to include rhododendrons and deciduous azaleas. Along the sunny edge of the woodland area more light and warmth penetrates, and a greater selection of plants will thrive, including low-growing perennials and dwarf shrubs which flower from late spring to autumn or have attractive foliage,

Opposite: View from the house.
Left: Three-dimensional view of the garden.

KEY TO PLANTING

1 *Hydrangea serrata* 'Bluebird'
2 *Iris foetidissima*
3 *Geranium renardii*
4 *Euonymus fortunei* 'Silver Queen'
5 *Hypericum* x *inodorum* 'Elstead'
6 *Rosa* 'Golden Showers'
7 *Rosa* 'New Dawn'
8 *Bergenia* 'Wintermärchen'
9 *Rhododendron* 'Praecox'
10 *Euonymus fortunei* 'Emerald Gaiety'
11 *Polygonatum multiflorum*
12 *Ilex aquifolium* 'Silver Queen'
13 Bulbs: bluebell, winter aconite, snowdrop, crocus,
narcissus, scilla
14 *Azalea* 'Gibraltar'
15 *Aucuba japonica* 'Crotonifolia'
16 *Lonicera periclymenum*
17 *Lamium maculatum* 'Chequers'
18 *Rubus idaeus* 'Aureus'
19 *Mahonia aquifolium*
20 *Clematis montana*
21 *Skimmia japonica* 'Obovata'
22 *Ilex* x *altaclerensis* 'Golden King'
23 *Skimmia japonica* 'Rubella'
24 *Persicaria amplexicaulis*
25 *Euphorbia amygdaloides* var. *robbiae*
26 *Dicentra eximia*
27 *Dryopteris felix-mas*
28 *Prunus laurocerasus* 'Otto Luyken'
29 *Anemone nemorosa*
30 *Digitalis purpurea*
31 *Sarcococca confusa*
32 *Epimedium* x *rubrum*
33 *Geranium phaeum*
34 *Melissa officinalis* 'Aurea'
35 *Vinca minor* 'Argenteomarginata Alba'
36 *Pyracantha* 'Orange Glow'
37 *Berberis thunbergii* 'Red Chief'
38 *Achillea* 'Moonshine'
39 *Hemerocallis* 'Stafford'
40 *Ceanothus impressus*
41 *Erica carnea* 'King George'
42 *Ilex aquifolium* 'Flavescens'
43 *Euonymus fortunei* 'Sunspot'
44 *Garrya elliptica* 'James Roof'
45 *Lamium maculatum* 'Aureum'
46 *Buxus sempervirens* 'Elegantissima'
47 *Hedera helix* 'Goldheart'
48 *Tilia cordata*
49 *Prunus avium*
50 *Quercus robur*

providing continuing interest following the spring display under the trees.

Away from the woodland itself, space for planting is limited by the extent of the paving, and wall shrubs and climbers are, therefore, used for screening and softening the boundary fences and walls, with smaller shrubs and perennials in front of them where space allows. A selection of tubs and containers of annuals or permanent planting such as dwarf rhododendrons or Japanese maples (such as *Acer palmatum* 'Dissectum Garnet') can be placed on the patio to give additional interest and can, of course, be moved around as desired.

THE FEATURES

The main paved area is of pale cream, reconstituted stone flags, which contrast with the relatively dark, shady area beneath the tree canopy. These are laid stretcher bond across the garden to emphasize the width and are carefully cut where they meet the lawn to maintain its perfectly circular shape.

DESIGN VARIATIONS

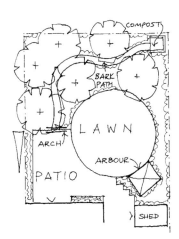

DIFFERENT ASPECT
The patio is positioned in the sunniest part of the garden, with the lawn moved back and to the side to accommodate it. The arbour is also repositioned so that it is in the sun, and the bark path passes under the arch, now becoming a woodland walk to the compost heap in the far corner.

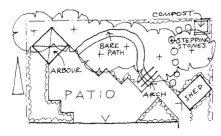

WIDE, SHALLOW PLOT
The patio is extended as far as the edge of the tree canopy and replaces the lawn. The arbour is positioned at one corner of the patio, which leads directly to it. The bark path, linking one end of the patio to the other, serves as a woodland walk, with the log path providing access to the compost heap in the corner.

TRIANGULAR PLOT
The lawn is moved forwards, away from the concentration of trees in the distant corner. The patio extends around the lawn, and the arbour is sited just on the edge of the tree canopy and reached by stepping stones from the patio or directly from the lawn. Another log path leads through the trees to the compost heap at the back.

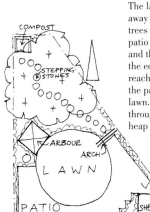

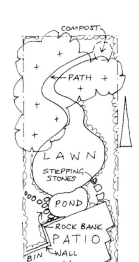

LONG, NARROW PLOT
Here, the trees are in the central section of the garden, which is, therefore, divided into the patio near the house and the lawn at the far end. The lawn is circular to mask the corner. The two areas are joined by a bark path, which passes under the trees, while the lawn is crossed by a diverging log path, one part of which leads to the arbour while the other part gives access to the compost heap.

At the far edge of the patio beyond the French windows a rustic arch, in peeled and treated larch poles, frames a timber-edged, bark-covered path leading through the trees to a small, square matching rustic arbour. The base of the path is covered with a porous membrane prior to surfacing it with the bark, so that it does not become contaminated with soil from below or need regular topdressing with fresh bark.

The arbour can also be reached from the other side of the garden via the flag paving, and at its rear a stepping-stone path made from slices of log, treated with preservative, leads through the bulbs and ground-cover planting to a compost area hidden away from view in the far corner of the garden.

Rhododendrons and bluebells will naturalize easily and quickly in a woodland setting.

A NEWLY DESIGNED GARDEN

THE DESIGN

An area of woodland in a garden can add greatly to its enjoyment, whether from the constantly changing effects of light and shade, the uplifting sight of spring flowers, starting right at the beginning of the year with snowdrops and winter aconites, or the rich colours of autumn leaves. Starting such a garden from scratch enables you to place an emphasis on any of these aspects that particularly appeal.

The aim of the design shown here is to create a garden that is fundamentally woodland in character but that also fulfils other needs. To achieve this, the plot is broadly divided into three zones: a decorative patio area by the house, with very ornamental planting and a small pond backed by a rockery; a central lawn with planting on either side of slightly less ornamental perennials and shrubs; and a woodland zone at the end of the garden, reached via a rough grass path and underplanted with bulbs for naturalizing, predominantly native shrubs and ground-cover perennials.

Because this garden is developed from a bare plot, the establishment of understorey planting is likely to be much more successful than in a garden with existing trees. This is due in part to the small size of the trees and their root systems when first planted, but also to the care that can be taken in selecting them, avoiding species with vigorous root systems, such as ash (**Fraxinus excelsior**), or that cast dense shade, such as beech (**Fagus sylvatica**).

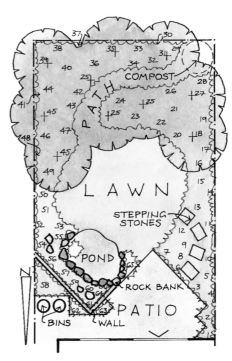

Garden 15.5m x 9.5m (51ft x 31ft)

1 *Caryopteris x clandonensis* 'Kew Blue'
2 *Iris unguicularis*
3 *Choisya ternata* 'Sundance'
4 *Jasminum officinale* 'Argenteovariegatum'
5 *Lavandula angustifolia*
6 *Helianthemum* 'Henfield Brilliant'
7 *Thuja orientalis* 'Rosedalis'
8 *Erica vagans* 'Lyonesse'
9 *Chamaecyparis lawsoniana* 'Minima Aurea'
10 *Iris sibirica* 'Tropic Night'
11 *Berberis thunbergii* 'Rose Glow'
12 *Geranium x cantabrigiense* 'Cambridge'
13 *Abelia x grandiflora*
14 *Hedera helix* ssp. *helix* 'Green Ripple'
15 *Lupinus* 'Gallery Yellow'

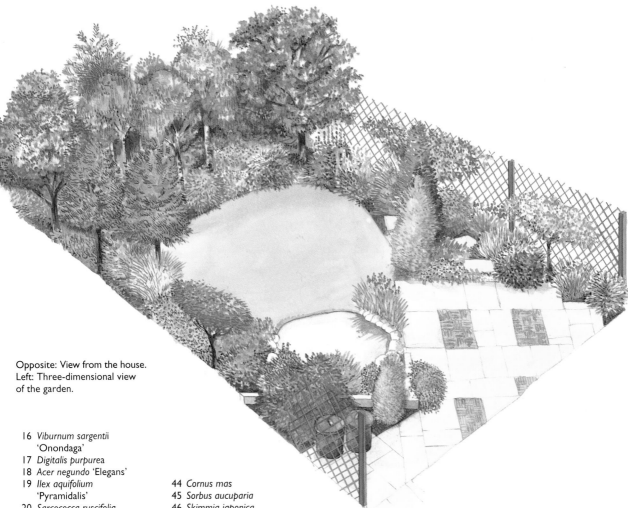

Opposite: View from the house.
Left: Three-dimensional view
of the garden.

16 Viburnum sargentii
    'Onondaga'
17 Digitalis purpurea
18 Acer negundo 'Elegans'
19 Ilex aquifolium
    'Pyramidalis'
20 Sarcococca ruscifolia
21 Viburnum opulus
    'Compactum'
22 Anenome nemorosa
23 Skimmia laureola
24 Iris foetidissima
25 Betula pendula
26 Vinca minor
27 Crataegus laevigata
28 Taxus baccata
29 Euphorbia amygdaloides
    var. robbiae
30 Lonicera periclymenum
    'Graham Thomas'
31 Sorbus intermedia
32 Aucuba japonica 'Variegata'
33 Polygonatum multiflorum
34 Viola odorata
35 Prunus padus 'Watereri'
36 Cornus sanguinea
37 Clematis montana
    'Elizabeth'
38 Prunus laurocerasus
    'Camelliifolia'
39 Acer campestre
40 Rubus cockburnianus
41 Lonicera periclymenum
42 Dryopteris felix-mas
43 Geranium macrorrhizum

44 Cornus mas
45 Sorbus aucuparia
46 Skimmia japonica
    'Fragrans'
47 Skimmia japonica 'Nymans'
48 Hedera helix 'Cristata'
49 Aruncus sylvester
50 Escallonia 'Apple Blossom'
51 Geranium sanguineum
    'Album'
52 Clematis macropetala
53 Pinus mugo 'Mops'
54 Euonymus fortunei
    'Silver Queen'
55 Sisyrinchium idahoense
56 Bergeris thunbergii
    'Atropurpurea Nana'
57 Helianthemum 'Wisley
    Primrose'
58 Viburnum x burkwoodii
59 Erica arborea
    'Albert's Gold'
60 Dianthus deltoides
    'Flashing Light'
61 Erica carnea 'Springwood
    Pink'
62 Thuja occidentalis 'Rheingold'
63 Juniperus horizontalis
    'Hughes'
64 Contoneaster congestus
65 Iris pallida 'Variegata'

THE PLANTING

Perennials and dwarf shrubs chosen for their ornamental flowers and foliage are deliberately restricted
to the area immediately around the patio. They provide eye-catching foreground interest, especially in
the height of summer, while in the middle distance
taller perennials, shrubs and climbers in less vivid
colours give height on either side of the lawn and disguise the boundary fence. At the far end of the garden
a selection of trees is planted to simulate the edge of
a woodland, creating areas of light and shade.
Underplantings of large evergreen shrubs break up
the views directly beneath the tree canopy and screen
the end of the garden, thereby giving the impression
of a larger area beyond. A range of bulbs and
ground-covering perennials, selected specifically
for the ultimately cool, shady conditions, are
allowed to intermix and naturalize, adding to the
effect. The bulbs are scattered throughout the garden
and they are not, therefore, shown on the plan.

165

In the early years, the lawn extends into a narrow, closely mown grass path leading to a compost area in the far corner of the woodland area. However, as the tree canopy matures and creates more shade, this path can be planted with more bulbs and, if cut only infrequently, will encourage more of a woodland flora to develop.

THE FEATURES

The patio of old stone flags mixed with terracotta-coloured paving bricks is set at an angle to the house, diverting attention away from the rectangular shape of the garden and focusing interest on the grass path leading to the woodland area beyond the lawn. A few matching flags are also dotted through the planting at the side of the patio as an alternative route on to the lawn.

In the left foreground off the patio an informal pond constructed from a flexible liner, with a simple fountain powered by a submersible pump, provides a stimulating feature. On the shallow side of the pond, nearest the lawn, the liner is carefully hidden by the grass edge giving a soft, informal feel, as well as helping wildlife such as frogs and toads to migrate in and out of the water. On the opposite side of the pond a rock bank takes advantage of the warm, sunny aspect. Because the garden is virtually level, the rear of the rock bank has been artificially raised by the use of a low brick wall, with a stone coping to match the patio flags.

In woodland where shade and competition from trees are
controlled, a wider range of plants can be introduced.

Design Variations

DIFFERENT ASPECT

The patio is moved away from the house, leaving a small paved area for access, and linked to it by stepping stones arranged in low planting. The trees are positioned so that the edge of the canopy forms a diagonal line that runs parallel to the edge of the patio and so that there is a long sweep of lawn, turning into a woodland path.

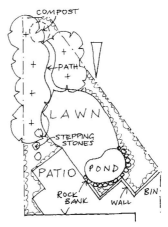

TRIANGULAR PLOT

The pond is brought forwards so that it is almost directly in front of the patio, while the centrally placed lawn is curved to help draw attention from the angular nature of the plot. The woodland extends further down the eastern side of the garden to compensate for the limited width at the far end.

LONG, NARROW PLOT

The patio here runs across the full width of the garden, and the pond is immediately in front of the patio. The lawn and the grass path weave in and out of the woodland area to give an impression of greater width.

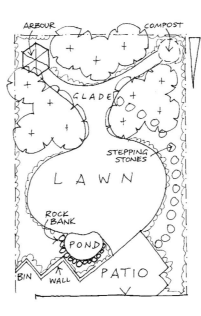

LARGER PLOT

The extra space available here not only makes it possible to accommodate a larger lawn and more generous border planting but also enables the trees to be positioned to create a woodland glade, with mown grass paths and wildflower areas. There is also space to include an arbour in the opposite corner from the compost area, with a path of log sections through the planting leading back to the patio.

FRONT GARDENS

Front gardens can legitimately be separated from other types of garden because more often than not they serve no other purpose than as a setting around the entrance to a house or other building.

The first example shows a tiny front garden, which might belong to a flat or small terrace house. This type and size of garden might frequently be put down to slabs or concrete, but here the design uses a range of materials and plants to produce a dramatic, low-maintenance feature, which would suit anyone who has little time to spend on garden chores.

In the second garden access for a car or other vehicle is considered, but in such a way that it does not detract from an attractive design. This is particularly suitable for small front gardens in which the area taken up for vehicle access is relatively large.

Even the tiniest of front gardens can be transformed with a little imagination.

A TINY,
LOW-MAINTENANCE PLOT

THE DESIGN

By their nature, a great many front gardens are open to public view, both from passing strangers and from visitors to your home. Add to this the fact that if you have a reasonable back garden you are unlikely to spend much leisure time in the front, and it is evident that a successful front garden needs to look good at all times with the minimum of input.

This tiny front garden to a terraced house has been especially designed as a striking feature that requires virtually no maintenance apart from an annual tidy up, and it is ideal if there is little time to spare for basic gardening chores.

A more interesting approach to the front door is created simply by relocating the gate in the opposite corner, making the path to the front door that bit longer. The design of this path makes a striking feature in its own right, but also blends in particularly well with the remainder of the garden. This is put down to gravel with limited, well-spaced planting and decorative features consisting of rocks and ornamental pots.

THE PLANTING

The shared boundary on one side of the garden is planted with a low, narrow box hedge (**Buxus sempervirens** 'Elegantissima') which is neatly trimmed on a regular basis to make a green 'wall'. A selection of larger shrubs along the boundary with the pavement generates a degree of enclosure,

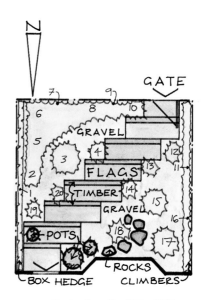

Garden 7m x 7m (23ft x 23ft)

KEY TO PLANTING
1 *Buxus sempervirens* 'Elegantissima'
2 *Taxus baccata* 'Fastigiata Aurea'
3 *Mahonia aquifolium* 'Apollo'
4 *Cotoneaster congestus*
5 *Hypericum* 'Hidcote'
6 *Phormium tenax* 'Purpureum'
7 *Hedera helix* 'Tricolor'
8 *Hydrangea paniculata* 'Kyushu'
9 *Hedera helix* 'Sagittifolia'
10 *Elaeagnus pungens* 'Dicksonii'
11 *Hedera helix* 'Ivalace'
12 *Helianthemum* 'Henfield Brilliant'
13 *Hebe pimeloides* 'Quicksilver'
14 *Thymus x citriodorus* 'Silver Posie'
15 *Koeleria glauca*
16 *Trachelospermum jasminoides* 'Variegatum'
17 *Hebe armstrongii*
18 *Yucca gloriosa* 'Variegata'
19 *Hebe pinguifolia* 'Pagei'
20 *Helianthemum* 'Wisley Primrose'

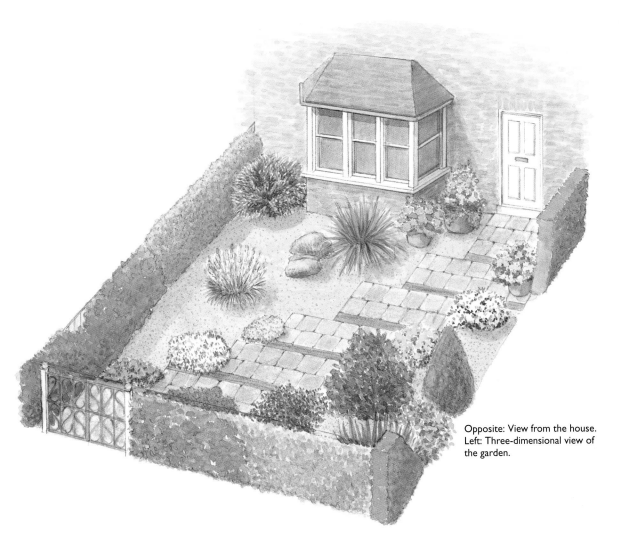

Opposite: View from the house.
Left: Three-dimensional view of
the garden.

while elsewhere within the garden plants chosen for their individual ornamental qualities are planted through the gravel mulch, with a strong emphasis on evergreens for ease of maintenance and year-round effect.

A few low-growing and prostrate shrubs and alpines are planted to soften the path edge and make a strong contrast to the angular paving style. The fences along the pavement and other side boundary support relatively slow-growing and easily managed climbers, including trachelospermum and small-leaved ivies (**Hedera helix** vars.), to screen the boundaries and act as an evergreen backdrop to the individual shrubs in front.

THE FEATURES
The striking path is made from very pale, rectangular concrete flags laid in a broadly stretcher-bond style alternated with lengths of pressure-treated timber, stained dark brown.

The remainder of the garden is covered with a small-grade, round gravel or pea shingle in shades of brown, buff and warm grey, laid on top of a porous, weed-suppressing membrane. As well as conserving moisture, the membrane prevents the soil and gravel from mixing, and is therefore an important labour-saving feature of the garden construction.

In front of the window a small, sculptural group of rock pieces is set into the gravel as a backdrop to a specimen variegated yucca (**Y. gloriosa** 'Variegata'), while several terracotta pots close to the front door can be used for brilliant displays of annuals during the summer months, with additional interest provided by scented plant varieties such as nicotiana.

171

DESIGN VARIATIONS

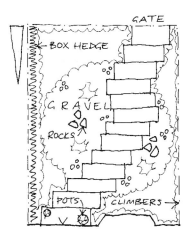

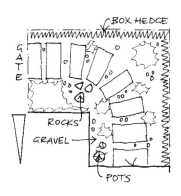

CORNER PLOT

The path is made to curve around the corner by spacing the flag and timber strips with additional gravel.

LARGER PLOT

The path is laid in a slightly meandering style, with the gravel concentrated in a central, circular area, broken only by the path and rock features on each side. Outside the circle, planting is denser and more generous.

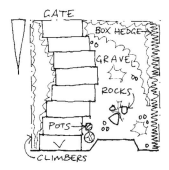

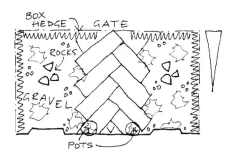

GATE OPPOSITE FRONT DOOR

The flag and timber strips are laid in a slight curve, with extra planting introduced on the narrow side. A block of planting in the far corner diverts the eye from the boundary and towards the gate.

WIDE, SHALLOW PLOT

Laying the path herringbone-style makes it more eye-catching. Perimeter planting is entirely box hedging, but with some low-growing individual plants in the gravel area.

A surprising amount of interest is provided in this tiny front garden by the combination of paving materials, which are set off by a relatively simple planting plan.

A GARDEN WITH
VEHICLE ACCESS

THE DESIGN

All too often, front gardens can be dominated by hard, unsympathetic driveways in order to pull the car off the road into a garage, car port or parking bay. With careful planning, however, it is possible to turn these paved areas into positive features that will add to the attraction of the garden, rather than detract from it.

This modest, shallow-fronted plot is typical of many such front gardens, with access required into a garage at the side of the house. Because of the limited depth of the garden, the only realistic location for the entrance gates is more or less directly in line with the garage. In order, therefore, to divert attention from what could be a dull, straight driveway, gravel is used for the finished surface, spreading it in an interesting and undefined way beyond the absolute minimum area required for vehicle access and linking together the other pedestrian areas in the garden.

The perfectly circular lawn, with its crisp, brick mowing edge, makes a striking contrast to the irregular gravel area, while the generous planting in the sweeping border helps to emphasize the characters of both.

THE PLANTING

The perimeter borders around the lawn, and at the side of the drive, are planted predominantly with shrubs for both flower and foliage, including a high proportion of evergreens and several varieties of ground-covering junipers (such as *Juniperus* x *media* 'Gold Coast'). This selection of plants is chosen not only to provide year-round interest, but also to keep maintenance requirements to a minimum.

The warm, protected house wall is used to advantage, and is planted with several choicer plants that might not be reliable in a colder, more exposed spot. A Japanese maple (*Acer palmatum* 'Katsura'), underplanted with ground cover, provides a break between the lawn and drive, creating an attractive approach to the front door while

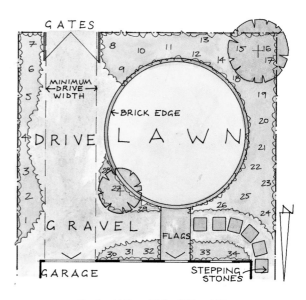

Garden 11.5m x 13.5m (38ft x 44ft)

174

Opposite: View from the house.
Above: Three-dimensional view of
the garden.

KEY TO PLANTING

1 *Taxus baccata* 'Repens Aurea'
2 *Juniperus chinensis* 'Blue Alps'
3 *Erica erigena* 'W.T. Rackliff'
4 *Miscanthus sinensis* 'Variegatus'
5 *Physocarpus opulifolius* 'Luteus'
6 *Elaeagnus* x *ebbingei*
7 *Ilex aquifolium* 'Argentea Marginata'
8 *Escallonia* 'Apple Blossom'
9 *Potentilla fruticosa* 'Princess'
10 *Buddleia* 'Lochinch'
11 *Osmanthus heterophyllus* 'Variegatus'
12 *Ilex crenata* 'Golden Gem'
13 *Cotoneaster horizontalis*
14 *Hydrangea paniculata* 'Kyushu'
15 *Elaeagnus pungens* 'Maculata'
16 *Acer negundo* 'Elegans'
17 *Viburnum tinus* 'Purpureum'
18 *Juniperus* x *media* 'Gold Coast'
19 *Weigela florida* 'Variegata'
20 *Erica* x *darleyensis* 'Molten Silver'
21 *Thuja plicata* 'Stoneham Gold'
22 *Caryopteris* x *clandonensis* 'Heavenly Blue'
23 *Ceanothus* 'Blue Mound'
24 *Abelia* x *grandiflora*
25 *Juniperus horizontalis* 'Blue Chip'
26 *Euonymus fortunei* 'Emerald Gaiety'
27 *Acer palmatum* 'Katsura'
28 *Tellima grandiflora* 'Purpurea'
29 *Persicaria affinis* 'Donald Lowndes'
30 *Convolvulus cneorum*
31 *Lavandula stoechas*
32 *Hebe andersonii* 'Variegata'
33 *Choisya* 'Aztec Pearl'
34 *Phygelius* x *rectus* 'African Queen'

at the same time discouraging people from cutting across the lawn edge.

THE FEATURES

The areas of pedestrian paving and driveway are constructed from fine-grade gravel or pea shingle laid on top of well-compacted hardcore blinded with a covering of fine ash or sand. By not having any edging to the drive, the gravel is allowed to spread into and under the planting, making a soft and informal boundary between the planting and the drive, and avoiding rigidly straight lines.

From the front door a series of square, reproduction stone flags are laid as stepping stones in the gravel for additional interest, and lead to the side gate.

To emphasize the circular shape of the lawn it is edged with a mowing strip of dark brown paving bricks laid in header bond, and the whole grass area is raised slightly above the surrounding gravel, helping to prevent the stones from spreading on to it and damaging the mower blades.

DESIGN VARIATIONS

The edge of this turning circle is completely masked by the gravel, which covers the ground and continues under the border planting. A hardy, deciduous tree, such as Sorbus 'Joseph Rock', could be used in place of the central palm and bedding plants as a permanent feature.

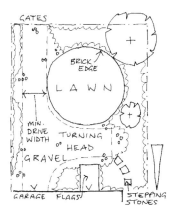

LONGER PLOT WITH TURNING AREA

The extra length of the garden makes it possible to include a turning area between the lawn and the front door. The small bed of acers is omitted, and the planting at the end of the turning area is irregular, to match the edge of the main drive.

TRIANGULAR PLOT

The shape of the garden makes it impossible to include a circular lawn, so a semicircular one is used instead. If space is severely restricted, the border behind the lawn can be replaced by a narrow hedge of, for example, yew or beech.

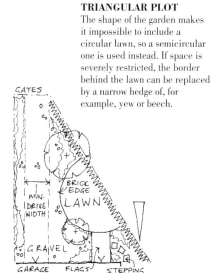

NARROW PLOT

The size makes including a lawn impracticable, and the extra space is put down to gravel, with an acer planted in the centre. Stepping stones lead from the edge of the drive proper to the front door.

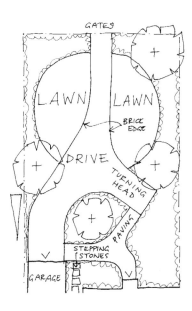

LARGER PLOT

In this larger area the drive passes through the circular lawn and sweeps around to the garage. The paved entrance to the house is surrounded by generous planting, with a tree forming both a focal point and a screen when viewed from the garden.

ROOF GARDENS

Often rooftops are the only opportunity that some people have to create a garden of their own. Building a garden in this situation has its limitations, however. The first and most critical is the ability of the roof in question to support soil, plants, paving and even lawn or water. Second, climatic conditions on rooftops can be quite different from those at ground level, with strong, swirling winds and extremes of temperature creating potential problems for plants.

The design in the first example is for a small garden where very little weight can be applied to the roof, and so lightweight paving is used with plants in containers, and the main load is carried on the walls rather than the floor (or roof). The small scale of the planting is made up for by the interesting floor and screen features.

In the second garden, weight is not a problem and so the design treats it very much as a patio garden that can be used as an overspill from the house, and is ideally suited for rooftop entertaining.

Lightweight timber decking and plants in pots and perimeter troughs have been used to transform this small city roof garden into an oasis of green.

A SMALL GARDEN OF LIMITED WEIGHT

THE DESIGN

One of the first factors to consider when building a roof garden is how much weight it can take safely, and the best way to find this out is to consult an architect or engineer. This information will then help determine the size and scale of the design.

In this example, the load-bearing capacity of the roof is very limited, and the bulk of the planting is contained in glass-fibre troughs. These are supported on brackets attached to the surrounding parapet wall, so that none of the weight is carried directly by the roof itself.

An interesting floor pattern is created by using a lightweight decking of thin timber slats set at an angle to the building and sitting among a layer of gravel, on which is placed a number of ornamental pots of annual and perennial plants, with sufficient space on the deck for a couple of chairs and a table.

The garden is sheltered from the cold winds by a trellis screen with climbers, which is fixed directly to the parapet wall, and a simple but effective irrigation system waters the troughs at the turn of a tap.

THE PLANTING

Roof gardens can at times be inhospitable places for plants, with greater extremes of temperature and exposure than are sometimes found down at ground level.

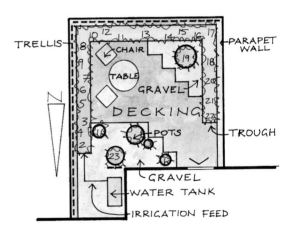

Garden 6.5m x 7m (21ft x 23ft)

Plants for this garden are therefore chosen to take account of these extremes, as well as being suitable for growing in the limited space available for root development, and include lavenders (*Lavandula* spp.), ivies (*Hedera* spp.) and junipers (*Juniperus* spp.). Climbers on the trellis are a mixture of permanent plants such as *Clematis macropetala* and annuals such as *Eccremocarpus scaber* for splashes of summer colour.

Opposite: View from the house.
Above: Three-dimensional view
of the garden.

KEY TO PLANTING

1 Annuals
2 *Juniperus procumbens* 'Nana'
3 *Helianthemum* 'The Bride'
4 *Hedera helix* 'Goldchild'
5 *Festuca glauca*
6 *Hedera helix* 'Congesta'
7 *Lavandula angustifolia* 'Alba Nana'
8 *Erica* x *darleyensis* 'Ghost Hills'
9 *Eccremocarpus scaber*
10 *Geranium ibericum*
11 *Euonymus fortunei* 'Emerald 'n' Gold'
12 *Clematis macropetala* 'Markham's Pink'
13 *Erica erigena* 'Irish Salmon'
14 *Linum narbonense*
15 *Aristolochia durior*
16 *Juniperus squamata* 'Blue Star'
17 *Fuchsia* 'Mrs Popple'
18 *Artemisia* 'Powis Castle'
19 *Phormium* 'Sundowner'
20 *Hebe vernicosa*
21 *Lavandula angustifolia* 'Hidcote'
22 *Genista hispanica* 'Compacta'
23 *Yucca filamentosa* 'Bright Edge'

To get the best out of these plants, use a good-quality, lightweight potting compost initially, coupled with regular liquid feeding or annual topdressing with controlled-release fertilizer.

THE FEATURES

The lightweight decking consists of thin, pressure-treated wooden slats screwed or nailed on to wide, shallow bearers sitting directly on the roof floor. The chevron pattern of the slats is repeated in the trellis panels, which are fixed partly to the top of the parapet wall and partly to square posts, which are themselves fixed with anchor bolts to the face of the wall.

Perimeter planting is contained in fibre-glass troughs supported on galvanized brackets attached to the wall, so that there is no weight on the roof structure itself. The troughs, which must have drainage holes, are watered by a simple arrangement of porous pipe laid in the compost and gravity fed from a water tank, situated right in the corner of the roof garden where there is sufficient strength to take its weight.

As a final decorative touch, a number of ornamental pots are placed on the gravel alongside the timber deck, and contain both permanent plants such as **Yucca filamentosa** 'Bright Edge' and annuals for bright colour during the summer.

181

DESIGN VARIATIONS

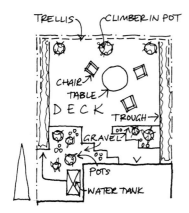

DIFFERENT ASPECT

The main decking is concentrated in an area as near to the far wall as possible. The end planting trough is omitted, and climbers in pots are trained to clothe the trellis there. The trellis itself is restricted to the north wall and to about one-third of each of the adjoining boundaries.

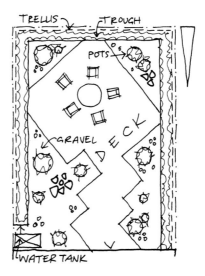

LARGER PLOT

A more generous area of decking is possible here, and it is set at an angle to the walls to introduce variety. Troughs are still restricted to the edge of the roof, and any planting in the extra space that is available has to be confined to pots and containers.

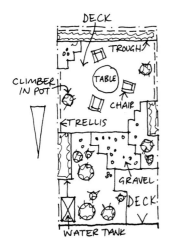

LONG, NARROW PLOT

The paving is divided into a deck near the doorway, with a connecting gravel path, and a main deck beyond for sitting. Smaller troughs placed against the side walls are staggered so that they do not restrict access, and climbers in pots are used to give maximum height in the smallest possible area.

TRIANGULAR PLOT

The shape of the decking follows that of the roof to give as much usable area as possible. The water tank is positioned on the strongest point of the roof – that is, at the intersection of the building walls – and the trellis is restricted to the ends of the long parapet wall.

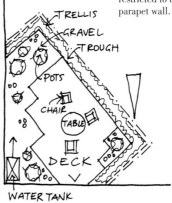

A dramatic change in level has been created on this roof garden by the use of a 'wedding cake', made of stained wooden planking, which adds less to the overall load carried by the roof than flagstones and steps.

A ROOFTOP PATIO GARDEN

THE DESIGN

Where there is adequate space and greater load-bearing capacity on a flat roof, it is possible to create a patio garden that is as impressive as any found at ground level.

The living room of this apartment opens on to a square roof space, which is designed as a patio garden. There is room to sit out either in the sun or in the shade cast by a pergola, with screen fencing along the two side boundaries providing wind protection but retaining a view across the landscape beyond.

A raised bed around the perimeter of the garden contains a substantial amount of planting, including some small trees and large shrubs, with pots of annuals and herbs adding extra plant interest on the patio areas.

A curving brick path leads from the pergola to a raised timber deck, which forms the edge of a shallow ornamental pool, making a striking feature when viewed from either the garden or the living room of the apartment.

THE PLANTING

With the extra strength of the roof, a greater depth of growing medium is possible in the raised beds, allowing small trees and large shrubs to be grown successfully. Those planted here include *Elaeagnus* x *ebbingei* 'Gilt Edge', *Hebe* 'Great Orme' and *Thuja plicata* 'Atrovirens'.

Permanent climbers on the pergola and screens, including ivy (*Hedera colchica* 'Sulphur Heart') and *Akebia quinata*, are supplemented with annual sweet peas and *Cobaea scandens* to extend the season of interest and provide scent.

A selection of pots dotted throughout the garden contain a mixture of plants such as geraniums (*Pelargonium* vars.), chives (*Allium schoenoprasum*) and sage (*Salvia officinalis* 'Tricolor'), with one particularly striking terracotta urn housing a specimen *Cordyline australis*.

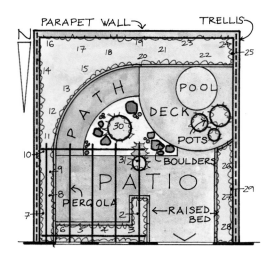

Garden 9.5m x 9.5m (31ft x 31ft)

Opposite: View from the house.
Above: Three-dimensional view of
the garden.

KEY TO PLANTING

1 *Cobaea scandens*
2 *Cotoneaster microphyllus*
3 *Genista lydia*
4 *Lavandula angustifolia* 'Hidcote Pink'
5 *Phormium* 'Yellow Wave'
6 *Phygelius capensis*
7 Sweet peas
8 *Hebe* 'Midsummer Beauty'
9 *Aster novi-belgii* 'Little Pink Beauty'
10 *Vitis vinifera* 'Apiifolia'
11 *Osmanthus heterophyllus* 'Gulftide'
12 *Pulmonaria officinalis* 'Sissinghurst White'
13 *Geranium* x *riversleaianum* 'Russell Prichard'
14 *Hedera colchica* 'Sulphur Heart'
15 *Helianthemum* 'Wisley Pink'
16 *Thuja plicata* 'Atrovirens'
17 *Diervilla* x *splendens*
18 *Ceanothus* 'Blue Mound'
19 *Stipa calamagrostis*
20 *Hemerocallis* 'Stella de Oro'
21 *Weigela* 'Victoria'
22 *Elaeagnus* x *ebbingei* 'Gilt Edge'
23 *Carex comans* Bronze Form
24 *Hebe* 'Great Orme'
25 *Akebia quinata*
26 *Potentilla fruticosa* 'Tilford Cream'
27 *Abelia schumannii*
28 *Hebe* 'Alicia Amherst'
29 *Hedera helix* 'Goldheart'
30 *Cordyline australis*
31 *Ipomaea purpurea*

THE FEATURES

The main paving in front of the patio doors and beneath the pergola is constructed from terracotta-coloured quarry tiles, with a non-slip finish. Leading on from this area, a curving path is laid in thin, dark brown paving bricks ('brick slips') in a running bond, contrasting with the red tiles.

At the end of this path, a raised deck made from pressure-treated softwood planks, stained silver-grey and screwed or nailed to rectangular timber bearers, provides a surround to a shallow, prefabricated, circular fibreglass pool, containing a submersible pump that supplies a single jet fountain.

The perimeter raised planting bed is retained along its front edge by a low palisade wall made from softwood planks, stained and finished to

185

match the decking. An automatic spray irrigation system is fitted within the planting bed, and this is controlled from within the apartment by a preset timer, so that watering can take place at night or any other convenient time.

In contrast to the deck and palisade, the pergola and screen are constructed from white-painted posts, rails and laths, to provide protection from sun and wind while retaining a light, airy feeling within the garden.

As a final touch, the large urn containing the cordyline sits in an area of mixed boulders, cobbles and gravel between the patio, decking and brick path.

DESIGN VARIATIONS

DIFFERENT ASPECT

The basic design is effectively turned through 180 degrees so that the main patio area is positioned in the sunniest part of the roof. The planting area is reduced slightly, because of the extra paving that is needed outside the patio doors to provide a link with the rest of the garden.

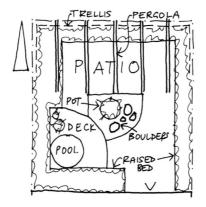

TRIANGULAR PLOT

Here, the garden is divided into two by enclosing the patio area with raised beds, leaving a small entrance into the furthest corner, where a pool sits at the back of the seating area. The trellis is restricted to the ends of the parapet wall, leaving an uninterrupted view out through the centre.

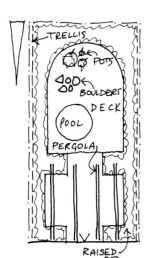

LONG, NARROW PLOT

The main patio is slightly smaller, but this is compensated for by an increase in the decking area. The pool forms a feature in the middle distance, with boulders and pots positioned behind it for additional interest. Trellis is used on the side parapet walls only.

WIDE, SHALLOW PLOT

In this area the patio and decking are set at an angle of 45 degrees to the building and are linked by a short path. The trellis is interrupted along the long parapet wall to allow distant views from the garden, and there is greater depth for taller planting in the far corners of the raised beds.

On a much stronger roof there is plenty of scope for paving, furniture, ornaments and even one or two small trees.

Part Two

GARDEN

FEATURES

POOLS, STREAMS AND WATER FEATURES

Water always adds an extra dimension to a garden, especially if it is moving, as in a fountain or stream. It can be used to make a central feature in its own right, or it can be used to complement other key elements, including planting, structures such as gazebos and bridges, and paving.

STYLES

Water features in a garden setting can take many forms, ranging from large ponds and lakes in estates of many acres to tiny pools, perhaps only large enough for birds to bathe in or drink from. They can range from the crisply edged and symmetrical pools and canals that are found in formal gardens to entirely natural-looking, boggy ponds or streams in gardens where wildlife interest is of maximum importance. Water can even be made to emerge from the centre of a millstone, a large granite boulder or a wall-mounted lion's head mask before disappearing through a pile of rocks or cobbles into a concealed underground reservoir.

MATERIALS AND TECHNIQUES

Whatever style is preferred, the basic requirement of any water feature, whether it is moving or still, is that there must be a container that will hold

AN ORNAMENTAL WATER OUTLET

A gentle trickle of water emerges from an old clay pipe into a tiny, semicircular pool. The pipe could easily be replaced by, say, a stone lion's head or other ornament. The water outlet is built into the brick wall feature.

KEY TO PLANTING
1 *Cotoneaster congestus*
2 *Hosta* 'Krossa Regal'
3 *Hedera helix* 'Tricolor'
4 *Acer palmatum*
  'Dissectum Garnet'
5 *Juniperus procumbens* 'Nana'
6 *Thuja plicata* 'Rogersii'
7 *Saponaria ocymoides*
8 *Iris laevigata*

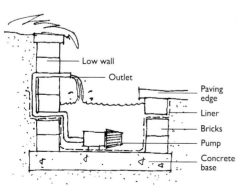

Low wall
Outlet
Paving edge
Liner
Bricks
Pump
Concrete base

sufficient water for the intended purpose without leaking. The options available for construction cover a wide spectrum of materials and techniques, starting with a simple hole in the ground in naturally impervious clay soil, through a whole array of products, including sheets of flexible pool liners, concrete, glass fibre, bentonite (clay) mat and pre-formed plastic.

Each material and technique has its own particular merits in terms of both ease of construction and cost. Pond liners are, in general, ideal if you want to install your own feature because they are flexible, relatively easy to use and quite economical. Some of the cheaper, poorer quality liners may, however, have a limited life, and they are more prone to punctures than the better quality ones. In contrast, a concrete construction, although requiring greater skill and increased expense, will, if carried out correctly,

A FORMAL PATIO POOL

This square, crisply detailed pool blends in well with the formal patio. It can be crossed by stepping stones cemented to the top of piers made from bricks or concrete blocks.

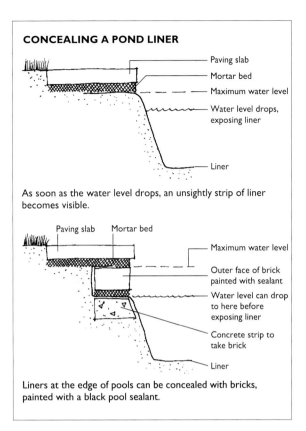

CONCEALING A POND LINER

Paving slab
Mortar bed
Maximum water level
Water level drops, exposing liner
Liner

As soon as the water level drops, an unsightly strip of liner becomes visible.

Paving slab   Mortar bed
Maximum water level
Outer face of brick painted with sealant
Water level can drop to here before exposing liner
Concrete strip to take brick
Liner

Liners at the edge of pools can be concealed with bricks, painted with a black pool sealant.

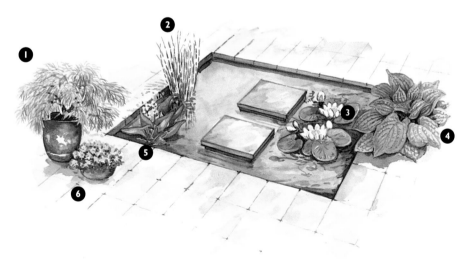

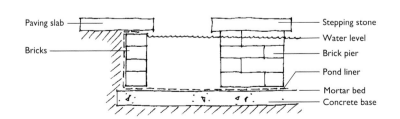

Paving slab
Bricks
Stepping stone
Water level
Brick pier
Pond liner
Mortar bed
Concrete base

KEY TO PLANTING
1 *Acer palmatum* 'Dissectum Atropurpureum'
2 *Scirpus lacustris* ssp. *tabernaemontani*
3 *Nymphaea* 'Marliacea Chromatella'
4 *Hosta sieboldiana* var. *elegans*
5 *Sagittaria sagittifolia*
6 *Saxifraga*

result in a water feature that will last almost indefinitely.

Ultimately though, the choice will be largely governed by the cost of materials and by the cost of labour if you intend to employ skilled help, or your own level of skill if you propose to do the work yourself. The size and extent of the water feature will also influence the cost, and you should bear in mind that if you are excavating for a pond, the larger it is, the more surplus material there will be to dispose of. As a rule, if you have a limited budget or are not confident of working with concrete and intend this to be a do-it-yourself project, one of the better quality pond liners, which should ideally have a 20 or 30 year guarantee, or a pre-formed, fibreglass pool should be seriously considered.

Right: A stream will bring life and movement into a garden.

A POOL ON TWO LEVELS

This traditional water features comprises two adjacent pools constructed with flexible liner and edged with crazy paving. Water from the upper pool cascades over one of the rocks into the lower pool.

KEY TO PLANTING

  1 *Juniperus communis* 'Repanda'
  2 *Iris pseudacorus* 'Variegata'
  3 *Hebe albicans* 'Red Edge'
  4 *Cotoneaster procumbens*
  5 *Azalea* 'Gibraltar'
  6 *Pinus mugo* var. *pumilio*
  7 *Cornus alba* 'Elegantissima'
  8 *Carex comans*
  9 *Berberis thunbergii* 'Dart's Red Lady'
10 *Astilbe* 'Snowdrift'
11 *Iris laevigata*

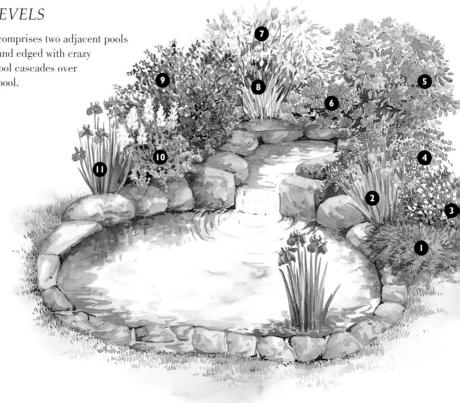

A NATURAL-LOOKING STREAM

A natural-looking stream, which is, in fact, artificial, meanders between rocks and over pebbles before entering an informal pond. Stones and marginal planting disguise the liner to create a natural effect.

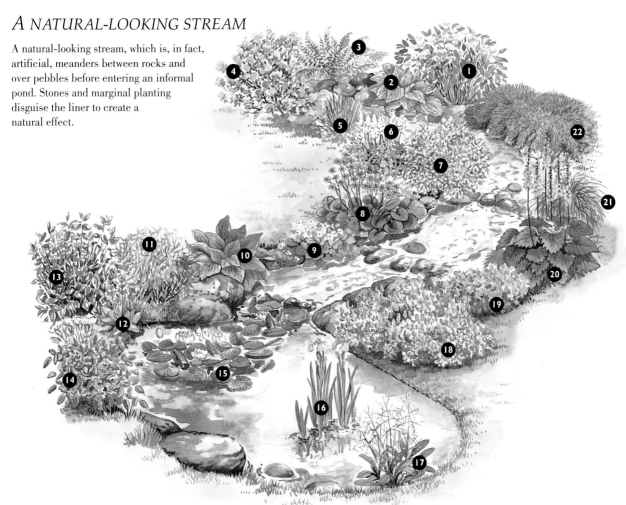

KEY TO PLANTING

1 *Cornus alba* 'Sibirica'
2 *Hosta* 'Royal Standard'
3 *Matteuccia struthiopteris*
4 *Azalea* Mollis Group
5 *Molinia caerulea* ssp. *caerulea* 'Variegata'
6 *Astilbe* 'Irrlicht'
7 *Salix purpurea* 'Nana'
8 *Ligularia dentata* 'Desdemona'
9 *Caltha palustris* var. *alba*
10 *Hosta* 'Frances Williams'
11 *Pleioblastus auricomus*
12 *Primula* (Candelabra hybrid)
13 *Cornus alba* 'Sibirica Variegata'
14 *Filipendula ulmaria*
15 *Nymphaea alba*
16 *Iris pseudacorus*
17 *Alisma plantago-aquatica*
18 *Salix lanata*
19 *Mimulus guttatus*
20 *Ligularia* 'The Rocket'
21 *Carex comans* Bronze form
22 *Juniperus* x *media* 'Mint Julep'

STREAM DETAILS

A 'shell' of thin plywood strips can be lined with overlapping sheets of pond liner to create the basic shape of the stream.

Strips of thin plywood, 150mm (6in) wide, treated with preservative, fixed to stakes.

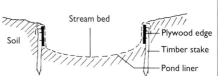

Stream bed

Soil — Plywood edge
— Timber stake
— Pond liner

A section through a stream.

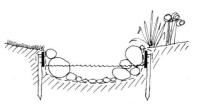

A section through an established stream. Stones on the liner create a natural effect, while the thin plywood means that planting can be brought right up to the water's edge.

ROCK GARDENS

Rockeries or rock gardens are intended to be re-creations of naturally occurring landscape features that are found all over the world, wherever underlying rock formations outcrop on sloping hillsides and thereby create suitable conditions for particular types of plant to become established. When they are constructed with their origins in mind and when serious consideration is given to the choice of site and to the selection of suitable materials and plants, rock gardens can be dramatic and garden worthy features.

ROCKERIES

Whenever possible, the rock garden should be built from pieces of locally occurring stone, and it should be sited on sloping ground so that a completely natural-looking setting is created into which appropriate plants can be placed. A rock garden can be built in association with streams and pools, and although an existing slope is ideal, a rock garden can also be created on a level site by regrading the ground to form an artificial gradient.

Most rock gardens are seen at their best when they are located in an open, reasonably sunny position, although sites with a northerly aspect can be equally successful, as long as the planting and placing of rocks take this into account. For maximum effect, a rock garden is best designed as an integral part of a complete garden rather than being a random feature, isolated in the middle of a large lawn as is sometimes seen.

SCREE GARDENS

Scree gardens also simulate a particular landscape feature – one that is usually found on the lower slopes of mountainous and alpine regions, where

A ROCK GARDEN ON LEVEL GROUND

Thin, flat stones are used to make an attractive rock outcrop on level ground, following the same rules regarding strata lines as for rockeries on a slope. Some taller, narrow planting provides a useful contrast.

KEY TO PLANTING
1 *Thuja orientalis* 'Aurea Nana'
2 *Helianthemum* 'Henfield Brilliant'
3 *Berberis thunbergii* 'Bagatelle'
4 *Arabis ferdinandi-coburgi*
5 *Juniperus communis* 'Compressa'
6 *Erica carnea* 'King George'

7 *Thymus serpyllum* var. *coccineus*
8 *Salix* 'Boydii'
9 *Cotoneaster congestus*
10 *Iberis sempervirens* 'Little Gem'
11 *Hypericum polyphyllum* 'Grandiflorum'
12 *Aubretia* 'Maurice Prichard'

13 *Dianthus* 'Pike's Pink'
14 *Hebe buchananii* 'Minima'
15 *Campanula carpatica* 'Chewton Joy'
16 *Geranium cinereum* 'Ballerina'

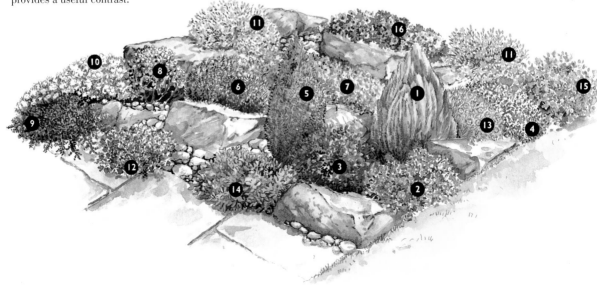

A well-made rockery should strike a nice balance between the rocks, the planting and the gravel. This one even manages to incorporate a little sink garden to one side.

ROCK GARDENS ON FLAT GROUND AND ON SLOPES

When a rock feature is introduced into a flat area, the planting should include species with a strong, upright habit to contrast with the site. The rocks should be tilted slightly to suggest a shallow, naturally occurring outcrop with the strata lines parallel.

Existing levels retained

Wide, thin rocks tilted

The strata lines in all rocks incorporated into a slope must be kept parallel. Tilt the rocks back slightly, making sure that they are all at the same angle. Rocks placed across a slope must also be positioned so that they are all at the same angle and so that the strata lines are parallel.

Rocks tilted back into slope

Line of existing slope

Rocks tilted across the slope

small fragments of rock fall from the upper slopes, accumulate and, in doing so, generate a particular set of growing conditions. These conditions are suited to specialized types of plant, predominantly those with tight, bushy or cushion-like habits, which are generally known as alpines. Like rock gardens, scree gardens look best on naturally sloping sites, but they can also be used in a wide variety of situations, including raised beds and small sink or trough gardens, although the planting must always be in scale with the container.

Because of their slightly more specialized nature, scree gardens can often be successful as features in their own right. They can, therefore, be developed as particular focal points, perhaps sited off the edge of a patio or in other suitable positions, such as the lower level of a larger rock garden.

As long as a few basic rules and principles are followed, both rock and scree gardens are relatively easy to construct. They are not necessarily costly, particularly if the rock, which is likely to be the main expense of such a project, is used sparingly and with thought.

USING ROCKS OF DIFFERENT DEPTHS

The most successful rock gardens are made of rocks that are a fairly uniform depth. If you have to use rocks that are different depths, try to bury them so that the tops are at the same level.

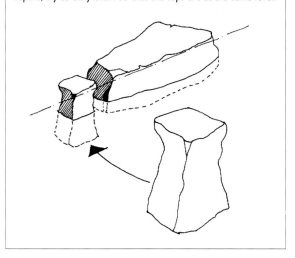

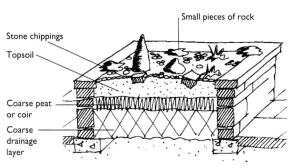

Stone chippings

Topsoil

Small pieces of rock

Coarse peat or coir

Coarse drainage layer

A RAISED SCREE BED

A small raised scree bed, built from stone, is planted with alpines and dwarf conifers. Scree beds must have good drainage, and this is generally easier to install in a raised bed. Alpines and dwarf conifers benefit from a mulch of stone chippings.

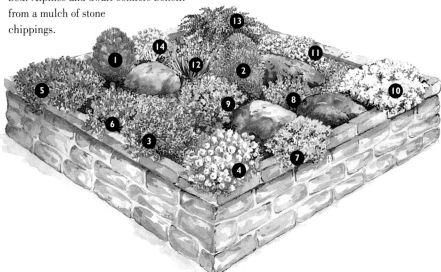

KEY TO PLANTING

1 *Chamaecyparis lawsoniana* 'Green Globe'
2 *Picea glauca* 'Alberta Globe'
3 *Hebe* 'Emerald Green'
4 *Campanula carpatica* var. *turbinata* 'Snowsprite'
5 *Thymus serpyllum* 'Pink Chintz'
6 *Viola* 'Ardross Gem'
7 *Sedum spathulifolium* 'Cape Blanco'
8 *Diascia* 'Ruby Field'
9 *Hypericum polyphyllum* 'Grandiflorum'
10 *Phlox subulata* 'White Delight'
11 *Sempervivum* 'Snowberger'
12 *Sisyrinchium idahoense*
13 *Cotoneaster congestus*
14 *Achillea* x *lewisii* 'King Edward'

USING A RETAINING WALL

Soil mounded against a low brick wall forms the basis of a rock garden on what was a level area of ground. This not only allows the plants to be viewed more easily but also helps to increase drainage, especially on heavy soil.

KEY TO PLANTING
1 *Helianthemum* 'Wisley Pink'
2 *Arabis ferdinandi-coburgi* 'Variegata'
3 *Berberis thunbergii* 'Bagatelle'
4 *Dianthus* 'Pike's Pink'
5 *Erica carnea* 'Myretoun Ruby'

6 *Juniperus squamata* 'Blue Star'
7 *Campanula carpatica* var. *turbinata* 'Karl Foerster'
8 *Iberis sempervirens* 'Little Gem'
9 *Juniperus communis* 'Compressa'

10 *Erica vagans* 'Lyonesse'
11 *Hebe pimeloides* 'Quicksilver'
12 *Geranium sanguineum* 'Shepherd's Warning'
13 *Viola* 'Clementina'
14 *Pinus mugo* 'Humpy'
15 *Hebe armstrongii*

16 *Aubrieta* 'Doctor Mules'
17 *Picea pungens* 'Globosa'
18 *Lysimachia nummularia* 'Aurea'

CREATING AN ARTIFICIAL SLOPE

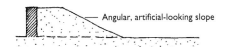

Angular, artificial-looking slope

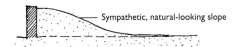

Sympathetic, natural-looking slope

Slopes created in the garden should be made to look as natural as possible.

When soil is moved in order to create a slope, it may be necessary to introduce drainage into the resulting depression, especially in areas of heavy ground or where the water table is high. Existing soil is moved from A to B and drainage may be needed where the new ground level is created at A.

If additional soil is used to create a slope, it can be placed against a low retaining wall.

PERGOLAS AND ARCHES

Pergolas originated many centuries ago when they were simply a means of supporting grape vines over a large area, so that the fruits could be picked easily. They were also built to provide welcome shade. Nowadays, however, the word pergola conjures up images of a wide range of structures, although strictly it should be used to describe a series of two or more interconnecting arches, leading from one part of a garden to another. The most basic function of a pergola is, therefore, to provide a pedestrian link between different areas of a garden. However, it can also be used to frame a view, as well as to divide a garden into two or more sections, to provide shade and a sense of privacy or enclosure, and to create a framework for planting in a confined area.

Materials that can be used for the construction of both pergolas and arches include wood, brick, real or artificial stone and metal, all of which can be used either individually or in combination with each other.

DESIGNS

Numerous designs are possible, ranging from simple, rustic larch poles to formal dressed stone columns topped with heavy, carved, oak beams. Although most ready-made pergolas are suitable for enclosing straight or rectangular paths and spaces, they can be designed and built to suit almost any shape, such as curves, circles or fan-shapes. These more unusual shapes are,

BUILDING A SIMPLE WOODEN PERGOLA

Joining together two identical arches with side rails creates a simple pergola framework that can be made more elaborate by adding extra cross rails to match the arch tops. The side rails provide the main support and should be fixed securely to the face of the posts with screws, while the cross rails are fastened on top by skew nailing. Overhang the cross and side rails by 150mm (6in) for best effect.

Two simple arches, made from lengths of timber.

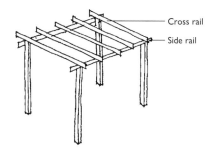

Cross rail

Side rail

Link two timber arches with side and cross rails to create a pergola.

AN OAK AND BRICK PERGOLA

Although it is relatively expensive, oak is an outstanding material for building arches and pergolas. This pergola uses piers of old red bricks, which not only provide support but also are in keeping with the general character of the structure.

KEY TO PLANTING
1 *Vitis coignetiae*
2 *Humulus lupulus* 'Aureus'

The luxuriant planting of perennials and climbing roses completely transforms this pergola, which is made from simple larch poles, nailed together.

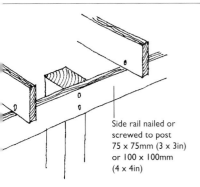

Fix the cross rail to the side rail by skew nailing or screwing or by small brackets. The timber uprights can be concreted into the ground.

Side rail nailed or screwed to post 75 x 75mm (3 x 3in) or 100 x 100mm (4 x 4in)

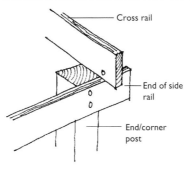

Cross rail

End of side rail

End/corner post

A detail of the corner section of a pergola.

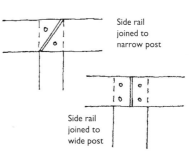

Side rail joined to narrow post

Side rail joined to wide post

A detail of the side section of a pergola.

AN ELEGANT WROUGHT IRON ARCH

Wrought iron has many uses in the garden, and here it has been used for an elegant ogee arch providing an archway through a closely clipped yew hedge.

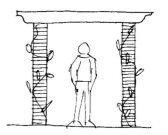

DIMENSIONS OF A PERGOLA OR ARCH

A low, narrow pergola, built from heavy timbers and with thick brick piers gives a grotto-like, enclosed character to the feature.

A tall, wide pergola, made from light-weight, slender elements, looks open and inviting.

however, much less likely to be available off-the-shelf, and they may require a fairly high level of skill to construct.

DIMENSIONS

The height and width of a pergola or arch can have a profound effect on the sensations experienced when walking under it. A low, narrow structure may cause a sense of enclosure, almost to the point of claustrophobia, so that you will want to hurry through as quickly as possible. A wider, taller framework, on the other hand, may engender a far more spacious feeling, and you are more likely to want to stroll beneath it in a leisurely manner. These particular sensations can be heightened still further by adjusting the dimensions of the materials used for the posts and rails and by changing the style of planting. A narrow, low pergola made from heavy stone piers and large oak beams that is covered in masses of foliage can create an almost grotto-like effect, whereas a taller, wider structure, made from slender, cast-iron arches and covered in delicate climbers, may seem very light and airy.

Although cost and ease of construction are the two factors that will ultimately influence your choice of materials and the style, you should also consider whether the arch or pergola can be made to complement other materials or structures in or around the garden. For example, a pergola made from unpeeled larch poles, crudely sawn and nailed together, might easily look out of place in the garden of a brand new, modern house, although it would be ideal for the garden of an old cottage, covered in rambling roses and honeysuckle.

A LEAN-TO PERGOLA

This lean-to pergola not only makes a pleasant sitting area but also helps to disguise a blank wall. One side rail of this pergola is supported on posts in the usual way and the other is fixed directly to the house wall.

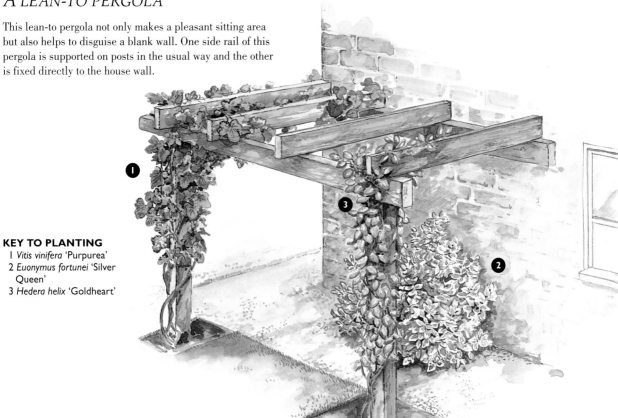

KEY TO PLANTING
1 *Vitis vinifera* 'Purpurea'
2 *Euonymus fortunei* 'Silver Queen'
3 *Hedera helix* 'Goldheart'

CONSTRUCTING ARCHES

Wires or thin wooden laths can be used to support climbers when more than one arch is used.

Arches can be linked by wires or laths over a curved path. This creates the impression of a pergola but no complicated construction is involved.

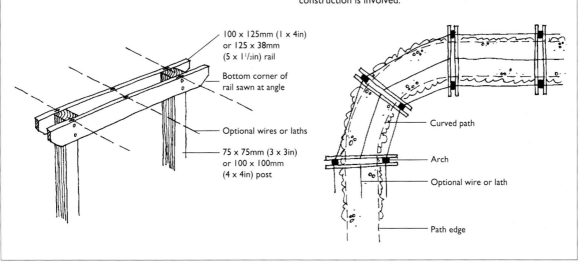

100 x 125mm (1 x 4in) or 125 x 38mm (5 x 1½in) rail

Bottom corner of rail sawn at angle

Optional wires or laths

75 x 75mm (3 x 3in) or 100 x 100mm (4 x 4in) post

Curved path

Arch

Optional wire or lath

Path edge

SUMMERHOUSES, GAZEBOS AND ARBOURS

Summerhouses, gazebos and arbours are all names for garden structures that are intended to provide shelter or to enclose sitting areas from where the garden can be viewed in varying degrees of comfort. The principal structural difference between these features is that summerhouses are basically small garden buildings that are completely enclosed and weatherproof and that have doors and glazing, while gazebos and arbours, although built on a similar scale, have open sides, may have a solid or an open roof and will provide only a limited degree of shelter. All three of these garden features can be made from a range of materials, including wood, brick, metal and real or artificial stone.

Gazebos and arbours are also available in kit form in a range of shapes and styles, and they are usually less demanding to erect than a summerhouse. If you are a do-it-yourself enthusiast, it is quite possible to produce your own simple, but very effective and unique feature.

ARBOURS AND GAZEBOS

An arbour can enclose a small sitting area anywhere within a garden, but it is usually in a private, secluded space and is often hidden from the rest of the garden by walls, fences or dense planting. In the true sense of the word, a gazebo is normally positioned in a more open situation so that a particular view or aspect of the garden is seen from within it.

SUMMERHOUSES

Wooden summerhouses are often supplied in prefabricated sections by specialist manufacturers, and they can be relatively quickly assembled on site, on a previously prepared hardstanding or base. They can range in style and quality from what is little more than a glorified garden shed to extremely expensive, high quality structures with cedar shingle roofs, double glazing, and even heating and lighting for winter or evening use.

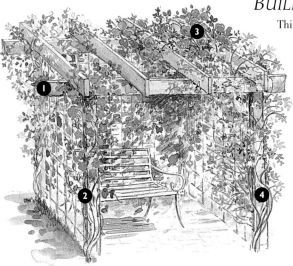

KEY TO PLANTING
1 *Lonerica periclymenum*
  'Graham Thomas'
2 *Clematis* 'Ville de Lyon'
3 *Rosa* 'Paul's Scarlet Climber'
4 *Jasminum* x *stephanense*

BUILDING A SIMPLE ARBOUR

This rectangular arbour is merely a simple pergola made from pieces of sawn timber, with standard trellis panels used to form the back and sides. A wrought iron and wooden bench provides an attractive seating area.

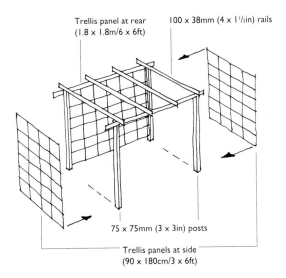

Trellis panel at rear (1.8 x 1.8m/6 x 6ft)

100 x 38mm (4 x 1¹/₂in) rails

75 x 75mm (3 x 3in) posts

Trellis panels at side (90 x 180cm/3 x 6ft)

SUMMERHOUSE SHAPES

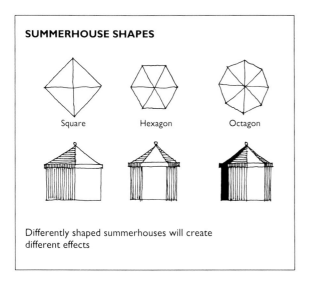

Square   Hexagon   Octagon

Differently shaped summerhouses will create different effects

PLANTING EFFECTS

Close planting around the summerhouse gives a low key, almost secretive feeling. The threshold of the building is as low as possible.

When tall planting is kept away from the building, which is raised on a wide plinth or terrace, the summerhouse becomes the focus of attention.

SUMMERHOUSE PLANTING

Planting should integrate a decorative building into the garden setting. The trees, shrubs and perennials around this hexagonal summerhouse have been carefully chosen to complement its elegant shape.

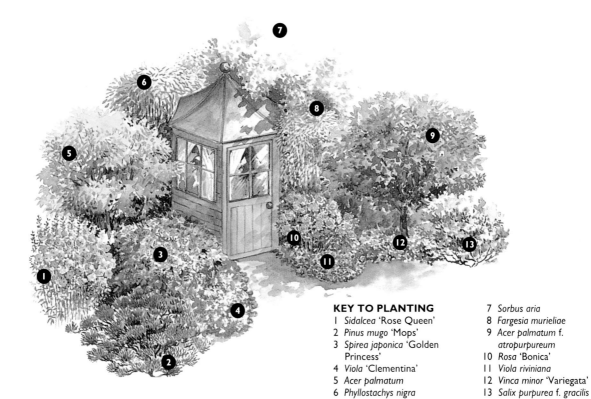

KEY TO PLANTING

1 *Sidalcea* 'Rose Queen'
2 *Pinus mugo* 'Mops'
3 *Spirea japonica* 'Golden Princess'
4 *Viola* 'Clementina'
5 *Acer palmatum*
6 *Phyllostachys nigra*
7 *Sorbus aria*
8 *Fargesia murieliae*
9 *Acer palmatum* f. *atropurpureum*
10 *Rosa* 'Bonica'
11 *Viola riviniana*
12 *Vinca minor* 'Variegata'
13 *Salix purpurea* f. *gracilis*

Summerhouses built in heavier materials, such as brick or stone, perhaps with slate or stone roofs, must be purpose built. They can be elaborate structures, with the same standard of internal finishes as you would expect to find in a house, and they are ideal for gardens that include an outdoor swimming pool because they can be used as changing rooms as well as housing the filtration systems for the pool itself.

Because of its generally solid appearance a summerhouse needs to be positioned carefully, particularly where space is at a premium, so that it does not dominate the whole garden. Ideally it should be sited to make the best use of available sunlight, and it should be linked to the rest of the garden and the house by suitable paths or paving, giving easy and reasonably direct access. Equally, gazebos and arbours must also be placed with care, although their size and generally lighter structure tend to be less overpowering than a summerhouse.

A SECLUDED ARBOUR

This striking arbour, with a seat, is made from round timber poles of varying heights set in the ground. Leave small gaps between the poles so that the foliage can grow through.

KEY TO PLANTING
1 *Potentilla fruticosa* 'Goldstar'
2 *Fargesia murieliae* 'Simba'
3 *Buddleia* 'Lochinch'
4 *Photinia* x *fraseri* 'Red Robin'
5 *Philadelphus coronarius* 'Aureus'
6 *Mahonia* x *media* 'Winter Sun'
7 *Lavandula angustifolia*

SITING A SUMMERHOUSE

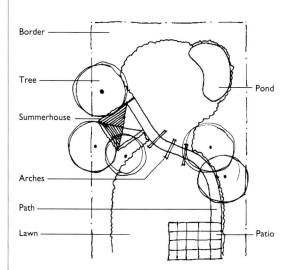

This summerhouse is deliberately screened from the house and looks out over what is, in effect, a 'secret' garden.

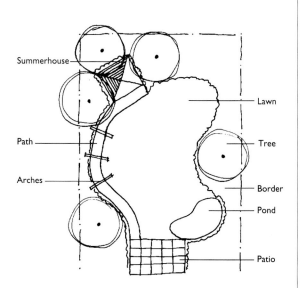

In this garden the same elements have been positioned in such a way that the summerhouse is now a major feature of the design.

AN OPEN-ARCHED GAZEBO WITH OLD-FASHIONED PLANTING

This delicate gazebo, sited at the junction of gravel paths, is made from a kit using nylon-coated steel tubing. There are climbing roses on all four pillars and a lavender hedge at the corners provides both a beautiful scent and a degree of enclosure without creating a claustrophobic effect.

KEY TO PLANTING

1 *Rosa* 'Pink Perpétué'
2 *Lavandula angustifolia* 'Munstead'

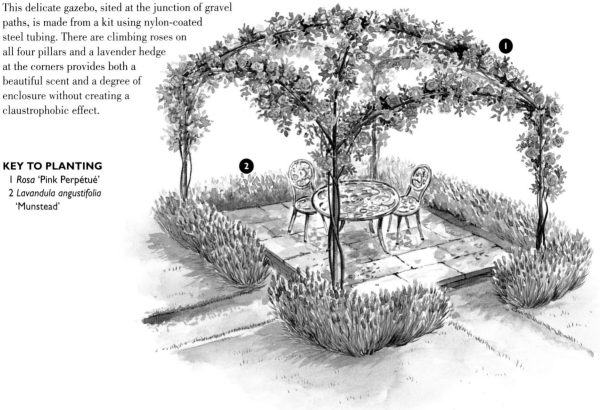

SITING A GAZEBO

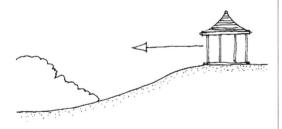

Positioning the gazebo on top of a mound or hill emphasizes the change in level and permits views to the distance, over the top of nearby planting.

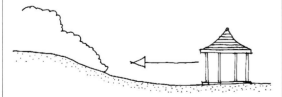

When a gazebo is sited in a low spot, not only are views out of the garden interrupted but also the gazebo's impact on its surroundings is diminished.

CHOOSING COMPLEMENTARY PLANTING

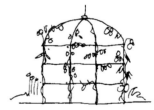

Lightweight, slender structures need to be complemented by light and elegant climbers, such as roses and jasmine, and by more delicate low planting around the base.

Heavier gazebos, with more robust proportions, need bold climbers such as vines and clematis while the surrounding planting should be on a scale to match.

PATIOS AND PAVING

These days the concept of a patio bears little resemblance to the word's original meaning of 'an inner courtyard open to the sky'. The term is now used to refer to virtually any reasonably sized, paved area that provides an essential link between the house and garden and allows the various activities of either area to spill over on to the patio so that it becomes a transitional zone between the two. In small gardens, particularly in urban areas, the patio can sometimes take up almost the entire garden area, and its detailed design and the materials chosen to build it are, therefore, important if it is to be successful. Apart from patios and other sitting areas, paving is also necessary in a garden for more practical reasons, the principal and obvious one being the ability to get from one part of the garden to another comfortably and in all weathers.

LOCATION

Not only the size but also the location and choice of material for a patio are important factors in its ultimate success. Providing a relatively large expanse of paving can be one of the most expensive items in a garden, and paying a little attention to these details in the planning stages can save a lot of wasted effort, time and money. In more temperate climates patios and sitting areas will tend to

PATIO SHAPES AND SIZES

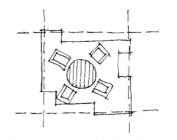

A square patio, 3 x 3m (10 x 10ft), can be made to look less severe simply by removing a few slabs. However, this will make seating cramped.

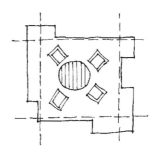

Adding a few slabs to a square patio, 3 x 3m (10 x 10ft), will break up the outline without using up seating space.

A BRICK-EDGED PATIO

Brick is particular effective when combined with other materials. In the patio shown below crazy paving is combined with brick semicircles, which match the wall and the house. When patios or paths are finished with brick, the concrete support for the back of the brick edge should be kept to a minimum, or close planting will not be possible.

KEY TO PLANTING

1 *Choisya ternata*
2 *Lavandula angustfolia*
3 *Hedera helix* 'Goldheart'
4 *Clematis* 'The President'
5 *Acer palmatum* 'Dissectum Atropurpureum'
6 *Rosa* 'New Dawn'
7 *Festuca glauca*
8 *Berberis thunbergii* 'Atropurpureum Nana'
9 *Armeria maritima*
10 *Pulsatilla vulgaris*
11 *Thymus vulgaris*
12 *Liriope muscari*
13 *Cistus* 'Silver Pink'
14 *Alchemilla mollis*
15 *Sempervivum ciliosum*

be most effective where they can make maximum use of available sunlight, particularly during the summer months; in warmer climates, on the other hand, the opposite view is sometimes taken and they might need to be situated in a part of the garden that is in cool shade, at least during the hottest part of the day.

MATERIALS

A wide range of materials is available for patio and paving construction. The factors governing the selection of one rather than another is that it must be able to provide an even, well-drained and weatherproof area for year-round use. The style of a patio can be determined by the choice of a particular material; alternatively, the choice of material can be determined by the style of patio. Uniform, square-edged concrete or new stone flags lend themselves to a geometric or formal arrange-

ment, for example, while old sandstone crazy paving or perhaps second-hand paving bricks are better suited to a more informal, possibly cottage-garden style. Many patios are successful and attractive because they copy or complement materials found elsewhere in or around the garden.

CONSTRUCTION

Although the basic cost of a patio or paved area will be determined by its size and the choice of material for its construction, another factor to be considered is whether the garden is level or on a slope, when you might need to support one or more edges of the patio with a retaining wall. The same considerations will affect the ease with which paving can be constructed and will determine whether you are able to carry out the work yourself or whether you will need to employ skilled help, with the additional cost that this entails.

RAISED TIMBER DECKING

Wood is a durable and attractive material in the right setting. Here it is used for a raised timber deck patio next to a pool, where it not only complements the planting but also provides a crisp, dark edge to the water.

KEY TO PLANTING

1 *Phormium cookianum* ssp. *hookeri* 'Tricolor'
2 *Escallonia* 'Apple Blossom'
3 *Acer palmatum* 'Bloodgood'
4 *Geranium ibericum*
5 *Hypericum* 'Hidcote'
6 *Euphorbia amygdaloides* var. *robbiae*
7 *Miscanthus sinensis*
8 *Robinia pseudoacacia* 'Frisia'
9 *Iris laevigata*

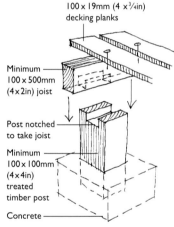

100 x 19mm (4 x ¾in) decking planks

Minimum 100 x 500mm (4 x 2in) joist

Post notched to take joist

Minimum 100 x 100mm (4 x 4in) treated timber post

Concrete

The decking planks are nailed or screwed to the joists.

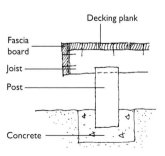

Decking plank

Fascia board

Joist

Post

Concrete

The fascia board is nailed or screwed to the ends of the joists.

A 'SOFT' PAVED AREA

Paved areas do not need to be large, blank expanses of brick, stone or concrete. Here stone flags are combined with gravel and plants to create a striking small front garden that is economical to build and easy to look after.

KEY TO PLANTING

1 *Hydrangea serrata* 'Diadem'
2 *Hebe pinguifolia* 'Pagei'
3 *Pinus mugo* 'Ophir'
4 *Potentilla fruticosa* 'Primrose Beauty'
5 *Miscanthus sinensis* 'Silver Feather'
6 *Lonicera nitida* 'Baggesen's Gold'
7 *Yucca gloriosa* 'Variegata'
8 *Helianthemum* 'Wisley Primrose'
9 *Prunus laurocerasus* 'Otto Luyken'
10 *Ophiopogon planiscapus* 'Nigrescens'
11 *Picea glauca* var. *albertiana* 'Conica'
12 *Thymus serpyllum*
13 Annual container plants

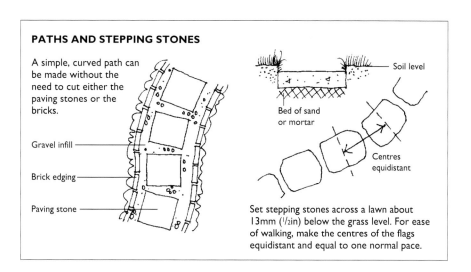

PATHS AND STEPPING STONES

A simple, curved path can be made without the need to cut either the paving stones or the bricks.

Gravel infill

Brick edging

Paving stone

Soil level

Bed of sand or mortar

Centres equidistant

Set stepping stones across a lawn about 13mm (1/2in) below the grass level. For ease of walking, make the centres of the flags equidistant and equal to one normal pace.

STEPS, SLOPES AND CHANGES IN LEVEL

Few gardens are exactly level, even if they may look it, and the smallest of slopes can be used to advantage to create changes of level with steps and retaining walls, which add interest to a flat site. In addition, it is also possible to create a more dramatic outlook by further altering existing ground levels or even simply by the skilled use of planting. At the other extreme, a steeply sloping garden can often suffer from one or more problems, including soil erosion, lack of usable level areas, poor access and either severe drying out of planting areas or permanently wet spots, caused by water accumulating at the bottom of slopes.

The same techniques – the use of steps, terracing and retaining walls – that are used to transform a flat garden into one with the interesting changes in level can also reduce or eliminate the problems caused by a steep slope, although incorporating these features does usually increase the cost compared to a similar plot where they are not needed.

BUILDING SIMPLE STEPS ON A LOW SLOPE

Simple timber and gravel steps are often all that are needed to rise up a low bank or slope. The risers may be light, slender planks nailed or bolted to stakes concealed behind, for an elegant appearance. Risers can also be much thicker, heavier timber held in place with stakes at the front to give a more utilitarian appearance.

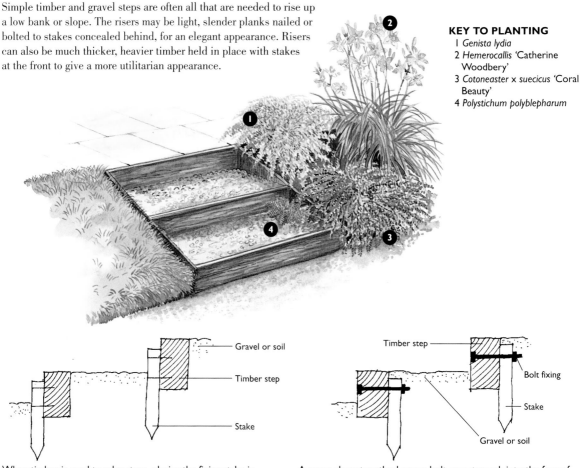

KEY TO PLANTING
1 *Genista lydia*
2 *Hemerocallis* 'Catherine Woodbery'
3 *Cotoneaster* x *suecicus* 'Coral Beauty'
4 *Polystichum polyblepharum*

Gravel or soil
Timber step
Stake

When timber is used to edge steps, placing the fixing stake in front of the timber gives a strong support, though not the neatest appearance.

Timber step
Bolt fixing
Stake
Gravel or soil

A more elegant method uses a bolt, countersunk into the face of the step, and passed through a concealed stake behind.

Constructing steps does not have to involve great feats of engineering and the complicated use of bricks and concrete. Here simple yet effective steps have been built from railways sleepers and gravel.

STEPS ON A GRASS BANK

Typical steps for a grass bank. Because mowing against the edges of the steps is difficult, use a mowing strip of bricks as an edge or plant a narrow border.

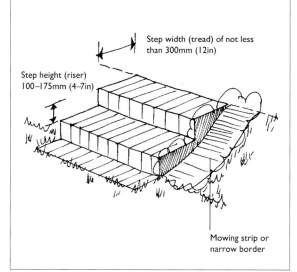

Step width (tread) of not less than 300mm (12in)

Step height (riser) 100–175mm (4–7in)

Mowing strip or narrow border

Even when expense is a limiting factor, however, it is still possible to remedy some of these problems by, for example, the careful selection of planting, by mulching planted areas or by using cheaper materials, such as treated timber edging in the place of brick or stone.

STEPS

Steps provide a means of access from one level area of a garden to another. They must not only be attractive and interesting, but must at the same time be safe and practical to use. Materials used for step construction should be similar to those used for paving and patios, where both appearance and practicality must be considered.

SLOPES

As an alternative to steps, gently sloping paths or ramps can be used to allow access to and around the garden for people with limited mobility or where garden machinery, such as lawnmowers and wheelbarrows, needs to be moved from one level to another.

TERRACES

In a sloping garden level areas or terraces, linked by steps or ramps, can be created by the construction of retaining walls and edges, which are made from basically the same materials as are found in normal wall construction, including a wide range of bricks, stone and wood. Simple, low retaining walls and edges can be constructed with only a relatively modest amount of practical know-how. However, as the slope increases, the height of any necessary retaining wall increases accordingly, and the point will be reached where expert or professional advice should be sought to avoid costly, possibly disastrous mistakes.

A RAMP FOR EASY ACCESS

Access to different levels of the garden can be made easy for everyone if ramps, rather than steps, are used. Here a half-landing makes for easier manoeuvrability.

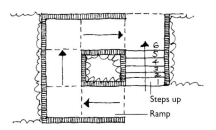

RAMP DESIGNS

A 'hairpin' ramp can provide gentle access up a steep slope. The retaining wall could be of log, brick, concrete block or stone.

A flight of steps can be combined with an alternative ramp to provide access for wheelchairs, prams and garden equipment such as wheelbarrows.

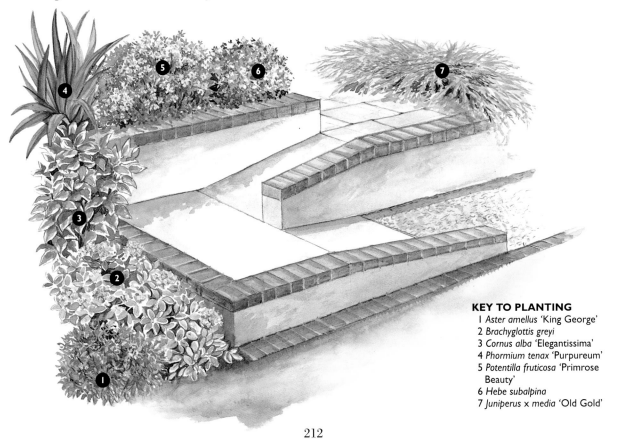

KEY TO PLANTING
1 *Aster amellus* 'King George'
2 *Brachyglottis greyi*
3 *Cornus alba* 'Elegantissima'
4 *Phormium tenax* 'Purpureum'
5 *Potentilla fruticosa* 'Primrose Beauty'
6 *Hebe subalpina*
7 *Juniperus* x *media* 'Old Gold'

A TERRACED BANK

When a slope has to be modified so that plants can become established, timber can be used as an edging for simple terraces. Both the timber board and the stake must be treated with preservative. The planting on the terraced bank illustrated below uses varieties that are suitable for a sunny, well-drained position.

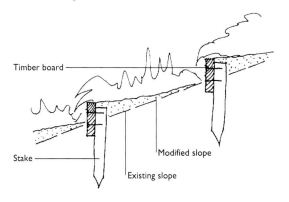

Timber board

Stake

Modified slope

Existing slope

KEY TO PLANTING

1 *Cotoneaster* x *suecicus* 'Coral Beauty'
2 *Genista lydia*
3 *Lonerica nitida* 'Baggesen's Gold'
4 *Cistus* 'Silver Pink'
5 *Linum narbonense*
6 *Helianthemum* 'Henfield Brilliant'
7 *Artemisia* 'Powis Castle'
8 *Taxus baccata* 'Semperaurea'
9 *Sarcococca confusa*
10 *Brachyglottis greyi*
11 *Helichrysum* hybrids
12 *Lavandula stoechas*
13 *Euonymus fortunei* 'Emerald 'n' Gold'
14 *Iberis commutata*
15 *Sedum aizoon* 'Aurantiacum'
16 *Santolina rosmarinifolia* ssp. *rosmarinifolia*
17 *Cytisus* x *praecox*

CUTTING AND FILLING ON A STEEP SLOPE

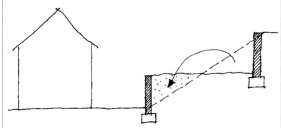

On steep slopes the creation of large, usable areas by cutting and filling requires major and costly engineering work.

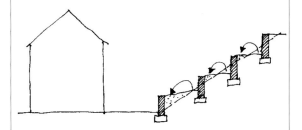

A solution to the problem of cutting and filling is to create a number of smaller usable areas. This method involves less disruption and expense, and it also results in a more attractive appearance.

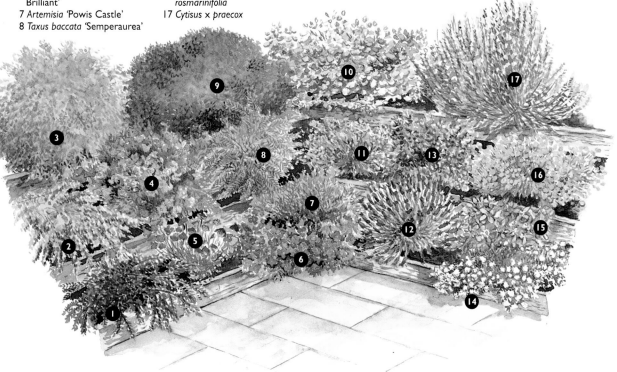

WALLS AND FENCES

Boundary walls and fences are necessary to mark on the ground the limits of a garden for both practical and legal reasons, and they can, of course, be used to provide varying degrees of security or privacy. In a large, new garden it is quite possible for the construction of these boundary markers to take up a large proportion of the budget. Even in an older garden, existing walls and fences may not have been well maintained and may need repair or even replacement, again at possibly significant cost. It is, therefore, important that walls or fences are made as attractive as possible within the available budget, so that they represent good value for money.

MATERIALS
Garden walls are normally built from traditional materials, such as brick, stone and various types of concrete blocks, while fences are most likely to be made from timber or metal. Frequently, however, combinations of the two are used, and metal railings are mounted on top of a low brick wall or wooden fencing panels are fixed between brick or

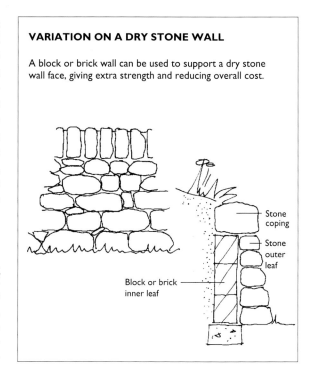

VARIATION ON A DRY STONE WALL

A block or brick wall can be used to support a dry stone wall face, giving extra strength and reducing overall cost.

Stone coping

Stone outer leaf

Block or brick inner leaf

A DRY STONE BOUNDARY WALL

Curving boundary walls are often more sympathetic than straight ones, and when they are built in dry stone they can be outstanding features, especially if plants are grown in the joints. Thick stones are used in the lower courses and thinner ones in the upper courses.

KEY TO PLANTING
1 *Arabis ferdinandi-coburgi*
2 *Sedum spathulifolium* 'Cape Blanco'
3 *Campanula carpatica*
4 *Polystichum polyblepharum*

ADDING TEXTURAL INTEREST TO A WALL

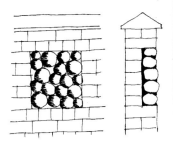

Cobbles or flints can be cemented into the space created by omitting a panel of bricks on one side of a 225mm (9in) wall.

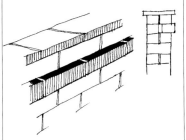

Textural interest can also be added by having one or more courses of bricks, blocks or stone jutting out slightly.

This old red brick and flint wall is a feature in its own right and is further enhanced by Rosa *'Compassion' and* R. *'Phyllis Bide'.*

ENHANCING BRICK WALLS

Plain brick walls can be made more attractive in various ways. Here, for example, contrasting bricks are used for the coping, damp proof course and ornamental panels.

DISADVANTAGES OF CURVED WALL COPINGS

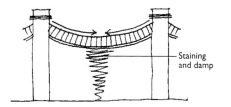

Rainfall tends to accumulate in the centre and run down the wall causing staining and damp.

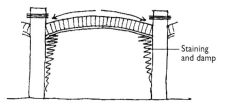

Coping that curves in the other direction will cause water to run away from the centre, creating staining and damp near the piers.

stone piers, for example. The choice of styles available for walls and fences is wide, and the final selection may well be influenced by the theme of the garden, materials in the fabric of the house or garden that might be complemented and the overall cost of materials and labour. This cost will to some degree be determined by the simplicity or complexity of the particular structure.

CONSTRUCTION

Building a free-standing wall which is not more than 750–900mm (2ft 6in–3ft) high is quite possible if you have a reasonable working knowledge of building techniques. For walls over this height, however, professional or expert structural advice and possibly also assistance in the construction should be sought. It is important to bear in mind that there may well be planning restrictions or guidelines on the heights and even the material of walls in some areas.

The construction of a simple fence, on the other hand, is within the capabilities of a much larger

A WINDOW FEATURE

A striking window feature in this wall uses special tapered key bricks to form a circle. The bricks in the top course are turned at an angle to create an attractive 'dogtooth' effect.

proportion of garden owners, although again you must be aware of any legal limitations that might apply, especially where the boundary adjoins a public highway.

Well-built walls, constructed from hard, durable brick or stone, where careful attention is paid to the pointing of joints and copings, and possibly including a damp-proof course, will require little long-term maintenance. Fences, on the other hand, particularly those made of the more economical, ready-made wooden panels and also some metal designs, may require a degree of regular maintenance. This may take the form of staining or painting to prevent rot or rust, and should be considered together with the factors already mentioned when the final choice of fence material is made.

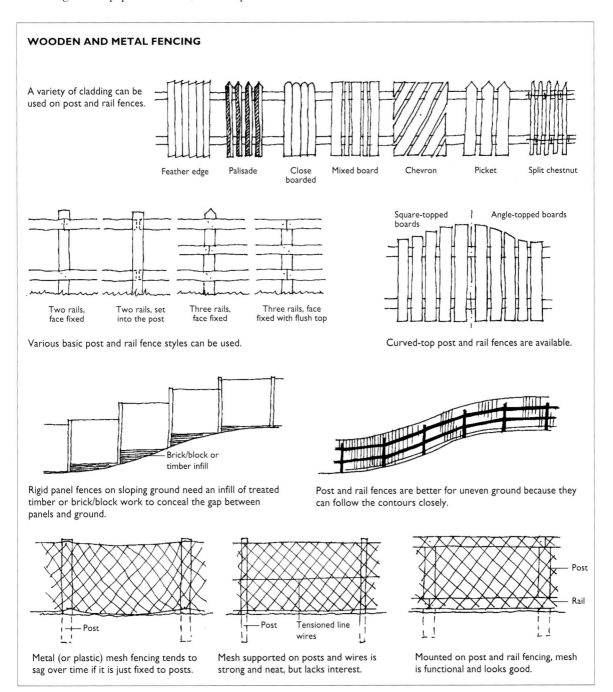

WOODEN AND METAL FENCING

A variety of cladding can be used on post and rail fences.

Feather edge   Palisade   Close boarded   Mixed board   Chevron   Picket   Split chestnut

Two rails, face fixed   Two rails, set into the post   Three rails, face fixed   Three rails, face fixed with flush top

Various basic post and rail fence styles can be used.

Square-topped boards   Angle-topped boards

Curved-top post and rail fences are available.

Brick/block or timber infill

Rigid panel fences on sloping ground need an infill of treated timber or brick/block work to conceal the gap between panels and ground.

Post and rail fences are better for uneven ground because they can follow the contours closely.

Post

Metal (or plastic) mesh fencing tends to sag over time if it is just fixed to posts.

Post   Tensioned line wires

Mesh supported on posts and wires is strong and neat, but lacks interest.

Post

Rail

Mounted on post and rail fencing, mesh is functional and looks good.

TRELLISES AND SCREENS

Trellis can be – and often is – used for boundary fences in a garden, but it is more often regarded either as a means of providing a decorative support for climbing plants, of dividing a garden into separate areas without creating a solid barrier or of screening views both into or out of the garden to give privacy. Screening and division can be achieved in other ways than by the use of traditional trellis, and the careful positioning of various other structures or features, including plants, can be equally effective.

When they are used as vertical support for plants, trellis and perforated screens make it possible to enclose an area with greenery and flowers without taking up too much valuable ground space, which might be needed for a patio, for example.

They also provide an instant means of dividing a garden into separate areas, and they can be used to give shade or, in an exposed position, provide shelter from the wind.

STYLES

The most popular types of trellis, which tend to be predominantly made of timber, come in a range of designs and quality. Some are basic panels, with square or diamond-shaped spaces, made from economical, sawn softwood; others are carefully detailed and finely finished ornamental panels made from the best quality wood. Screens and trellis made from wrought iron or metal in other forms are also available. It is possible to obtain some ready-made pieces, but these are more likely to be

USING TRELLIS TO CONCEAL A VIEW

A broken line of trellis panels creates a focal point in the garden and can also be used to block an unattractive view, while still allowing access to the garden beyond.

KEY TO PLANTING
 1 *Clematis* 'Jackmanii Superba'
 2 *Hedera canariensis*
   'Variegata'

 3 *Lonicera* 'Dropmore Scarlet'
 4 *Jasminum officinale* f. *affine*
 5 *Alchemilla mollis*
 6 *Geranium renardii*

MAKING WALL TRELLIS

Making your own trellis from, for example, roofing battens, allows you to tailor the size and shape to your own requirements. The horizontal battens are screwed to the wall, and the upright battens are nailed or screwed to the wall-mounted strips. The trellis supports *Clematis* 'The President'.

Below: This trellis panel is a striking feature and it is further enhanced by the ivy which frames, rather than covers, it.

SUPPORT FOR CLIMBERS

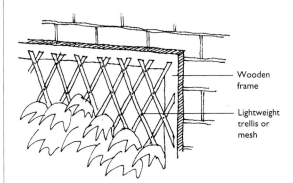

Wooden frame

Lightweight trellis or mesh

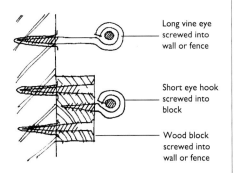

Long vine eye screwed into wall or fence

Short eye hook screwed into block

Wood block screwed into wall or fence

Lightweight trellis and mesh to support climbing plants are best fixed to a wooden frame, which is mounted on the wall. This gives room for the plants to develop and provides space for wildlife.

Wires to support climbers are best held in place with vine eyes. Long vine eyes, fixed directly to wall or fences, or short eye hooks, screwed into wall-mounted wooden blocks, give extra room – a gap of 50–70mm (2–3in) – behind for stems to develop.

A PALISADE SCREEN

A screen such as this palisade can be easily made from a row of wooden posts. These should be treated to prevent rot. Since the posts are so close together, they can simply be fixed by digging out a narrow trench and setting the posts in a 100mm (4in) bed of concrete. Light can penetrate through the palisade, which does not become a solid barrier.

KEY TO PLANTING
1 *Berberis* x *stenophylla*
2 *Heuchera micrantha* 'Palace Purple'
3 *Geranium renardii*
4 *Aesculus parviflora*

SCREENS FOR EXTRA PRIVACY

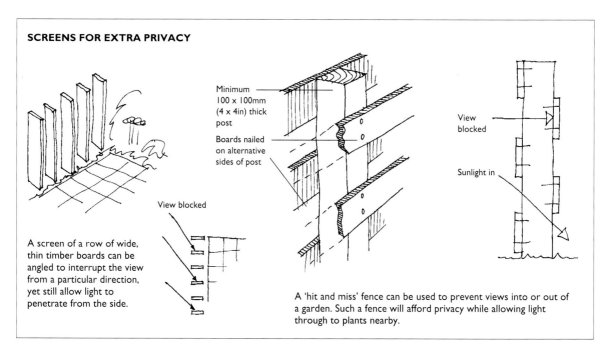

Minimum 100 x 100mm (4 x 4in) thick post

Boards nailed on alternative sides of post

View blocked

View blocked

Sunlight in

A screen of a row of wide, thin timber boards can be angled to interrupt the view from a particular direction, yet still allow light to penetrate from the side.

A 'hit and miss' fence can be used to prevent views into or out of a garden. Such a fence will afford privacy while allowing light through to plants nearby.

specially made to meet specific requirements. Although they are more costly than the most popular softwood panels, wrought iron trellis or screen systems can compare quite favourably with the best wooden equivalents.

In addition to wood and metal, perforated concrete block and brick walls can be used to give the same effect, and these have the added advantage of requiring little or no maintenance. Plastic in various forms, such as netting or rigid sections, is also available. Although it requires no maintenance in the short term, the long-term life of plastic products does not compare favourably with, say, a brick screen wall, and the range of colours and finishes available can sometimes be limited and not always sympathetic to the garden design.

MAINTENANCE

As with boundary fences and walls, the long-term maintenance of the various structures should be considered before a final choice is made, and this is especially important if they are going to support plants. Wooden trellis panels and screening systems bought pre-assembled or in kit form are usually pressure treated by the manufacturer, and any subsequent maintenance is likely to be for cosmetic purposes only. If, however, you will be making your own trellis or screen from untreated timber, it will be necessary not only to treat the finished structure when it is newly erected, but also to treat it every two or three years thereafter, especially where the wood comes into contact with the ground.

CONSTRUCTION

Apart from any maintenance considerations, building a trellis or screen, especially to a simple design, is within the capability of many gardeners, and will give double pleasure by not only being your own work but also by being a feature found in no other garden. Building tall, perforated screen walls in bricks, concrete blocks or stone is, however, not to be recommended for general home construction, principally because they lack the stability of a solid wall and need greater skill to build safely.

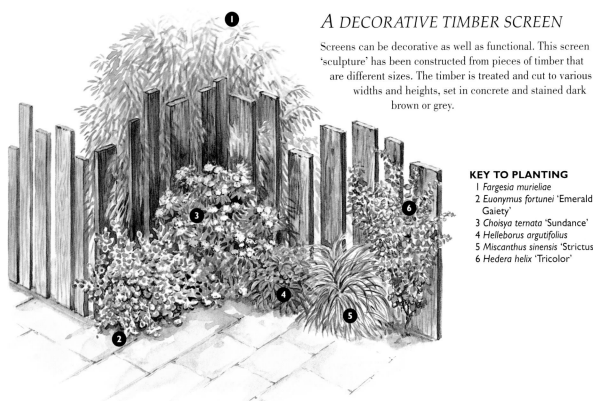

A DECORATIVE TIMBER SCREEN

Screens can be decorative as well as functional. This screen 'sculpture' has been constructed from pieces of timber that are different sizes. The timber is treated and cut to various widths and heights, set in concrete and stained dark brown or grey.

KEY TO PLANTING
1 *Fargesia murieliae*
2 *Euonymus fortunei* 'Emerald Gaiety'
3 *Choisya ternata* 'Sundance'
4 *Helleborus argutifolius*
5 *Miscanthus sinensis* 'Strictus'
6 *Hedera helix* 'Tricolor'

BEDS AND BORDERS

If a planting scheme is to be successful, the plants within it must be arranged in such a way that they not only create the desired visual effects in terms of colour, texture, light and shade but also suit the physical conditions to be found in the part of the garden where they are planted. Even within the limited space of an individual garden, the nature of the soil, its moisture content and the amount of sun, wind or shade can vary enormously from one area to another. With all these variables to consider it is little wonder that so many gardeners find planting design very frustrating, especially when a wrongly positioned and expensive plant fails to thrive or even dies.

PROBLEM AREAS
Apart from these general considerations, many gardens have a particular problem area as far as plants

are concerned. This may be the result of heavy shade under a tree, dry, poor soil next to a high wall or a badly drained, permanently wet spot, for example, and although identifying such places can be relatively straightforward, coming up with an adequate planting solution is not always so easy.

PLANTING SUGGESTIONS

In this chapter are ideas and planting suggestions not only for those situations where conditions favour the growth of a wide range of plants, but also for the more difficult spots, for which the selection of the right plants is far more critical.

PLANTING A WINTER BORDER

This border has been planted to provide interest from late autumn to early spring, when other parts of the garden may be lacking in colour.

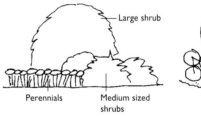

BALANCING THE PROPORTIONS OF PLANTS

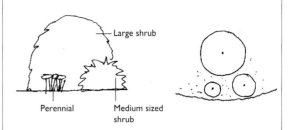

Large shrub

Perennial   Medium sized shrub

When they achieve maturity this large shrub, perennial and medium sized shrub planted together will not be in proportion to each other, and there will be a large area of bare soil to maintain.

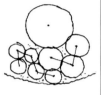

Large shrub

Perennials   Medium sized shrubs

Larger groups of smaller plants within a planting scheme will help to maintain the overall proportions and reduce the amount of bare soil that is visible.

KEY TO PLANTING
1 *Prunus* x *subhirtella* 'Autumnalis Rosea'
2 *Viburnum* x *bodnantense*
3 *Viburnum tinus* 'Eve Price'
4 *Iris foetidissima* 'Variegata'
5 *Lonicera fragrantissima*
6 *Mahonia* x *media* 'Winter Sun'
7 *Hebe pinguifolia* 'Pagei'
8 *Choisya ternata*
9 *Erica erigena* 'W.T. Rackliff'
10 *Cotoneaster* x *suecicus* 'Coral Beauty'
11 *Cornus alba* 'Sibirica'
12 *Skimmia japonica* ssp. *reevesiana*
13 *Juniperus squamata* 'Blue Swede'
14 *Bergenia* 'Abendglut'
15 *Erica* x *darleyensis* 'Molten Silver'
16 *Carex hachijoensis* 'Evergold'

AN EASY-CARE ISLAND BED

Traditional, easy-care perennials are displayed to best effect in an island bed such as this one. As a general rule, taller plants are placed towards the middle of the bed, and the minimum width of the bed should be at least twice the height of the tallest plant for the best effect.

KEY TO PLANTING
1 *Leucanthemum* x *superbum* 'Snowcap'
2 *Bergenia cordifolia* 'Purpurea'
3 *Dicentra* 'Luxuriant'
4 *Euphorbia polychroma*
5 *Iris* 'Jane Phillips'
6 *Helleborus corsicus*
7 *Eryngium variifolium*
8 *Doronicum* 'Miss Mason'
9 *Aster novi-belgii* 'Lady in Blue'
10 *Achillea* 'Moonshine'
11 *Campanula persicifolia*
12 *Crocosmia* 'Lucifer'
13 *Scabiosa caucasica* 'Clive Greaves'
14 *Geranium* x *oxonianum* 'Wargrave Pink'
15 *Geum* 'Borisii'
16 *Koeleria glauca*
17 *Iris* 'Green Spot'
18 *Solidago* 'Golden Thumb'
19 *Lavandula angustifolia* 'Nana Alba'
20 *Hemerocallis* 'Stella de Oro'

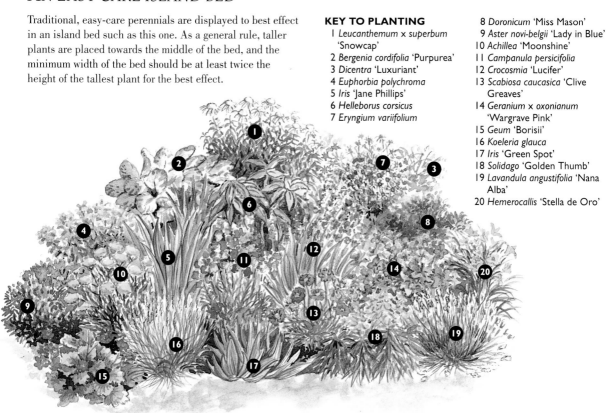

PLANTING PROBLEMS AND SOLUTIONS

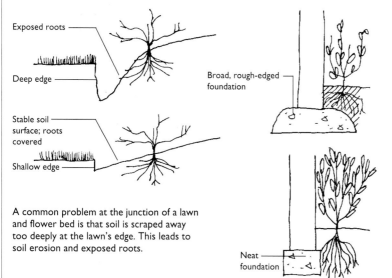

Exposed roots
Deep edge
Stable soil surface; roots covered
Shallow edge

A common problem at the junction of a lawn and flower bed is that soil is scraped away too deeply at the lawn's edge. This leads to soil erosion and exposed roots.

Broad, rough-edged foundation

Neat foundation

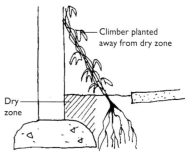

Climber planted away from dry zone

Dry zone

Over-generous wall foundations tend to create a zone of hot, dry, shallow soil where close-planted subjects cannot thrive. Ideally, the foundations should be square-edged to permit planting closer to the base. Climbers need to be planted so that their roots are away from the base of a wall where the foundation is very wide.

Planting based on a single colour theme – in this case, yellow – can often produce surprisingly stimulating results.

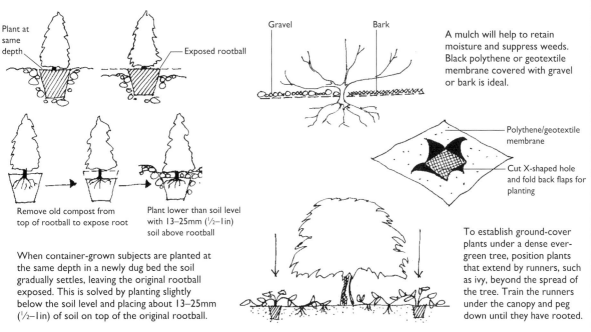

Plant at same depth

Exposed rootball

Remove old compost from top of rootball to expose root

Plant lower than soil level with 13–25mm (½–1in) soil above rootball

When container-grown subjects are planted at the same depth in a newly dug bed the soil gradually settles, leaving the original rootball exposed. This is solved by planting slightly below the soil level and placing about 13–25mm (½–1in) of soil on top of the original rootball.

Gravel   Bark

A mulch will help to retain moisture and suppress weeds. Black polythene or geotextile membrane covered with gravel or bark is ideal.

Polythene/geotextile membrane

Cut X-shaped hole and fold back flaps for planting

To establish ground-cover plants under a dense ever-green tree, position plants that extend by runners, such as ivy, beyond the spread of the tree. Train the runners under the canopy and peg down until they have rooted.

HERB GARDENS

Herbs have been used for culinary and medicinal purposes for centuries, but recently they have begun to be appreciated for their decorative value as well. Complete gardens based entirely on herbs are not often seen and are probably best suited to smaller plots, where other considerations such as providing space for children to run about or for hanging out the washing do not apply. More frequently, a herb garden is seen as part of a larger plot, sometimes in a rather formal or symmetrical style, or herbs are grown in raised beds and containers.

Where herbs form a regular part of the family diet, the herb garden should ideally be located close to, or with good all-weather access from, the kitchen. If you intend to devote part of a garden or border purely to herbs, a few additional ornamental shrubs will help to provide a permanent framework. These might include, for example, shrub roses (such as **Rosa glauca** or **R.** 'Nevada'), dwarf mock orange (**Philadelphus** 'Manteau d'Hermine'), **Viburnum** x **bodnantense** 'Dawn' and **Mahonia** x **media** 'Winter Sun'. The range of old fashioned and traditional herbs is extensive and includes many varieties that, while not necessarily of great practical value in the modern kitchen, nevertheless warrant inclusion because of their attractive leaves,

PLANTING HERBS IN A PAVED AREA

A colourful way of breaking up a bland paved area is to plant larger herbs, such as sage, in place of some of the flags. Low-growing or creeping herbs, such as thyme, can be planted in the joints of the paving.

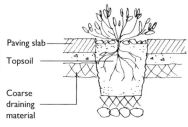

Paving slab
Topsoil
Coarse draining material

Planting in pockets between slabs.

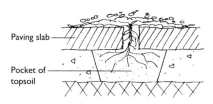

Paving slab
Pocket of topsoil

Planting in paving joints.

KEY TO PLANTING
1 *Allium schoenoprasum* (chives)
2 *Origanum vulgare* (oregano)
3 *Thymus vulgaris* (thyme)
4 *Mentha spicata* (spearmint)
5 *Chamaemelum nobile* (camomile)

226

*This herb garden is made all the more attractive by the
happy mixture of formality and informality. The occasional
ornamental plant, such as the iris, adds interest.*

A FORMAL HERB GARDEN

A formal and symmetrical herb garden can form part of a
larger garden, especially if the plot is long and narrow.

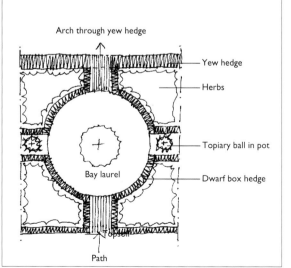

Arch through yew hedge

Yew hedge

Herbs

Topiary ball in pot

Bay laurel

Dwarf box hedge

Topsoil

Path

A HERB SQUARE

This simple yet eye-catching herb square
can form a feature at the centre
or corner of a patio or lawn.

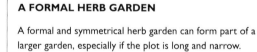

KEY TO PLANTING
1 *Thymus vulgaris* (thyme)
2 *Ruta graveolens* (rue)
3 *Laurus nobilis* (bay)

flowers or scent, including artemisia (especially forms such as *Artemisia* 'Powis Castle') and rue (*Ruta graveolens*).

DESIGNS

The traditional knot or parterre layout for a herb garden, although formal, is actually quite a sensible arrangement, giving easy access to different herbs that can be planted in groups of one species in separate areas according to their vigour and size. The loss of ground required by the paths dividing each section could well be offset by the improved productivity of such an area. Certain

herbs, particularly those that are long-lived perennials or of a shrubby nature such as rosemary, thyme, chives and sage, for example, are valuable additions to the mixed border, where they will serve the double purpose of being both decorative and of culinary value.

PLANTING AND CARE

Most herbs prefer to be in sun for at least part of the day, and they do best in a light, fertile soil with reasonable drainage, although there are exceptions to this – mint (*Mentha*) and parsley (*Petroselinum*), for example, which do better in a cooler, slightly

HERBS IN A MIXED BORDER

Herbs can be ornamental as well as culinary, and they are used here as an integral part of a mixed border.

KEY TO PLANTING

1 *Miscanthus sinensis* 'Silver Feather'
2 *Taxus baccata* 'Fastigiata Aurea'
3 *Elaeagnus* x *ebbingei*
4 *Weigela florida* 'Variegata'
5 *Laurus nobilis* 'Aurea'
6 *Iris* 'Jane Phillips'
7 *Thymus* x *citriodorus* 'Silver Posie'
8 *Hebe* 'Wingletye'
9 *Salvia officinalis* 'Aurea'
10 *Viburnum tinus* 'Eve Price'
11 *Erica carnea* 'Myretoun Ruby'
12 *Ruta graveolens* 'Jackman's Blue'
13 *Thymus* x *citriodorus* 'Aureus'
14 *Allium schoenoprasum* 'Forescate'
15 *Potentilla fruticosa* 'Tilford Cream'
16 *Aster novi-belgii* 'Little Pink Beauty'
17 *Foeniculum* 'Giant Bronze'
18 *Salvia officinalis* 'Purpurascens'
19 *Calluna vulgaris* 'H.E. Beale'
20 *Origanum vulgare* 'Aureum'
21 *Angelica archangelica*
22 *Helichrysum angustifolium*
23 *Hydrangea serrata* 'Preziosa'
24 *Hemerocallis* 'Stafford'

HERBS IN A RAISED BED

Many herbs appreciate the conditions created by raised beds, and here they form a pleasing contrast with the dark brown log edging.

Flexible rolls of half-round, treated logs make good raised beds for herbs. If a curved edge is needed, the log edging is best secured by concrete at the base.

KEY TO PLANTING

1 *Petroselinum crispum* (parsley)
2 *Allium schoenoprasum* (chives)
3 *Thymus vulgaris* (thyme)
4 *Salvia officinalis* 'Purpurascens' (purple sage)
5 *Chamaemelum nobile* (camomile)
6 *Rosmarinus officinalis* (rosemary)
7 *Origanum vulgare* 'Aureum' (oregano)
8 *Artemisia dracunculus* 'Sativa' (French tarragon)
9 *Salvia officinalis* 'Tricolor' (sage)
10 *Thymus citriodorus* 'Aureus' (thyme)
11 *Lavandula angustifolia* 'Hidcote' (lavender)
12 *Hyssopus officinalis* (hyssop)

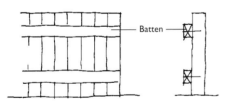

Above: Straight-sided raised beds can easily be made by fixing the edging to wooden battens.

Below: On badly drained ground excess moisture can drain through to the hardcore below the paving.

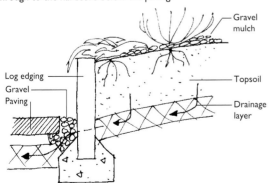

more shaded situation and in a heavier soil, and herbs with silvery or woolly leaves, such as rosemary (**Rosmarinus**), sage (**Salvia officinalis**) and helichrysum, prefer a well-drained, sunny or even hot situation. Vigorous herbs such as mint (**Mentha**) and lemon balm (**Melissa officinalis**) are best planted either in containers or in a spot where they cannot spread to other beds or borders. A single slab may, for example, be left out of a patio in order to house a mint bed.

Many herbs lend themselves to being grown in containers, particularly annual varieties such as basil (**Ocimum**), and this obviates the need to allocate space for them in the general borders, which would otherwise be very patchy for much of the year. Container-grown herbs will respond well if given regular attention by watering, feeding and trimming, although they will never be quite so productive as plants given the same attention grown in the open ground. Maintenance is important, for many herbs are vigorous and require regular pinching and trimming, so that they do not rapidly outgrow their space and become leggy and tall or run to seed prematurely.

POTS AND CONTAINERS

There has been an upsurge of interest in container gardening in recent years, not only in the scale of its general popularity but also in the diversity of both plants and receptacles that gardeners are prepared to use. While annual species, such as geraniums, lobelias, petunias and the like, are still high on the list of many people's most popular container plants, the range of other varieties that can be successfully grown in pots is enormous. In fact, almost any plant can at some time be grown in a pot, from a tiny, encrusted alpine saxifrage to a potentially enormous oak or maple – even aquatic plants can be grown in suitable waterproof containers.

One of the beauties of a plant in a container is that it can be moved from place to place for different reasons at different times. If you want your collection to be mobile, however, do not make the mistake of using massive containers that cannot be moved once they are full of damp compost.

Unless it is to be used for aquatic plants, of course, the container must have drainage holes through which excess moisture can escape to prevent water logging, which can cause severe physiological problems to the plant and ultimately even its death. Because the plant roots are effectively trapped within the container, the compost must be the best

CONSTRUCTING A SIMPLE BRICK CONTAINER

A simple and attractive container constructed from old bricks is suitable for annuals or for small trailing plants, such as thyme and aubrieta.

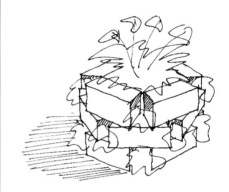

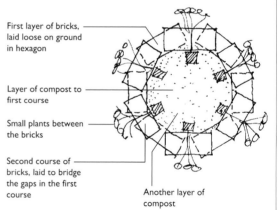

First layer of bricks, laid loose on ground in hexagon

Layer of compost to first course

Small plants between the bricks

Second course of bricks, laid to bridge the gaps in the first course

Another layer of compost

DISPLAYING A SPECIAL POT

A special pot, such as this one containing a Japanese maple, is worth showing off. Here the pot is enhanced by using a circle of tiles, granite setts and gravel set into a patio.

KEY TO PLANTING
1 Acer palmatum 'Dissectum Viridis'
2 Vinca minor 'Variegata'

Too often emphasis is placed on containers for
summer planting. Here, a selection of plants provides
striking winter interest.

available, and it must be supplemented with regular liquid feeding during the growing season.

Even if the plants are in containers, they should not be simply placed together in one spot on the patio. Every plant should be treated as it would be if it were being planted in the ground, with sun lovers, such as hebe and agapanthus, placed in the hot, sunny parts of the garden. Choicer plants, such as Japanese maples and deciduous azaleas, must be kept out of the fierce heat, perhaps in a

position where they receive sun only in the morning or late afternoon.

CHOICE OF CONTAINER
Almost any material can be used as a container for plants provided that it is reasonably durable and will not contaminate the compost. Plastic, fibreglass, metal, wood, concrete, stone, brick, stoneware and terracotta, in all sorts of shapes and forms, can be used. The choice of material for the pot will, to some

231

SITING CONTAINERS

Some containers, especially dark, plastic ones, can become very hot if they stand in direct sunlight and this can lead to root scorch.

Containers can be screened from too much sun by piles of attractively arranged rocks, stones or shells.

A plant in a terracotta or stone pot will also screen a container from the sun.

degree, influence what is grown in it, and vice versa. Terracotta, for example, can be porous, which means that it is excellent for plants that do not like excessively damp soil, such as lavender or helianthemum, but it is not so good for those that do, such as astilbes or hostas, which might be happier in a fibreglass or stone pot. It is also important to remember that some materials, such as black plastic, heat up very quickly in direct sun, and this can cause root damage to plants such as Japanese acers, which prefer their roots to be cool, and which might, therefore, be happier in a well-insulated wooden tub.

PLANT CARE

In addition to ornamental plants, herbs, vegetables and fruit can all be grown in pots or containers, but do not expect the same yields as you might obtain

DRAINPIPE CONTAINERS

Sections of salt-glazed drainpipe can be used as containers for groups of plants. Place the empty pipes in position before filling with good quality potting compost, below which is a layer of coarse gravel or broken crocks for drainage.

KEY TO PLANTING
1 *Euonymus fortunei* 'Emerald Gaiety'
2 *Euphorbia cyparissias*
3 *Hedera helix* 'Spetchley'
4 *Festuca glauca*
5 *Spiraea japonica* 'Gold Mound'
6 *Ceanothus* 'Blue Mound'
7 *Viburnum davidii*
8 *Epimedium* x *youngianum* 'Niveum'
9 *Miscanthus sinensis* var. *purpurascens*

WINDOWBOX PLANTING

Windowboxes need not be restricted to traditional annual bedding plants. Here dwarf plants for permanent, year-round colour are used.

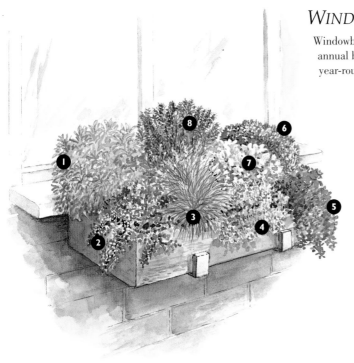

KEY TO PLANTING

1 *Euonymus japonicus* 'Microphyllus Palchellus'
2 *Cotoneaster congestus*
3 *Festuca glauca* 'Sea Urchin'
4 *Sedum spathulifolium* 'Cape Blanco'
5 *Hedera helix* 'Spetchley'
6 *Hebe cupressoides* 'Boughton Dome'
7 *Campanula carpatica* 'Snowsprite'
8 *Erica carnea* 'Vivelli'

PLANTING IN CONFINED SPACES

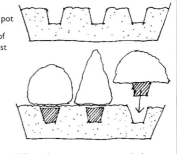

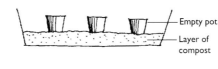

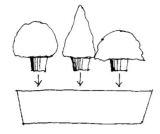

Empty pot

Layer of compost

More compost added

When an instant effect in a confined space is required, the lack of space can make planting very awkward.

The planting process can be simplified by using the pots in which the plants were grown.

When the pots are removed, the plants can be dropped into the corresponding holes in the compost.

from the same plants grown in the ground. Again, for best results try to match the conditions in the container to those in which the plant would thrive if planted out.

When they are grown in new compost, plants such as annuals and salad crops will get through a season with no more than regular watering and a fortnightly liquid feed from early summer through till early autumn. Permanent plantings, however, especially woody plants and perennials such as rhododendrons and hostas, will need to be repotted or potted-on at least every other spring, and

although growth will never be quite so prolific as on a similar plant in the ground, pruning should still be carried out to maintain the health, vigour and quality of flowers and foliage.

The reasons for growing plants in pots and tubs are many and varied – lack of space, poor ground conditions or purely as ornamental features, for example – but perhaps the greatest attraction of container gardening is that, in a tiny space, it is possible to grow a selection of plants to provide year-round interest, from tiny spring bulbs through to summer-flowering perennials and winter-flowering shrubs.

Part Three

PLANT

DIRECTORY

Among the many thousands of plants now available to gardeners from nurseries and garden centres, there are some varieties that are likely to be bought on impulse because of their instant appeal, often the result of their flamboyant and striking flowers. Although this is understandable, quite often the immediately obvious attraction of a particular plant can be more than outweighed by one or more less obvious disadvantages that may not be evident at the time of purchase. One of these might be that the plant flowers for only a few days and for the rest of the year is nothing more than an innocuous mound of greenery – and not even that if it is a deciduous shrub or an herbaceous perennial. Another drawback could be that the plant needs a specific combination of soil, moisture and light conditions in order to achieve its full potential.

Some perennials, such as **Dicentra spectabilis** (bleeding heart or Dutchman's trousers) are delightful in both flower and leaf but die away completely in midsummer leaving a conspicuous patch of bare ground. Others, such as some varieties of **Aster novi-belgii** (Michaelmas daisy) regularly fall victim to disfiguring attacks of mildew and other ailments.

In a large garden a plant that may add to the overall picture only briefly can sometimes be tolerated because of the number of other plants around it to continue the interest. In a more modest garden, however, there really is no place for varieties that may contribute little in relation to the amount of space that they occupy. In such a situation it would be much better to select your plants from varieties that could be said to provide value for money.

The problem, of course, is to define a 'value-for-money' plant. The most obvious first choice might be one such as **Dicentra** 'Luxuriant', that flowers over a long period, or perhaps a plant such as **Eranthis hyemalis** (winter aconite), which makes an impact at a time of year when the garden is lacking interest.

Even better are plants that give double value at different times – **Cornus alba** 'Aurea', for example, has golden leaves throughout spring and summer, and these fall in autumn to reveal beautiful red stems for the winter.

The directory that follows gives a selection of the more popular 'value-for-money' plants used in the garden designs of Part 1.

The success of this herbaceous border lies in the fact that it is laid out along traditional lines using well-proven, reliable plants.

PERENNIALS

Achillea 'Moonshine'
Height: 60cm (24in); planting
distance: 45cm (18in)
Silvery grey, deeply cut foliage with
flat heads of sulphur yellow flowers
in late summer. Prefers full sun and
good drainage. Excellent for cutting.

Agapanthus 'Bressingham White'
Height: 90cm (36in); planting
distance: 45cm (18in)
Long, strap-like leaves with round
clusters of white, funnel-shaped
flowers in summer. Prefers sunny,
sheltered position with good
drainage.

Artemisia 'Powis Castle'
Height: 60cm (24in); planting
distance: 60cm (24in)
A mound of silver filigree foliage on
woody stems. Good foil to other
plants. Needs full sun and good
drainage. Cut back hard in early
spring, with a light trim in midsummer to keep in shape.

Aster amellus 'King George' (Michaelmas daisy)
Height: 60cm (24in); planting
distance: 45cm (18in)
Lavender blue, daisy flowers with
yellow centre over grey-green
foliage in late summer. Prefers good
soil in an open position away from
shade. Good cut flower.

Astilbe x arendsii 'Bressingham Beauty'
Height: 90cm (36in); planting
distance: 60cm (24in)
Spikes of feathery, pink flowers
above glossy, pinnate foliage in
summer. Does best in rich, moist
soil in partial or dappled shade.
Good cut flower.

Aster amellus 'King George'

Dicentra 'Luxuriant'
Height: 30cm (12in); planting
distance: 30cm (12in)
Bright red, heart-shaped flowers
dangle over fresh green, ferny
leaves from late spring to early
autumn. Does best in fertile,
organic-rich soil, ideally in a spot
sheltered from cold wind and
severe frost.

Epimedium x youngianum 'Niveum'
Height: 25cm (10in); planting
distance: 45cm (18in)
Low mounds of semi-evergreen,
red-veined, heart-shaped leaves
make excellent ground cover.
Small, white, starry flowers in late
spring. Prefers good, rich soil in
light shade. Cut back old leaves in
early spring, before flowers appear.

Euphorbia characias ssp. wulfenii (spurge)
Height: 1.2m (4ft); planting
distance: 1.2m (4ft)
Bushy, evergreen, sub-shrub with
narrow, blue-green leaves and long
panicles of yellow-green flowering
bracts in early summer. Any
reasonable soil in sun or light
shade, but needs good drainage.
Cut off old flower stems at their
base after flowering. Good for floral
arrangements.

Euphorbia griffithii 'Fireglow' (spurge)
Height: 1m (3ft 3in); planting
distance: 90cm (36in)
Thick, fleshy stems with narrow
leaves tinged red with silver
midrib. Clusters of orange flowering
bracts for long period during summer.

Grow in any reasonable soil in full sun for best colour. Cut off dead stems at ground level in late autumn.

Ferula 'Giant Bronze' (bronze fennel)

Height: 1.8m (6ft); planting distance: 90cm (36in)

Tall, hollow stems covered in a haze of wiry, soft bronze-coloured foliage and flat heads of tiny yellow flowers in summer. Grow in any reasonable, well-drained soil in full sun. Cut back to ground level in early spring.

Geranium himalayense 'Plenum' (syn. G. grandiflorum)

Height: 25cm (10in); planting distance: 45cm (18in)

Grey-green, deeply cut leaves with a succession of double lavender blue to mauve flowers in early summer. Any reasonable soil, but prefers full sun for best flowering.

Geranium renardii

Height: 25cm (10in); planting distance: 30cm (12in)

Rounded, felty, grey-green leaves form a low clump above which pale lavender flowers with purple veins appear in early summer. Prefers ordinary soil in full sun, but tolerates light shade.

Helleborus lividus var. corsicus (Lenten rose)

Height: 60cm (24in); planting distance: 60cm (24in)

Leathery, spiny edged, evergreen leaves with pale green, cup-shaped

flowers in spring. Does best in good, well-drained soil, in full sun or light shade, sheltered from cold, drying winds. Remove flower stems after flowering. Good for floral arrangements.

Heuchera micrantha 'Palace Purple'

Height: 30cm (12in); planting distance: 30cm (12in)

Glossy, dark purple leaves act as a contrast to long sprays of tiny, white flowers in early summer. Colours best in good, rich soil in full sun or very light shade.

Hosta 'Krossa Regal'

Height: 60cm (24in); planting distance: 45cm (18in)

Green-blue, wavy edged leaves on upright stems, arching outwards. Lilac, tubular flowers on long stalks in summer. Prefers heavy, rich soil in full sun or light shade. Dislikes dry conditions.

Iris foetidissima 'Variegata'

Height: 45cm (18in); planting distance: 45cm (18in)

Long, evergreen, sword-shaped leaves are variegated white, springing from ground level. Small purple flowers in early summer are followed by large seedheads, which open to reveal bright orange seeds in winter. Grows in any well-drained soil in sun or part shade.

Lamium maculatum 'Aureum'

Height: 30cm (12in); planting distance: 30cm (12in)

Neat clumps of pale gold, nettle leaves with pink flowers in early summer. Needs light shade, out of direct sun, and prefers rich soil.

Ligularia 'The Rocket'

Height: 1.2m (4ft); planting distance: 45cm (18in)

Large, heart-shaped leaves with jagged edges, surmounted by tall, black stems and spikes of brilliant yellow flowers. Does best in heavy, moisture-retentive soil in sun or light shade.

Liriope muscari

Height: 30cm (12in); planting distance: 30cm (12in)

Broad, grass-like, evergreen leaves form good ground-covering clumps. Small spikes of mauve-lilac flowers, resembling those of the grape hyacinth, and borne from late summer to early autumn.

Ferula 'Giant Bronze'

Liriope muscari

Lamium maculatum 'Aureum'

Matteuccia struthiopteris

Matteuccia struthiopteris (ostrich fern, ostrich-feather fern)

Height: 90cm (36in); planting distance: 60cm (24in)
Fresh green fronds of foliage create a narrow shuttlecock effect in late spring before eventually assuming a broad vase shape. Prefers a lightly shaded position in good soil, but will tolerate full sun if the soil does not dry out. Cut dead fronds back to soil level in late autumn.

Osteospermum ecklonii

Height: 45cm (18in); planting distance: 60cm (24in)
Small, green leaves and tough stems make a wide-spreading plant covered in large, lilac-mauve daisy flowers with a blue centre from early summer to autumn. Flowers best in full sun in any reasonable soil.

Persicaria affinis 'Dimity'

Height: 20cm (8in); planting distance: 60cm (24in)
Simple, glossy leaves create a weed-suppressing mat interspersed with short pink spikes of long-lived flowers that fade to red–brown during summer. Any soil in sun or part shade.

Phormium tenax 'Purpureum'

Height: 1.5m (5ft); planting distance: 1m (3ft 3in)
Long, purple, sword-shaped leaves form a striking evergreen clump with spikes of dull red flowers, produced only occasionally in summer. Needs good, well-drained soil in full sun. Will not tolerate water-logged ground and requires protection from severe winter weather except in mild climates. Cut off dead leaves at the base in spring.

Phygelius x rectus 'African Queen'

Height: 90cm (36in) (more on a wall); planting distance: 60cm (24in)
A shrubby perennial with small leaves and long, salmon-red, fuchsia-like flowers with yellow throats from summer to early autumn. Needs full sun in a sheltered position in well-drained, ordinary soil. Will produce woody stems against a wall, but may be cut back to ground level if planted in the open; so treat as a perennial.

Pulmonaria officinalis 'Sissinghurst White'

Height: 25cm (10in); planting distance: 45cm (18in)
Large, oval, hairy leaves, marbled white, precede spikes bearing clusters of dainty, white flowers over a long period from spring to early summer. Prefers cool, moist soil in partial shade and is liable to wilt and scorch in hot, dry situations. Remove flower stems when flowering is finished.

Rudbeckia fulgida var. sullivantii 'Goldsturm'

Height: 75cm (30in); planting distance: 45cm (18in)
Small, pointed, hairy leaves on upright stems topped by large, bright yellow to orange, star-shaped flowers with contrasting brown centre throughout summer. Grows in any reasonable, well-drained soil, but needs full sun. Cut back to ground level in late autumn.

BULBS

Nerine bowdenii

Allium moly
Height: 30cm (12in);
planting distance: 10cm (4in)
Clusters of grey-green, strap-shaped
leaves followed by many stems
bearing clusters of yellow, star-
shaped flowers in early to
midsummer. Any reasonably fertile
soil, preferring good drainage and
full soil.

Anemone blanda
Height: to 15cm (6in);
planting distance: 10cm (4in)
Blue, daisy-like flowers emerge
before the deeply-cut, geranium-
like leaves in late winter to early
spring. White, mauve and pink
forms are available. Grow in any
good soil that does not dry out while
the leaves are active in spring, in
full sun or light shade such as
beneath deciduous trees or shrubs.

Cyclamen hederifolium (syn. C. neapolitanum)
Height: 10cm (4in);
planting distance: 10–15cm (4–6in)
Pale pink or mauve flowers with
recurved petals stand above
orbicular green leaves marked with
silver from late summer until late
autumn. The leaves remain until late
spring. Does best in organically rich
soil, disliking excessive wetness,
dryness or full sun.

Eranthis hyemalis (winter aconite)
Height: 10cm (4in);
planting distance: 5–10cm (2–4in)
Glossy, lemon-yellow, buttercup-
like flowers emerge before the
deeply cut mid-green leaves in late
winter. Grows best in a well-drained
soil provided there is adequate
moisture until the leaves die in

early summer. Good beneath
deciduous trees and shrubs.

Galanthus nivalis (common snowdrop)
Height: 10–20cm (4–8in);
planting distance: 5–15cm (2–6in)
Narrow, strap-shaped, blue-green
leaves. Drooping, six-petalled
(three large, three small), white
flowers with a green spot, carried
singly on short stalks in late winter.
Does best in light shade in a heavy
or organic-rich soil that does not
dry out.

Hyacinthoides non-scripta (syn. Scilla non-scriptus) (bluebell)
Height: 30cm (12in);
planting distance: 10cm (4in)
Strap-shaped, mid green leaves,
upright at first then spreading.
Clusters of bell-shaped, purple-blue
flowers at the end of straight,
upright stems are borne in late
spring. Does best in organically rich
soil that is not prone to drying out,
in full sun or light shade.

Narcissus 'February Gold'
Height: 20–30cm (8–12in);
planting distance: 10–15cm (4–6in)

Narrow, upright, mid-green leaves
and yellow flowers with long
trumpets and swept-back petals
appear in late winter and early
spring. Any good, well-drained soil
in full sun or light shade. Suitable
for naturalizing in fine grass or
among dwarf shrubs or perennials.

Nerine bowdenii
Height: to 60cm (24in);
planting distance: 15cm (6in)
Narrow, mid-green, strap-shaped
leaves emerge just after the
flowers, which are composed of
narrow, pink petals, often twisted or
curled, borne in loose clusters at
the ends of tall stems in late summer
through to late autumn. Does best in
a reasonable, well-drained soil, in full
sun but with some protection.

Tulipa tarda (syn. T. dasystemon) (tulip)
Height: 15cm (6in);
planting distance: 7.5–10cm (3–4in)
Strap-shaped, mid-green leaves
form a central rosette from which
emerge up to five lily-like, yellow
flowers with white tips to the petals
in late spring. Needs a well-drained
soil in a warm, sheltered spot.

SHRUBS

Abelia x grandiflora

Height: 1.5m (5ft); spread: 1.2m (4ft)

Small, glossy, semi-evergreen leaves on a twiggy bush, with clusters of small pink and white tubular flowers from summer to autumn. Any ordinary soil, in full sun, for best flowering, sheltered from cold, dry winds. Remove one-third of the old stems at ground level in early spring.

Acer palmatum 'Bloodgood'

Height: to 3.5m (11ft 6in); spread: to 3.5m (11ft 6in)

Blood-red, palmate leaves turn to dark purple during summer. Prefers good, rich, moisture-retentive soil, ideally neutral or slightly acid, in a position sheltered from cold wind in sun or light, dappled shade. Remove dead or damaged branches in spring.

Aucuba japonica 'Crotonifolia'

Height: 1.5m (5ft); spread: 1.5m (5ft)

Large, pointed, evergreen leaves with yellow spots and blotches. Any well-drained soil in sun or partial shade, but dislikes positions exposed to severe wind. Cut back in early spring if outgrowing its position.

Azalea 'Gibraltar'

Height: 1.2m (4ft) spread: 1.2m (4ft)

Young bronze-tinted leaves turn to pale green, followed by autumn colour. Large heads of orange, funnel-shaped flowers on old wood in late spring to early summer. Needs well-drained, acid soil, preferably enriched with organic matter, that does not dry out excessively. Best in light or dappled shade, out of strong wind. Trim lightly after flowering if required to keep to size.

Berberis thunbergii 'Dart's Red Lady'

Height: 60cm (24in); spread: 60cm (24in)

Rounded, purple-black leaves from early spring, turning red in autumn. Small, yellow-white flowers in late spring. Any good soil, but needs full sun for best colour. No regular pruning, but cut back hard in early spring if too large.

Caryopteris x clandonensis 'Heavenly Blue'

Height: to 100cm (3ft 3in); spread: to 100cm (3ft 3in)

Small, grey-green leaves on silvery stems with deep blue flowers on new growths in late summer. Any soil, but needs good drainage and full sun in a warm, sheltered spot. Cut hard back to healthy buds in spring.

Ceanothus 'Puget Blue'

Height: 3m (10ft); spread: 3m (10ft)

Tiny, glossy evergreen leaves on dense, twiggy growth. Masses of blue tufted flowers in late spring. Any good soil, except where alkalinity is very high. Prefers full sun for maximum flowering, and shelter from cold winds. Trim lightly after flowering.

Ceratostigma willmottianum

Height: 90cm (36in); spread: 90cm (36in)

Small, green leaves on slender, twiggy stems produce deep blue, saucer-shaped flowers from summer to early autumn, followed by grey-brown seedheads. Prefers good, rich soil in full sun; dislikes shade. Cut back to ground level in spring.

Acer palmatum 'Bloodgood'

Ceratostigma willmottianum

Aucuba japonica 'Crotonifolia'

Choisya ternata 'Sundance' (Mexican orange blossom)

Height: 1.5m (5ft); spread: 1.5m (5ft)

Yellow-green, evergreen, trifoliate leaves turn gold in winter. Clusters of white, sweetly scented flowers at tips of stems in late spring. Any good soil, if not excessively alkaline, in full sun or light shade. Needs protection from cold winter wind and severe frost. Cut back to required size after flowering.

Cornus alba 'Aurea'

Height: 1.8m (6ft); spread: 2m (6ft 6in)

Oval, golden yellow leaves on long, red stems. Small clusters of white flowers in late spring to early summer if plant is not pruned. Produces best leaves in rich, moisture-retentive ground in full sun. Dislikes very dry spots. Annual or biennial hard pruning produces vigorous, straight stems and larger leaves.

Cornus alba 'Sibirica Variegata'

Height: 1.2m (4ft); spread: 1.5m (5ft)

White variegated leaves, with red stems and white flowers in late spring, followed by purple-black berries in autumn. Full sun for best colour, in any soil, but especially if good, rich and moisture retentive. Prune hard annually or biennially in early spring for best leaf and stem colour (although this means loss of flower and berry).

Elaeagnus x ebbingei

Height: 1.8m (6ft); spread: 1.8m (6ft)

Shiny, silvery-green, pointed, evergreen leaves with tiny, sweetly scented, white flowers on unpruned plants in autumn. Any reasonable soil, but prefers full sun, although dislikes extremely wet or dry situations. Cut back as required in late winter to keep within bounds, or trim lightly in summer.

Erica x darleyensis 'Molten Silver'

Height: 60cm (24in); spread: 60cm (24in)

Dark green, thin leaves on dense, twiggy bush, with masses of tiny, tubular white flowers from late autumn to spring. Any neutral or acid soil, although tolerates small amount of lime, in full sun for maximum flowering. Trim off flowering spikes with shears in late spring.

Euonymus fortunei 'Emerald 'n' Gold'

Height: 60cm (24in); spread: 90cm (36in); to 2 x 1.5m (6ft 6in x 5ft) on a wall

Small, evergreen leaves splashed with gold on dense bush. Occasional inconspicuous green flowers and small red fruits on wall-grown plants. Any well-drained soil in sun or shade. Trim in early spring to keep within bounds.

Euonymus fortunei 'Emerald 'n' Gold'

Exochorda x macrantha 'The Bride'

Height: 1.2m (4ft); spread: 1.5m (5ft)

Smooth, narrow leaves on arching stems with racemes of large, white, saucer-shaped flowers in late spring. Occasional small red fruits. Best on a good, rich soil, in a sheltered position in sun or partial shade.

Hebe armstrongii

Height: 90cm (36in); spread: 90cm (36in)

Olive greeny-gold, whipcord shoots, conifer-like in growth, with tiny white flowers at the tips in summer. Needs good, rich, well-drained soil, not prone to water-logging or severe drought, in full sun.

Hebe 'Mrs Winder'

Height: 90cm (36in); spread: 90cm (36in)

Small, narrow, shiny purple leaves with spikes of bright mauve to blue flowers from summer to early autumn. Needs good drainage, preferably on a light soil in full sun for best flower production. Trim lightly to shape in late spring.

Hebe rakaiensis

Height: 75cm (30in); spread: 90cm (36in)

Tiny, oval, evergreen leaves on neat, dome-shaped bush, with spikes of tiny, white flowers sometimes produced in summer. Any reasonable soil, but needs good drainage and full sun. Trim lightly immediately after flowering to keep within bounds.

Hydrangea aspera Villosa Group

Height: 2m (6ft 6in); spread: 2m (6ft 6in)

Long, velvety, purple-green leaves on upright stems, with large lilac-blue flower heads in late summer on older wood. Prefers good, rich, neutral or slightly acid soil, sheltered from strong winds. Dislikes full sun. Remove one-third of main stems at ground level in spring.

Hydrangea serrata 'Preziosa'

Height: 90cm (36in); spread: 90cm (36in)

Green, pointed leaves with red tinges on reddish stems, with good autumn colour. Long-lasting, rose-pink florets forming rounded flower heads in summer, turning red-purple in autumn. Prefers acid soil; dislikes extremes of wet and dry, doing best in light shade. Remove old flowering stems in late spring.

Ilex aquifolium 'Handsworth New Silver' (holly)

Height: 3m (10ft); spread: 1.8m (6ft)

Glossy, silver-margined leaves on conical shrub or small tree. Insignificant clusters of small, white, female flowers in late spring need nearby male tree to produce red berries in late autumn. Tolerates any well-drained soil, but grows more strongly on good, rich ground in full sun or very light shade. Trim in spring to keep within bounds.

Ilex aquifolium 'J.C. van Tol' (holly)

Height: to 4m (13ft); spread: to 2m (6ft 6in)

Glossy, dark green, almost spineless leaves on an evergreen bush or small tree. Tiny white female flowers in late spring on unpruned wood, followed by clusters of red berries in autumn, if a male holly is nearby. Does best on good, fertile, well-drained soil in full sun or light shade. Cut back to required size in late winter or trim lightly in summer; there will be some loss of flower and fruit in both cases.

Choisya ternata 'Sundance'

Exochorda x macrantha 'The Bride'

Ilex aquifolium 'J. C. van Tol'

Mahonia x media 'Winter Sun'
Height: 2.5m (8ft 6in); spread: 1.5m (5ft)
Large, glossy, spiky, evergreen leaves on stout, upright stems. Clusters of upright spikes of scented yellow flowers from late autumn to spring. Prefers good, rich soil in a sunny position with shelter from wind. Cut back flowering stems by up to one-third immediately after flowering.

Osmanthus x burkwoodii (syn. x Osmarea burkwoodii)
Height: 3m (10ft); spread: 2.5m (8ft 6in)
Small, leathery, evergreen leaves with clusters of tiny, white, sweetly scented flowers in spring. Any good soil, preferably in light shade, but does not like water-logged ground. Trim lightly after flowering to keep in shape.

Photinia x fraseri 'Rubens'
Height: 1.2m (4ft); spread: 1.5m (5ft)
Spear-shaped, evergreen leaves open brilliant sealing-wax red, turning greener with age. Clusters of white flowers on older shoots in early summer. Does best on fertile, well–drained soil in full sun for best colour development and flowering. Dislikes cold, exposed positions. If too large, cut back to desired size in late spring.

Physocarpus opulifolius 'Dart's Gold' (ninebark)
Height: 1.8m (6ft); spread: 1.8m (6ft)
Golden, three-lobed leaves on brown stems with clusters of small, off-white flowers in summer. Prefers good, rich soil that does not dry out, in sun or light shade. Dislikes cold, dry wind. Remove one-third of old stems at ground level after flowering.

Potentilla fruticosa 'Tilford Cream'
Height: 45cm (18in); spread: 60cm (24in)
Small, grey-green leaves on twiggy bush with creamy white, saucer-shaped flowers from late spring to early autumn. Does best in any normal soil in full sun or very light shade, but dislikes extremes of wet and dry. Trim lightly in spring.

Prunus laurocerasus 'Otto Luyken' (laurel, cherry laurel)
Height: 1m (3ft 3in); spread: 1.2m (4ft)
Dark, glossy, evergreen pointed leaves with spikes of small, white flowers in spring. Prefers good, fertile soil in sun or partial shade, but dislikes water-logged ground. Cut back lightly after flowering to keep in shape, or hard back in late winter if outgrowing its space.

Pyracantha 'Orange Glow' (firethorn)
Height: 3m (10ft); spread: 1.8m (6ft)
Small, glossy, evergreen leaves on thorny stems with clusters of small, white flowers in early summer, followed by bright orange berries in the autumn. Prefers reasonably fertile soil, flowering and fruiting best in full sun. Trim lightly after flowering to just above the flowers to keep in shape.

Ribes laurifolium
Height: 60cm (24in); spread: 60cm (24in)
Leathery, elliptical evergreen leaves with pendulous clusters of green-white flowers in spring, followed by red fruits, which gradually turn black. Any reasonable soil in sun or light shade, but dislikes wet or exposed conditions. Trim lightly after flowering to keep in shape.

Rosa glauca (syn. R. rubrifolia)
Height: 2m (6ft 6in); spread: 1.5m (5ft)
Grey-purple leaves on upright blue-purple stems with single pink flowers in summer, followed by red hips. Any reasonable soil, as long as it is not water-logged, but needs to be in full sun for best effect. Remove one-third of old stems at or near ground level in late winter.

Mahonia x media 'Winter Sun'

Osmanthus x burkwoodii

Photinia x fraseri 'Rubens'

Prunus laurocerasus 'Otto Luyken'

Rosa 'Queen Elizabeth'

Height: to 1.8m (6ft); spread: to 1.2m (4ft)

Glossy, dark green leaves on strong, upright stems with large, slightly fragrant, clear pink flowers in early summer and sometimes early autumn. Best on good, rich, well-drained soil in full sun. Remove weak or dead stems and cut back others to between five and seven buds in early spring; prune lightly in late autumn to prevent winter wind rock.

Salix purpurea f. gracilis (purple osier)

Height: 1m (3ft 3in); spread: 1m (3ft 3in)

Small, narrow, grey-purple leaves on long, slender, shiny stems. Tolerates wide range of soils, but needs full sun for best foliage effect. Cut back to ground level annually or biennially in late winter.

Spiraea japonica 'Gold Mound'

Height: 90cm (36in); spread: 1.2m (4ft)

Small, pointed golden leaves on a dense twiggy bush, followed by clusters of small pink flowers in early summer. Will grow in any reasonable soil, but needs full sun for best colours and flowering. Trim lightly immediately after flowering or cut back hard in early spring for strong stems and better colour.

Ribes laurifolium

Viburnum x bodnantense 'Dawn'

Height: 2.5m (8ft 6in); spread: 1.8m (6ft)

Pointed, green, red-tinged leaves on strong upright stems with clusters of pink, sweetly scented flowers on the bare wood from late autumn to spring. Will tolerate any soil, but avoid extremes of dry and wet. Needs full sun for best flowering. Remove one-third of old wood at or near ground level in spring.

Viburnum japonicum

Height: 1.2m (4ft); spread: 1.5m (5ft)

Large, glossy, evergreen leaves with clusters of white, scented flowers on old wood in late spring. Any soil, as long as it is not water-logged, but prefers light shade for best effect. Trim lightly after flowering to keep bushy. Can prune hard in spring if getting too large.

Viburnum
x bodnantense
'Dawn'

Spiraea japonica
'Gold Mound'

Physocarpus
opulifolius
'Dart's Gold'

CLIMBERS

Actinidia kolomikta
Height: 1.8–2.4m (6–8ft)
Dark green, heart-shaped leaves,
with pink and cream splashes on
older plants, with slender, twining
stems. Small, white flowers in
summer on old wood. Any
reasonable soil, but does not grow
well on poor or badly drained sites.
Needs warm south- or west-facing
wall for best colour.

**Ampelopsis glandulosa var.
brevipedunculata 'Elegans'**
Height: 180cm (6ft)
Small vine leaves, mottled pink and
cream, on slender stems. Any
reasonable, well-drained soil, but
prefers warm south- or west-facing
wall. May be cut to ground level in
winter but sprouts again.

**Campsis x tagliabuana
'Madame Galen'**
Height: to 9m (30ft)
Light green leaflets on stiff stems,
with woody branches ultimately
producing aerial roots. Exotic,
salmon-red trumpet flowers
produced on racemes in late
summer. Best on good, fertile, well-
drained soil. Needs sheltered
position in full sun; best against a
wall. Some tip die-back in winter;
needs to be pruned off in spring.

**Celastrus orbiculatus
(syn. C. articulatus)
(staff vine, oriental bittersweet)**
Height: to 10m (33ft)
Large, toothed leaves on vigorous
twining stems, with tiny, green
flowers on older wood in summer
followed by hanging clusters of
brilliant orange/yellow fruits and
seed capsules. Any reasonable,
well-drained soil, but avoid

Clematis armandii

extremely wet or dry spots. Flowers
and fruits best in full sun,
preferably against west- or
south-facing wall.

Clematis armandii
Height: to 10m (33ft)
Long, glossy evergreen leaves on
vigorous stems. White, saucer-
shaped, scented flowers produced
in late spring. Best in good, fertile,
well-drained soil in full sun or light
shade. Needs protection of wall
except in mild climate. Remove any
unwanted growths immediately after
flowering.

Clematis orientalis
Height: to 9m (30ft)
Light green, deeply cut leaves on
tangles of rampant stems. Yellow,
star-shaped flowers on new wood
from late summer to early autumn,
followed by silky seed heads. Any
reasonable soil in full sun or light

shade. Cut back spindly growths or
unwanted stems in spring.

**Eccremocarpus scaber
(Chilean glory flower, glory
vine)**
Height: to 3m (10ft)
Dark green, semi-evergreen pinnate
leaves on slender twining stems.
Small tubular, orange-scarlet
flowers carried from late spring to
early autumn. Any reasonably
fertile, well-drained soil against
warm south- or west-facing wall.
Only evergreen in mild climates;
elsewhere, treat as a perennial or, in
extremely cold areas, as an annual.

**Hedera colchica
'Sulphur Heart'**
Height: to 5m (16ft) or more
Large, evergreen, ovate leaves,
splashed with gold centre on
vigorous climbing stems. Any well-
drained soil, but needs some sun for

best colour. Cut back to required size in early spring and during growing season if necessary.

Hedera helix 'Ivalace'
Height: to 3m (10ft) or more
Small, glossy leaves with attractive wavy edges, on well-branched stems. Any reasonable soil, in sun or shade, provided drainage is adequate. Trim back to size in spring and also during growing season if required. Also good as ground cover.

Lonicera periclymenum 'Graham Thomas' (honeysuckle)
Height: to 5m (16ft)
Pale green, ovate leaves on smooth, twining stems with clusters of very fragrant creamy-white to yellow flowers in summer. Prefers good, fertile well-drained soil. Best if roots are planted in shade, with stems allowed to grow into sun or light shade. In spring cut back weak and spindly side growths to leave strongest stems.

Parthenocissus henryana (syn. Vitis henryana)
Height: to 6m (20ft) or more
Dark green leaves of 3–5 leaflets, with striking white/pink variegations along the ribs, on self-clinging stems. Good autumn colour. Best in good, well-drained fertile soil. Needs protection of a south- or west-facing wall. Remove any unwanted growths in early spring.

Rosa 'Zéphirine Drouhin'
Height: to 3m (10ft)
Light green pointed leaflets, tinted red, with semi-double carmine pink flowers with a sweet scent through summer. Needs good, fertile soil, avoiding extremes of wet or dry, in full sun. In late winter remove one-third of old wood, plus any other unwanted branches.

Vitis coignetiae (crimson glory vine)
Height: 10m (33ft) or more
Large, heart-shaped leaves, felty beneath, on vigorous stems with tendrils. Small clusters of tiny green flowers in spring produce small, inedible, black 'grapes' on ripe wood. Needs good, fertile soil to produce the bold foliage in sun or light shade. Cut back to required size and thin out overgrown shoots in spring.

Vitis vinifera 'Purpurea'
Height: to 5m (16ft)
Purple vine leaves on stems with tendrils, followed by tiny green flowers and small black 'grapes' on ripe wood in a hot summer. Needs good, fertile, well-drained soil, preferably in sun to develop the best colour. Remove any straggly or unwanted growths in spring.

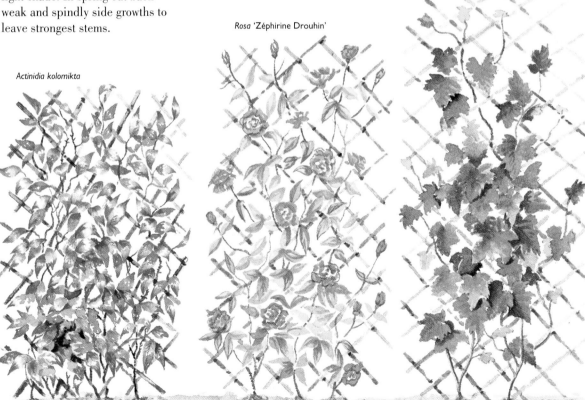

Vitis vinifera 'Purpurea'

Rosa 'Zéphirine Drouhin'

Actinidia kolomikta

GRASSES AND BAMBOOS

Fargesia nitida
(syn. Sinarundinaria nitida)
Height: 2m (6ft 6in); planting distance: 100cm (3ft 3in) or more
Elegant, slender, blue-green canes covered in a bloom, with small, narrow, grassy leaves. Any good, fertile soil, in sun or shade, but dislikes extremes of dry and wind. Remove-one third of old canes at ground level in spring.

Helictotrichon sempervirens
(syn. Avena candida,
A. sempervirens)
(blue oat grass)
Height: 45cm (18in); planting distance: 45cm (18in)
Dense clump of stiff, narrow, blue-grey leaves with taller stems of oat-like flower spikes to 90cm (36in) in summer. Any reasonable soil, but needs good drainage and full sun. Remove old flower stems in late autumn.

Miscanthus sacchariflorus
(Amur silver grass)
Height: 3m (10ft); planting distance: 90cm (36in)
Tall, straight, sugar-cane-like stems with long, narrow, arching leaves and silver midrib. Any reasonable soil, although does best in richer, moister conditions, in full sun. Cut back to ground level in spring before new growth appears.

Miscanthus sinensis
'Silver Feather'
Height: 2m (6ft 6in); planting distance: 60cm (24in)
Slender, upright canes with long, narrow, grassy leaves, topped by plumes of feathery pink-white flower heads in autumn. Does best in a good, fertile soil in full sun. Cut out dead canes at ground level in spring.

Sasa veitchii
(syn. S. albomarginata)
Height: 100cm (3ft 3in); planting distance: 90cm (36in) or more
Dwarfish bamboo with slender canes and pale green, grassy leaves becoming bleached in winter, giving a variegated appearance. Any reasonable soil, as long as it does not dry out, in sun or very light shade. Spreads to form good ground cover.

Stipa gigantea (golden oats)
Height: 180cm (6ft); planting distance: 60cm (24in)
Clumps of thin, spiky blue-grey foliage from which emerge tall stems with oat-like flower heads in summer. Any reasonably fertile soil, but needs good drainage and full sun. Cut dead stems down to ground level in spring.

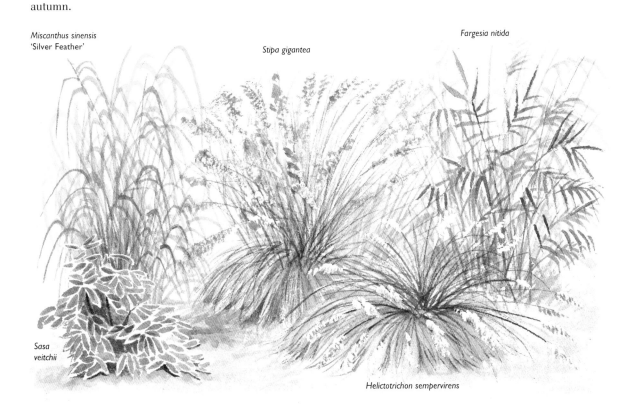

Miscanthus sinensis
'Silver Feather'

Stipa gigantea

Fargesia nitida

Sasa
veitchii

Helictotrichon sempervirens

TREES

Acer negundo 'Flamingo' (ash-leaved maple, box elder)

Height: 4m (13ft); spread: 3m (10ft)
Ash-like leaves, variegated pale green, pink and cream, on pale grey-green stems. Any reasonable soil, but dislikes extremes of wet, dry and alkalinity. Full sun produces best colour. Shorten long stems by one-third to one-half in spring to produce strong, well-coloured stems and leaves.

Acer saccharinum f. *lutescens* (silver maple)

Height: 6m (20ft); spread: 4m (13ft)
Large, lime green, palmate leaves with silver undersides, turn yellow in autumn. Any soil, as long as it is not water-logged. Produces best coloured leaves in open position in full sun.

Amelanchier lamarckii

Height: 5m (16ft); spread: 4m (13ft)
Small tree or large shrub with smooth, pale green, oval leaves and masses of white flowers in late spring. Orange-red autumn colours, with small red fruits. Any reasonable soil but flowers best in full sun. Remove low side branches in late winter to maintain a clear trunk.

Arbutus unedo f. *rubra* (strawberry tree)

Height: to 3m (10ft); spread: to 3m (10ft)
Small tree or, usually, large shrub, with leathery, oval, evergreen leaves and attractive, red-brown older wood. Arching clusters of small, bell-shaped pink flowers appearing slowly until late spring, followed by small, strawberry-like fruits in autumn. Prefers fertile, organic-rich

Betula utilis var. *jacquemontii*

soil in light shade; tolerates slight alkalinity.

Betula pendula 'Tristis' (silver birch)

Height: 10m (33ft); spread: 4m (13ft)
Small, triangular to oval leaves on slender twigs, with upright trunk and elegant, pendulous branches. White trunk with black diamond effect and good yellow autumn leaf colour. Any soil, but needs open position in full sun. Keep first 2m (6ft or so) of trunk clear of side branches in winter to prevent them dragging on the ground.

Betula utilis (Himalayan birch)

Height: 8m (26ft); spread: 3m (10ft)
Small, ovate, toothed leaves on slender twigs and branches. Creamy white bark, on older wood, with yellow autumn leaf colour. Any reasonable soil, except permanently water-logged. Needs an open, sunny position. Remove low branches in winter to 2m (6ft or so) above ground to accentuate white trunk.

Malus 'John Downie'

Height: 6m (20ft); spread: 4m (13ft)
Bright mid-green, oval leaves, with large, single white apple blossoms in late spring, followed by orange-

249

scarlet crab apples, ideal for jelly. Ordinary, well-drained soil, but best in full sun for maximum flowers and fruit. Shorten tips of main branches in early spring if outgrowing its space.

Prunus 'Pandora'

Height: 7m (23ft); spread: 3m (10ft) Young leaves emerge red-bronze, turning to green in summer and yellow in autumn. Shell pink cherry flowers in spring. Does best on a good, fertile soil in full sun; does not tolerate extreme dryness.

Prunus x schmittii

Height: 9m (30ft); spread: 3m (10ft) Young coppery foliage turns to green with pink cherry blossoms on old wood in spring. Upright stems form narrow crown, with trunk and main branches a glossy mahogany colour. Any reasonably fertile soil in sun or partial shade. Keep lower 2m (6ft or so) of trunk free from side branches

to enhance the appearance of bark in winter.

Prunus x subhirtella 'Autumnalis Rosea' (Higan cherry, rosebud cherry)

Height: 5m (16ft); spread: 4m (13ft) Small, oval, toothed leaves preceded by small clusters of pendulous rose-pink flowers continually from winter to spring. Does best on good, fertile, well-drained soil, in full sun.

Sorbus aucuparia 'Sheerwater Seedling' (mountain ash, rowan)

Height: 6m (20ft); spread: 2m (6ft 6in) Small, dark green leaflets on long stems give good autumn colour, with upright stems making this a narrow, conical tree. Clusters of small white flowers in late spring to early summer, followed by hanging,

orange berries in autumn. Any reasonable soil, in full sun for best flowers and berries.

Sorbus hupehensis (Hupeh rowan)

Height: 5m (16ft); spread 2.5m (8ft 6in) Small, grey-green leaflets on long stalks contrast with clusters of white flowers in late spring to early summer, followed by small, white, pink-tipped fruits in autumn. Any reasonable, well-drained soil, but is not happy in extremely alkaline conditions. For best flowers and fruit, needs open position in full sun.

Betula pendula 'Tristis'

Prunus 'Pandora'

Sorbus hupehensis

CONIFERS

Chamaecyparis lawsoniana **'Minima Aurea'**

Height: 60cm (24in); spread: 45cm (18in)

Very dense, conical bush of tight, golden, feathery foliage. Grows in any reasonable, well-drained soil; needs full sun. Good for raised bed or container.

Juniperus x *media* **'Old Gold'**

Height: 1m (3ft 3in); spread: 1.5m (5ft)

Dense, golden evergreen foliage on low, spreading bush. Grows in any soil, as long as it is not water-logged, preferring full sun for best colour. Cut back main stems by up to one-third in spring to keep within bounds or trim lightly in summer. Good ground-cover conifer.

Juniperus squamata **'Blue Star'**

Height: 60cm (24in); spread: 75cm (30in)

Dense, steel blue, prickly foliage on a rounded evergreen bush. Will grow in any soil, provided it is not water-logged, but needs full sun. Trim lightly in spring if outgrowing space. Good for raised bed or container.

Juniperus virginiana **'Sulphur Spray'**

Height: 75cm (30in); spread: 1m (3ft 3in)

Pale green evergreen foliage, tipped with white and sulphur yellow in summer, along arching stems. Does best on good, fertile soil; needs good drainage and full sun for best colour. Shorten main stems by up to one-third in early spring to keep within bounds.

Pinus mugo **'Ophir'**

Height: 90cm (36in); spread: 1.2m (4ft)

Dwarf pine of bushy growth with pale yellow-green needles, turning gold in winter. Occasional insignificant flowers produce small pine cones. Will grow in any reasonable soil, but needs good drainage and full sun. Remove overlong or unwanted branches in spring.

Pinus mugo **var.** *pumilio*

Height: 1m (3ft 6in); spread: 1.2m (4ft)

Dense clusters of needles on short, stiff stems, making a rounded bush. Occasional flowers in spring may produce small pine cones. Grows in any reasonable soil, but needs good drainage and full sun.

Pinus mugo 'Ophir'

Chamaecyparis lawsoniana
'Minima Aurea'

Juniperus squamata
'Blue Star'

Juniperus x media
'Old Gold'

INDEX

252

ACKNOWLEDGEMENTS

PHOTOGRAPHS
Garden Picture Library 71 (Mayer/le Scanff), 166 (Geoff Dann), 251 (John Glover); **Jerry Harpur** 38 (Designer: Keith R. Geller, Seattle, Wa.), 46 (Designer: Jerry Harpur), 51 (Designer: Mark Rios & Associates, Los Angeles), 61 (Designers: Brian Daly & Alan Charman, Chobham, Surrey), 133 (Designer & Constructor: Berry's Garden Company, Golders Green), 134 (Inverewe Garden, Ross & Cromarty, Scotland), 178 (Designer: Perry Guillot, New York City), 183 (Designer: Keith Corlet, New York City), 187 (Designer & Constructor: Tim Du Val, New York City), 206 (Designer: Mel Light, Los Angeles); **Harry Smith Collection** 85; **Andrew Lawson** 105, 195; **Clive Nichols** 2–3 (The Manor House, Upton Grey, Hampshire), 4–5 (Ashtree Cottage, Wiltshire), 6 (The Old School House, Essex), 7 (The Old Rectory, Sudborough, Northamptonshire), 8 (Designer: Vic Shanley), 9 (Glazeley Old Rectory, Shropshire), 12–13 (23 Beech Croft Road, Oxford), 14 (East Lambrook Manor Garden Nursery, Somerset), 18 (Designer: Anthony Noel), 23 (Tintinhull House Garden, Somerset/The National Trust), 26 (Designer: Sue Berger), 28 (The Chipping Croft, Gloucestershire), 33 (The Old Rectory, Sudborough, Northamptonshire), 36 (Barnsley House, Gloucestershire), 43 (Designer: Jill Billington), 53 (Designer: Jill Billington), 56 (Designer: Malley Terry), 74 (Chelsea 94), 76 (The Beth Chatto Gardens, Elmstead Market, Essex), 80 (Southview Nurseries, Hampshire), 88 (The

Beth Chatto Gardens, Elmstead Market, Essex), 91 (Chelsea 94), 94 (Designer: Richard Coward), 101 (Chelsea 94), 109 (Designer: Jill Billington), 115 (Carrog, Wales), 118 (Designer: Jill Billington), 125 (Designer: Vic Shanley), 129 (Designer: Jill Billington), 142 (40, Osler Road, Oxford), 149 (The Manor House, Upton Grey, Hampshire), 153 (Designer: Jill Billington), 157 (The Anchorage, Kent), 159 (Old Rectory Cottage, Berkshire), 163 (Duckyls, Sussex), 169 (Malvern Terrace, London), 173 (Designer: Jill Billington), 176 (40, Osler Road, Oxford), 188–189 (Vale End, Surrey), 198 (Ashtree Cottage, Wiltshire), 211 (Designer: Lucy Gent), 215 (Designer: Olivia Clarke), 219 (Designer: Anthony Noel), 225 (White Windows, Longparish, Hampshire), 227 (The Mill House, Sussex), 231 (Designer: Caroline Cordy), 234 (Designer: Malley Terry), 236 (Butterstream, Trim, Co Meath/Designer: Jim Reynolds), 249 (Carrog, Wales); **Hugh Palmer** 146; **Photos Horticultural** 62 (Capel Manor Institute); **Ward Lock** 67,99; **Wildlife Matters** 139.

ILLUSTRATIONS
Line illustrations and colour plans: **Tim Newbury**; colour artwork in Part 1: **Michael Shoebridge** and **Kevin Maddison**; colour artwork in Part 2: **Wendy Bramall**; colour artwork in Part 3: **Paul Staveley**.

The author would like to thank **Tony Fry** of Bressingham Plant Centre.